AF322737

Contents | Page

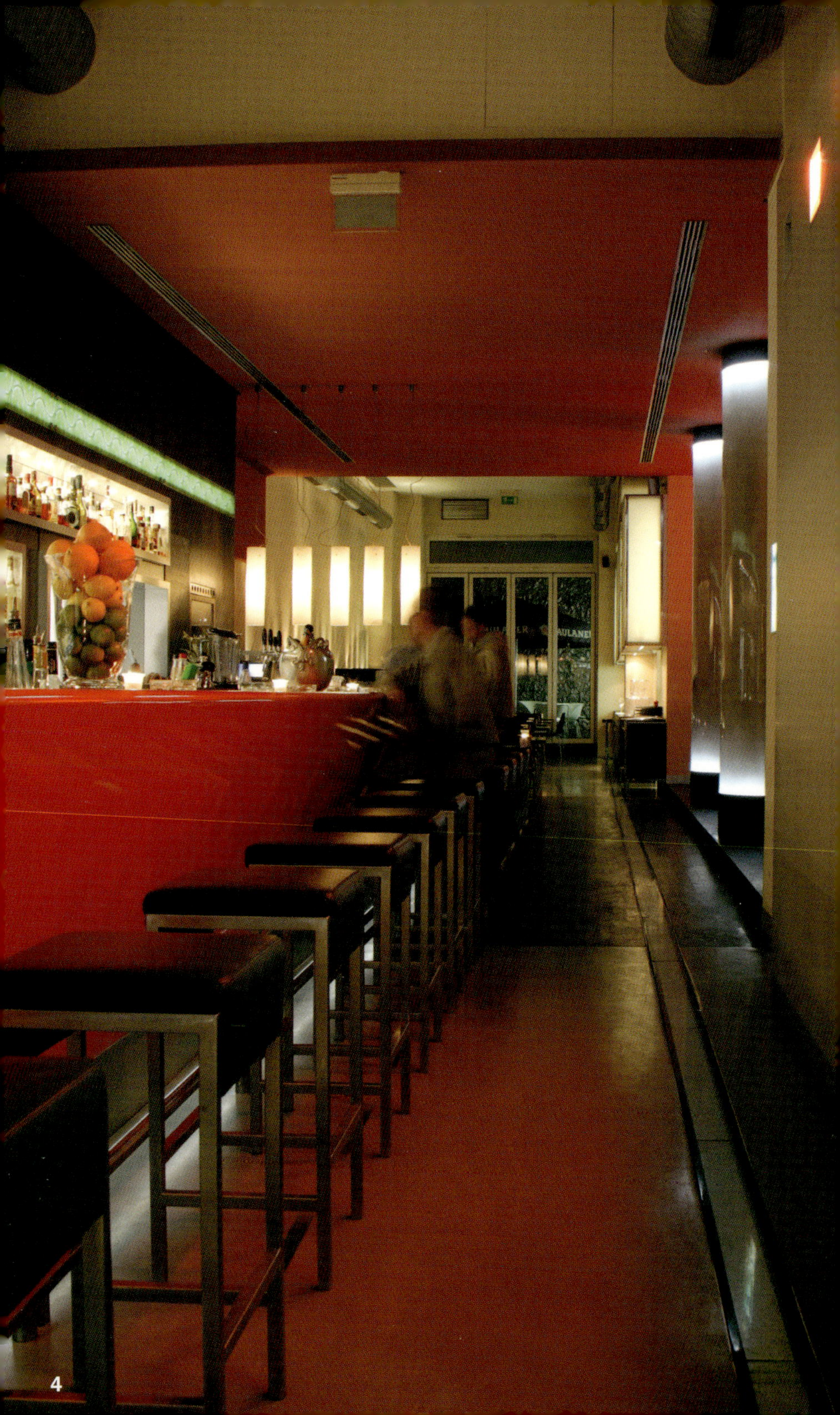

Cool Restaurants Frankfurt

teNeues

Imprint

Editor: Micky Rosen

Editorial coordination: Henrik Sauer

Photos (location): Friedrich Frey (cesar's), Fritz Busam (Coconut Groove), Klaus Setzer (King Kamehameha Club), Emanuel Raab (Micro, Silk), Stefan Minx (MoschMosch). All other photos by Roland Bauer.

Introduction: Gaby Adora

Layout & Pre-press: Thomas Hausberg, Jan Hausberg

Imaging: Jan Hausberg

Translations: SAW Communications, Dr. Sabine A. Werner, Mainz
Dr. Suzanne Kirkbright (English / introduction), Nina Hausberg (English / recipes), Céline Verschelde (French),
Silvia Gómez de Antonio (Spanish), Maria-Letizia Haas (Italian)

Editing English recipes: Karin Mahle

Produced by fusion publishing GmbH, Stuttgart . Los Angeles   www.fusion-publishing.com

Published by teNeues Publishing Group

teNeues Book Division
Kaistraße 18
40221 Düsseldorf, Germany
Tel.: 0049-(0)211-994597-0
Fax: 0049-(0)211-994597-40
E-mail: books@teneues.de

teNeues Publishing Company
16 West 22nd Street
New York, NY 10010, USA
Tel.: 001-212-627-9090
Fax: 001-212-627-9511

teNeues Publishing UK Ltd.
P.O. Box 402
West Byfleet
KT14 7ZF, Great Britain
Tel.: 0044-1932-403509
Fax: 0044-1932-403514

teNeues France S.A.R.L.
4, rue de Valence
75005 Paris, France
Tel.: 0033-1-55766205
Fax: 0033-1-55766419

teNeues Ibérica S.L.
c/Velázquez, 57 6.° izda.
28001 Madrid, Spain
Tel.: 0034-657-132133

teNeues
Representative Office Italy
Via San Vittore 36/1
20123 Milan
Tel.: 0039-(0)347-7640551

Press department: arehn@teneues.de
Phone: 0049-2152-916-202

www.teneues.com

ISBN-10: 3-8327-9118-3
ISBN-13: 978-3-8327-9118-6

Bibliographic information published by Die Deutsche Bibliothek.
Die Deutsche Bibliothek lists this publication in the Deutsche Nationalbibliografie;
detailed bibliographic data is available in the Internet at http://dnb.ddb.de.

Average price reflects the average cost for a dinner main course without beverages. Recipes serve four.

Einleitung

Frankfurt am Main ist großzügig mit Eindrücken für alle Sinne und vereint auf einzigartige Weise Gegensätze wie Beschaulichkeit und schillernde, internationale Dynamik. Architektonisch reicht die Spannbreite von Gassen mit Fachwerkhäusern über Villen aus der Gründerzeit bis zur Skyline mit über 80 Hochhäusern, die der Wirtschafts- und Finanzmetropole den Beinamen „Mainhattan" eingebracht hat. Als zentraler kontinentaleuropäischer Verkehrsknotenpunkt ist Frankfurt die ideale Handels- und Messestadt, die unter anderem die Internationale Automobil Ausstellung und die Frankfurter Buchmesse ausrichtet und seine Gäste mit der Zeil, der längsten Einkaufsmeile Europas, lockt. In der Stadt des Buches, die zahlreiche bedeutende Verlage sowie führende wissenschaftliche Institute beherbergt, gibt man den Künsten Raum zur Entfaltung. Einzigartig ist das Museumsufer mit 13 Museen allein auf der Sachsenhäuser Seite, bedeutend die Oper. So bleibt die Stadt bei aller Hektik und allem Wandel menschlich und unaufdringlich. Gastronomisch misst sich Frankfurt an der Welt. Ob mit oder ohne Sternekoch, ob mit heimischen oder internationalen Spezialitäten, die hier vorgestellten Restaurants überzeugen durch ihre Symbiose von Ambiente, Service und Qualität. Noch dazu sind sie zentral gelegen. Wie fast alles in Frankfurt. Typisch: Tagsüber trifft man Bänker und andere Geschäftsleute, abends auch die Szenegänger. Man kennt sich und weiß, wo man sich begegnet. Zum Beispiel in der neuen Bar 54, die auch am Abend Leben auf die „Fressgass" bringt, oder in den Restaurants Silk und Micro des Gesamtkunstwerks Cocoon Club. Schick, lecker und freundlich gibt sich auch das Biancalani als Adresse für optisch anspruchsvolle Genießer. Zu den Klassikern gehört die Villa Merton: Ein Esszimmer für alle, die Wert auf eine elegant lockere Atmosphäre legen und dabei eine Sterneküche schätzen. Das puristische Rama V mit goldenen Buddhas und Antiquitäten führt seit Jahren die Rangliste der besten Thaiküchen an.
Mit brillanten Farbfotos führt *Cool Restaurants Frankfurt* in 31 Restaurants und schaut mit einer Auswahl von Rezepten zum Nachkochen über die Schulter der Chefs.

Gaby Adora

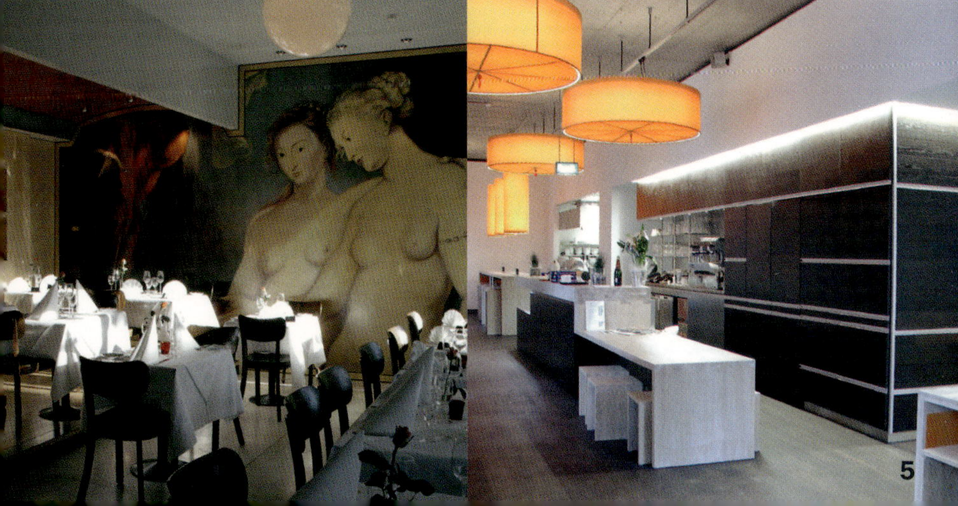

Introduction

Frankfurt am Main lavishes impressions on all the senses and has a unique way of uniting contrasts like tranquility and dazzling international dynamism. Architecturally, the range extends from alleys with half-timbered houses to late 19th century villas and to the skyline with over 80 high-rise buildings, which have earned the commercial and financial metropolis the nickname of "Mainhattan". As a central interchange for continental European travel, Frankfurt is the ideal trading and conference city, which hosts among others the International Automobile Exhibition and the Frankfurt Book Fair and tempts its guests with the Zeil—Europe's longest shopping mile. In this city, home of the book and numerous important publishing houses as well as leading scientific institutes, the arts are given the space to evolve. The "Museumsufer" is unique with 13 museums alone being located on the Sachsenhausen side of the river; and the opera is important. In spite of the hectic pace of life and constant change, the city remains human and unobtrusive.
Gastronomically, Frankfurt rates itself by international standards. Whether with or without a star-rated chef, whether boasting domestic or international specialties, the restaurants introduced in this guide are convincing because of their symbiosis of ambiance, service and quality. In addition, they are centrally located. This is like almost everything in Frankfurt. Typically, by day you meet bankers and other businessmen and by night you also see the fashionable trendsetters. Everyone knows one another and where to meet. For instance, in the new Bar 54, which by night also livens up the "Fressgass", or in the restaurants Silk and Micro in the complete artwork Cocoon Club. The Biancalani is also a chic, tasty and friendly venue for connoisseurs of sophisticated optical delights. The Villa Merton counts among the classics: A dining room for everyone valuing an elegant and relaxed atmosphere with an appreciation of star-rated chefs. The purist Rama V with golden Buddhas and antiques has topped the rankings of the best Thai cuisines for years.
Cool Restaurants Frankfurt features brilliant photos to introduce you to 31 restaurants and, including a selection of recipes to try out, it takes a look over the chef's shoulder.

Gaby Adora

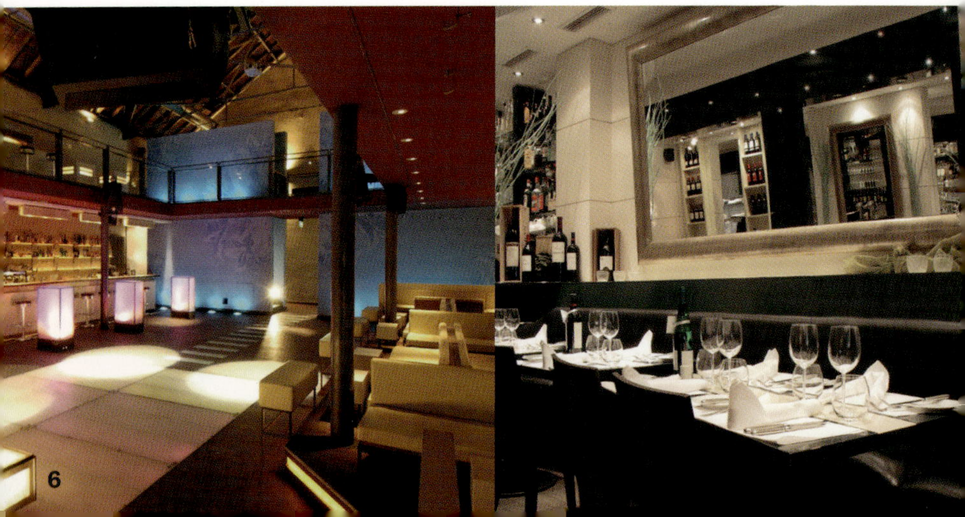

Introduction

Francfort sur le Main réveille tous les sens et réunit de manière unique des contraires tels que la tranquillité et le dynamisme trépidant et international. Du point de vue architectural, la diversité est grande : les ruelles aux maisons à colombage, les villas datant de l'expansion industrielle, la skyline comptant plus de 80 tours et qui est à l'origine du surnom de la métropole économique et financière, « Mainhattan ». Plaque tournante central de l'Europe continentale, Francfort est la ville commerçante et d'exposition idéale. Elle organise entre autres l'exposition internationale de l'automobile et le salon du livre de Francfort et attire les visiteurs avec la Zeil, la plus longue artère commerçante d'Europe. Cette ville du livre, qui héberge de nombreuses maisons d'édition significatives ainsi que des instituts scientifiques de premier plan, réserve également aux différents arts de s'épanouir. La berge des musées (« Museumsufer »), comptant 13 musées sur la seule rive Sachsenhäuser, est unique ; quant à l'opéra, il est exceptionnel. La ville, malgré son effervescence et toutes les transformations qu'elle subit, conserve ainsi son atmosphère de tranquillité et reste à dimension humaine.

Du point de vue gastronomique, Francfort rivalise avec le monde entier. Avec ou sans cuisinier étoilé, proposant des spécialités locales ou internationales, les restaurants présentés dans cet ouvrage nous séduisent par leur symbiose d'ambiance, de service et de qualité. Ils bénéficient en outre d'une position centrale, comme presque tout à Francfort. Fait typique : le jour, on y rencontre les banquiers et autres hommes d'affaires, et le soir, on y croise également les amateurs des lieux originaux et à la mode. On se connaît et on sait où se retrouver. Par exemple dans le nouveau Bar 54 qui, le soir aussi, redonne également vie à la ruelle « Fressgass » ou dans les restaurants Silk et Micro du Cocoon Club, chef-d'œuvre intégral. Chic, délicieux et sympathique, le Biancalani est une bonne adresse pour les gourmets qui accordent de l'importance à l'effet optique. La Villa Merton compte parmi les classiques : la salle à manger s'adresse à tous ceux qui recherchent l'association d'une atmosphère élégamment décontractée et d'une cuisine étoilée. Avec ses bouddhas dorés et ses pièces d'antiquité, l'établissement puriste Rama V occupe depuis des années la première place de la liste des meilleures cuisines thaïlandaises.

Avec des photos brillantes en couleur, *Cool Restaurants Frankfurt* nous fait découvrir 31 restaurants et nous permet de jeter un coup d'œil dans la cuisine des chefs avec une sélection de recettes à réaliser soi-même.

Gaby Adora

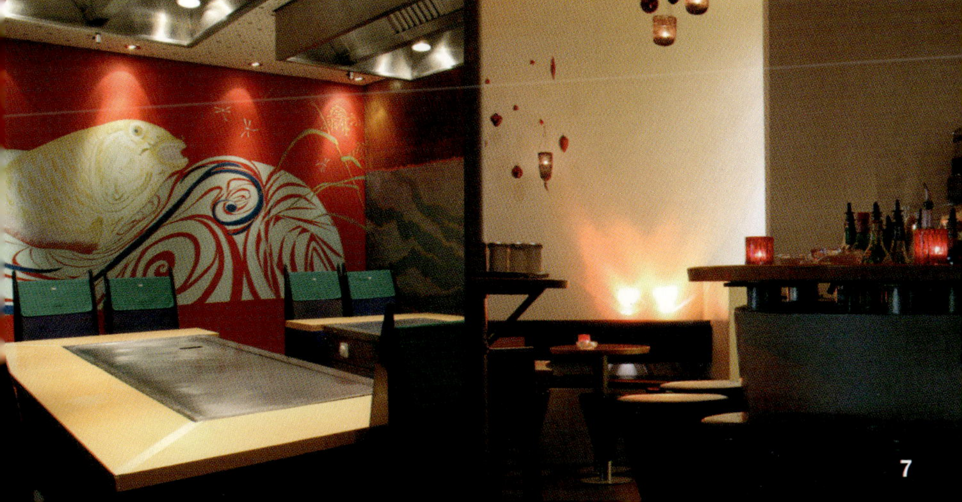

Introducción

Fráncfort del Meno ofrece impresiones para todos los sentidos y reúne de una forma única polos opuestos como la tranquilidad y el irisado dinamismo internacional. Desde el punto de vista arquitectónico, el espectro se extiende desde callejones con casas de paredes entramadas, pasando por villas del periodo fundacional hasta un perfil de la ciudad recortado por más de 80 rascacielos que han dado a esta metrópolis económica y financiera el apodo de "Mainhattan". Como nudo de comunicaciones situado en el centro de la Europa continental, Fráncfort es la ciudad ideal para el comercio y las ferias internacionales, entre ellas la exposición internacional del automóvil y la feria del libro. Además, este centro urbano atrae a sus visitantes con la Zeil, la calle comercial más larga de Europa. En la ciudad del libro, que alberga numerosas editoriales importantes además de instituciones cientificas líderes, los artistas tienen espacio suficiente para desarrollarse. Algo único es su orilla de museos ("Museumsufer"), con 13 museos situados sólo en el lado de la colina Sachsenhausen además del sobresaliente edificio de la ópera. Así, la ciudad sigue siendo un lugar humano y apacible a pesar del ajetreo y los cambios. Gastronómicamente, Fráncfort se mide con el mundo. Tanto con o sin cocinero estrella o con especialidades nacionales o internacionales, los restaurantes que aquí presentamos convencen por la simbiosis del ambiente con el servicio y la calidad. Además, todos están situados en el centro. Como casi todo en Fráncfort. Típico: durante el día uno se cruza con banqueros y personas de negocios por las calles, por la tarde se unen los amantes de la gastronomía. Se conocen entre ellos y saben dónde encontrarse. Por ejemplo en el nuevo Bar 54, que también llena de vida la "Fressgass", o en los restaurantes Silk y Micro, de la obra de arte total Cocoon Club. Elegante, delicioso y agradable se presenta también Biancalani, una dirección para sibaritas de aspecto exigente. Villa Merton pertenece a los clásicos: Un comedor para todos los que valoran una atmósfera elegantemente distendida y aprecian una cocina estrella. El purista Rama V, con budas dorados y antigüedades, posee desde hace años la mejor cocina tailandesa.
Con brillantes fotos a todo color, *Cool Restaurants Frankfurt* le lleva a 31 restaurantes y le presenta una selección de recetas de sus cocineros para que usted también las prepare en casa.

Gaby Adora

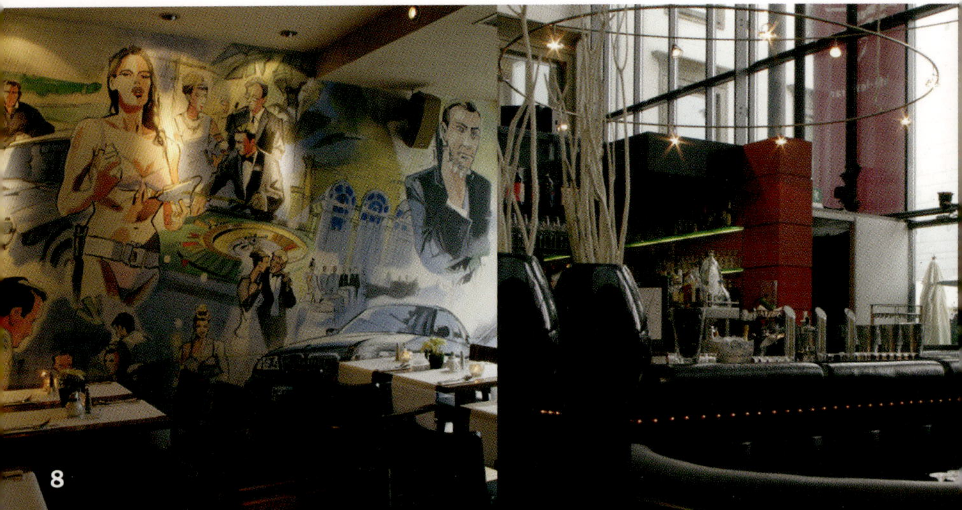

Introduzione

Francoforte sul Meno regala impressioni che coinvolgono tutti i sensi: è una città che unisce in modo unico elementi contrastanti come tranquilità e dinamismo internazionale e poliedrico. Dal punto di vista architettonico, si passa da vicoli su cui si affacciano case con travature a traliccio, a ville che risalgono al periodo di sviluppo economico-industriale del II Reich allo skyline con più di 80 grattacieli, che è valso alla metropoli economica e finanziaria l'appellativo di "Mainhattan". Nodo stradale e ferroviario al centro dell'Europa continentale, Francoforte è la città commerciale e fieristica per eccellenza, che ospita – tra l'altro – il Salone Internazionale dell'Automobile e la Frankfurter Buchmesse, la Fiera del Libro, attirando gli ospiti nella Zeil, lo shopping mile più lungo d'Europa. Nella città del libro, in cui hanno sede molte grandi case editrici ed importanti istituti scientifici, le arti trovano lo spazio necessario al loro sviluppo. Ne sono alcuni esempi lo straordinario "Museumsufer", la sponda del Meno su cui sono situati molti musei – 13 solo sulla riva Sachsenhäuser – ed il notevolissimo Teatro dell'opera. È per questo che Francoforte – pur così frenetica ed in continua trasformazione – riesce a conservare una dimensione umana e tranquilla.

Dal punto di vista gastronomico, Francoforte sta al passo con il mondo. Con o senza celebri cuochi, con specialità locali o menu internazionali, i ristoranti che presentiamo in questo volume conquistano per il perfetto equilibrio tra atmosfera, servizio e qualità. Essi sono inoltre situati in centro, come quasi tutto a Francoforte, una città che, di giorno, è punto d'incontro per banchieri e uomini d'affari, e di sera anche per coloro che animano il jet-set. Ci si conosce e si sa dove incontrarsi: per esempio al nuovo Bar 54, che anche di sera riempie di vita la "Fressgass", la via delle gozzoviglie, o nei ristoranti Silk e Micro, situati nell'opera d'arte totale Cocoon Club. Chic, squisito e cordiale è Biancalani, l'indirizzo giusto per buongustai dallo spiccato senso estetico. Tra i posti classici c'è il Villa Merton: una sala da pranzo per tutti coloro che prediligono un'atmosfera cordiale ed elegante e che apprezzano la cucina di classe. Il puristico Rama V, invece, arredato con pezzi d'antiquariato e Buddha dorati, è da anni il numero uno delle cucine tailandesi.

Le splendide foto a colori di *Cool Restaurants Frankfurt* guidano il lettore attraverso 31 ristoranti e lo invitano a cimentarsi in cucina, svelandogli alcune ricette degli Chef de Cuisine.

Gaby Adora

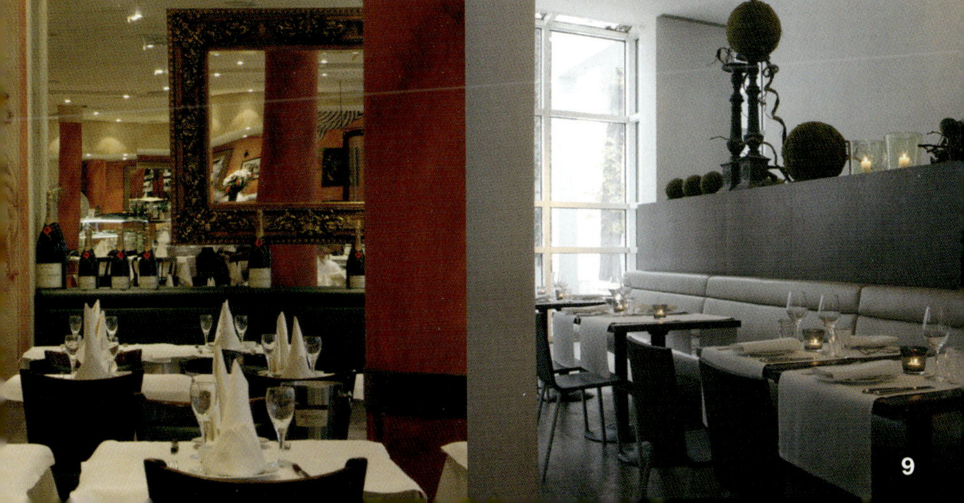

Bar 54

Design: Oana Rosen | Owners: Micky Rosen, Lior Ehrlich, Alex Urseanu

Große Bockenheimer Straße 54 | 60313 Frankfurt | Innenstadt
Phone: +49 69 92 88 68 48
www.bar-54.de
Subway: Alte Oper
Opening hours: Mon–Wed 8 am to 2 am, Thu–Sat 8 am to 4 am,
Sun 10 am to 1 am
Average cocktail price: € 10

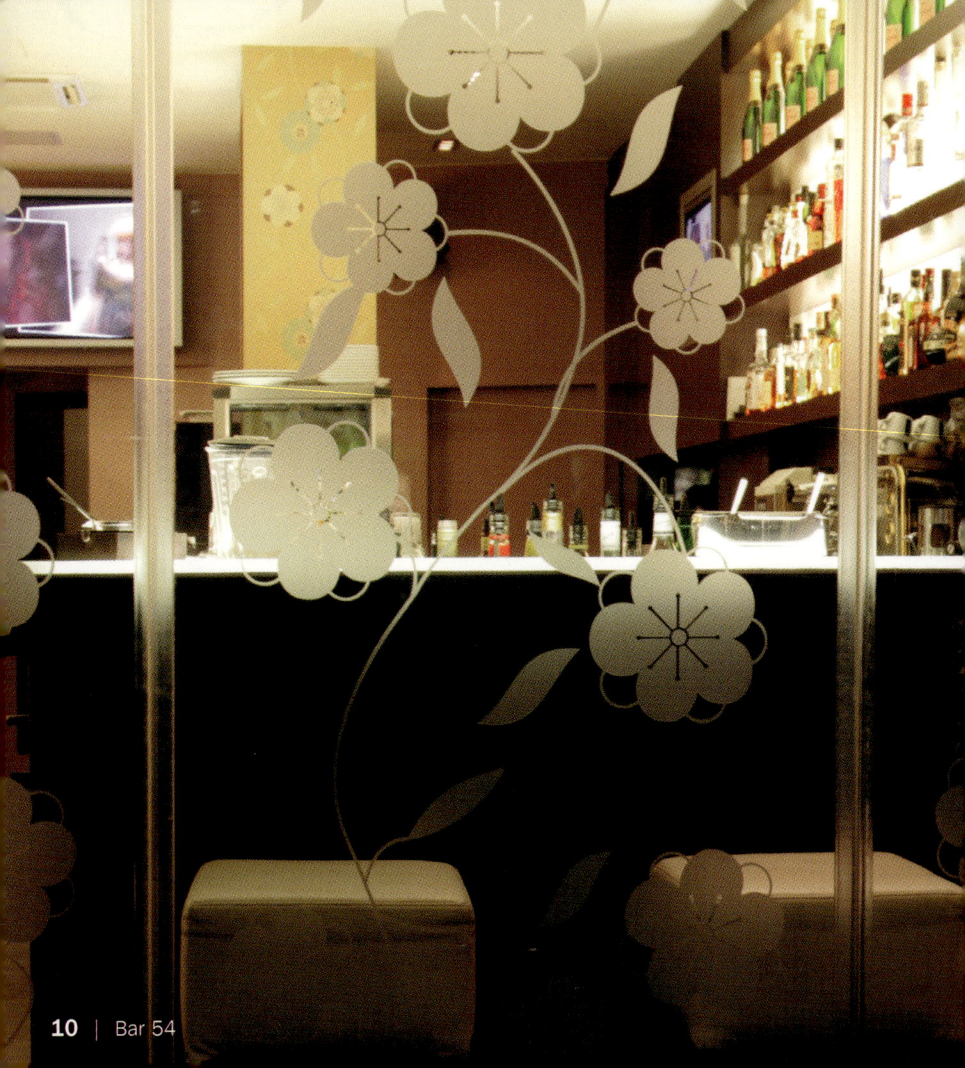

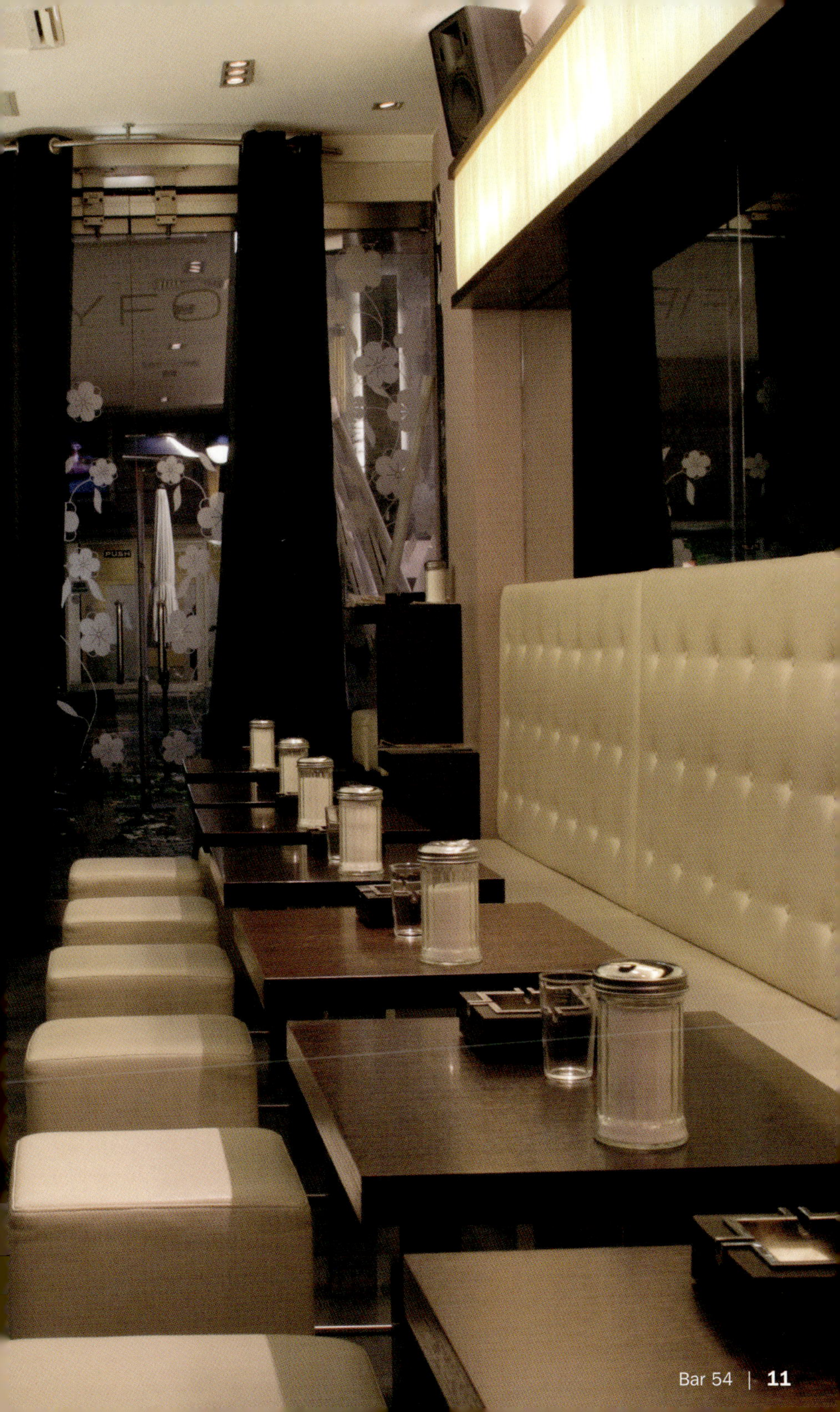

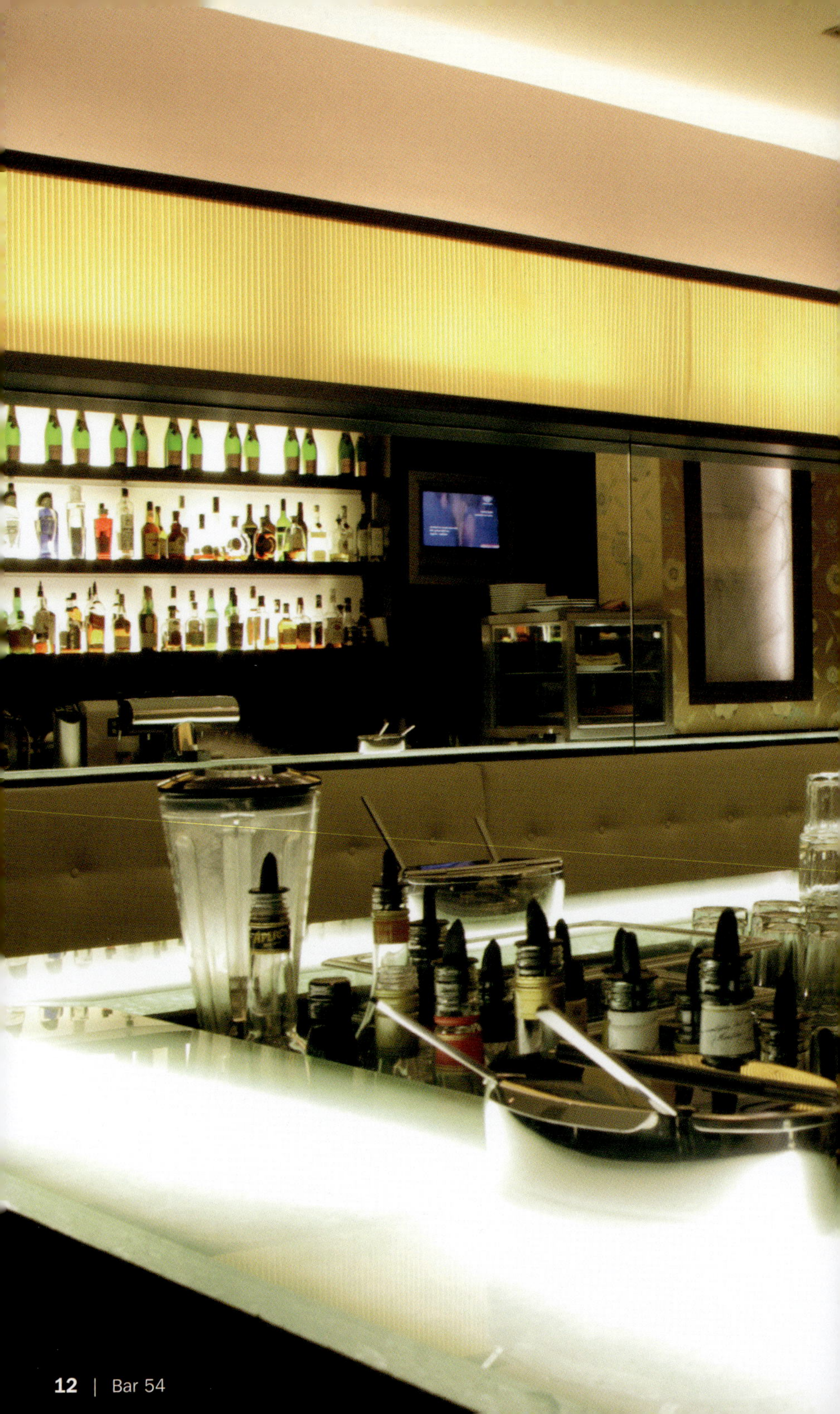

Vanilla Sky
Cocktail

4 cl vodka
2 ½ cl Vanillelikör
2 cl Haselnusssirup
10 cl Milch
1 Strohhalm
1 eingelegte Kirsche
1 Scheibe Ananas
Eiswürfel, eventuell Ananasgrün zur Dekoration

Die Zutaten in einen Shaker füllen und kräftig mischen. In ein Glas auf Eiswürfel gießen und mit Strohhalm, Kirsche, Ananasscheibe und Grün garnieren.

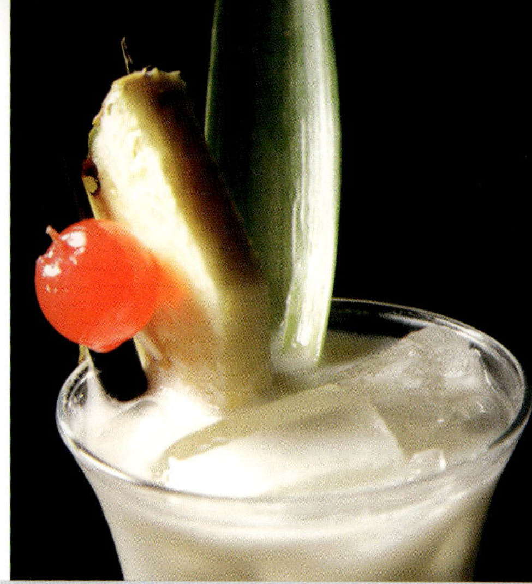

4 cl vodka
2 ½ cl vanilla liquor
2 cl hazelnut syrup
10 cl milk
1 straw
1 candied cherry
1 slice pineapple
Ice cubes, pineapple greens for decoration, if desired

Combine all ingredients in a shaker and shake well. Pour in a glass on ice cubes and garnish with straw, cherry, pineapple slice and pineapple greens.

4 cl de vodka
2 ½ cl de liqueur de vanille
2 cl de sirop de noisette
10 cl de lait
1 paille
1 cerise en conserve
1 tranche d'ananas
Glaçons, éventuellement des feuilles d'ananas pour décorer

Remplir les ingrédients dans un shaker et les secouer vigoureusement. Verser sur des glaçons dans un verre et garnir avec la paille, la cerise, la tranche d'ananas et les feuilles.

4 cl de vodka
2 ½ cl de licor de vainilla
2 cl de licor de avellana
10 cl de leche
1 pajita
1 cereza confitada
1 rodaja de piña
Cubitos de hielo, si lo desea una hoja de la piña para decorar

Mezcle bien los ingredientes en una coctelera. Vierta la mezcla en un vaso con hielo y decore con la pajita, la cereza, la rodaja de la piña y la hoja.

4 cl di vodka
2 ½ cl di liquore alla vaniglia
2 cl di sciroppo di nocciole
10 cl di latte
1 cannuccia
1 ciliegia conservata
1 fetta di ananas
Cubetti di ghiaccio, per la guarnizione: eventualmente, il ciuffo verde dell'ananas

Mettere gli ingredienti in uno shaker ed agitare con forza. Versarli in un bicchiere sui cubetti di ghiaccio e guarnire con la cannuccia, la ciliegia, la fetta ed il ciuffo di ananas.

Biancalani [CUCINA] [BAR] [ENO]

Design: Tom Bock | Chef: Thomas Haus
Owner: 3B Management GmbH & Co KG

Walther-von-Cronberg-Platz 7–9 | 60594 Frankfurt | Sachsenhausen
Phone: +49 69 68 97 76 15
www.biancalani.de
Subway: Südbahnhof
Opening hours: Mon–Fri noon to 3:30 pm and 6 pm to open end,
Sat 6 pm to open end
Average price: € 15
Cuisine: Mediterranean

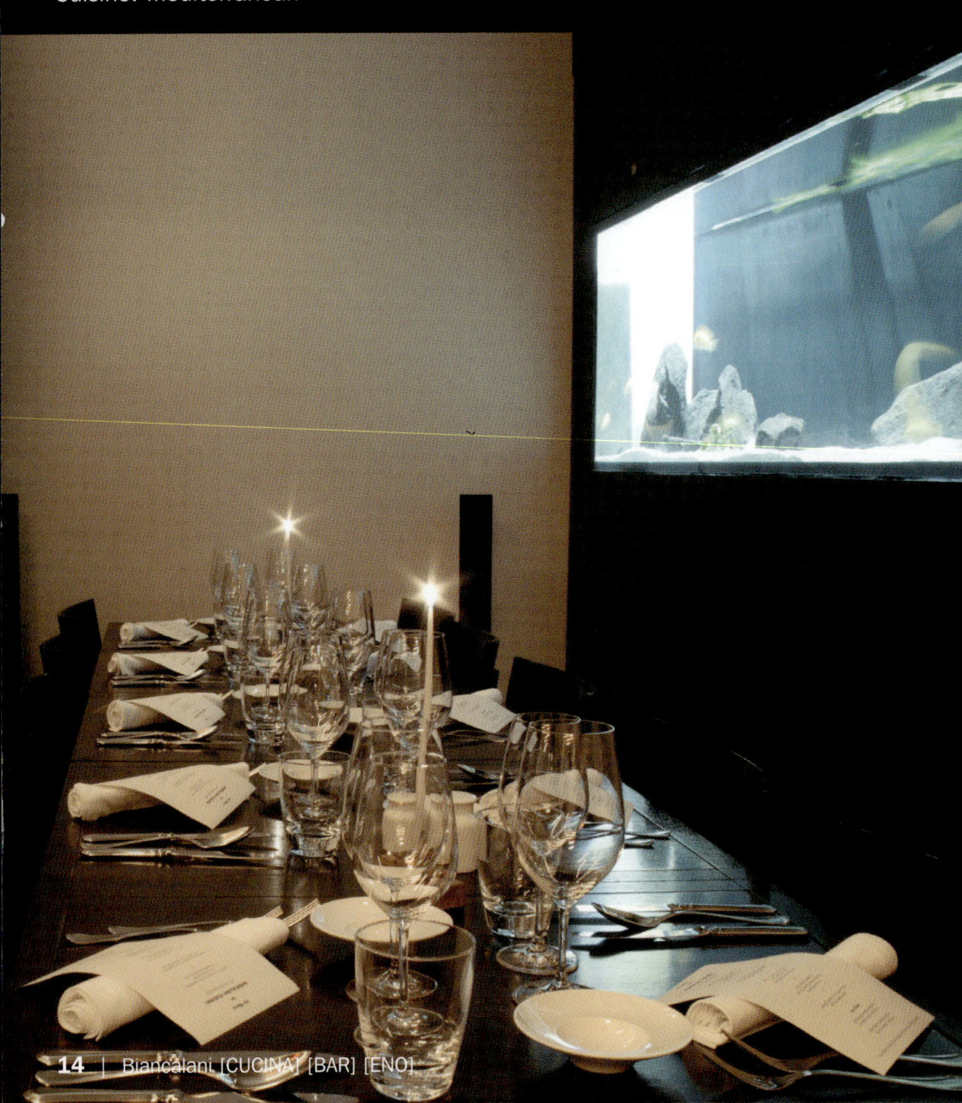

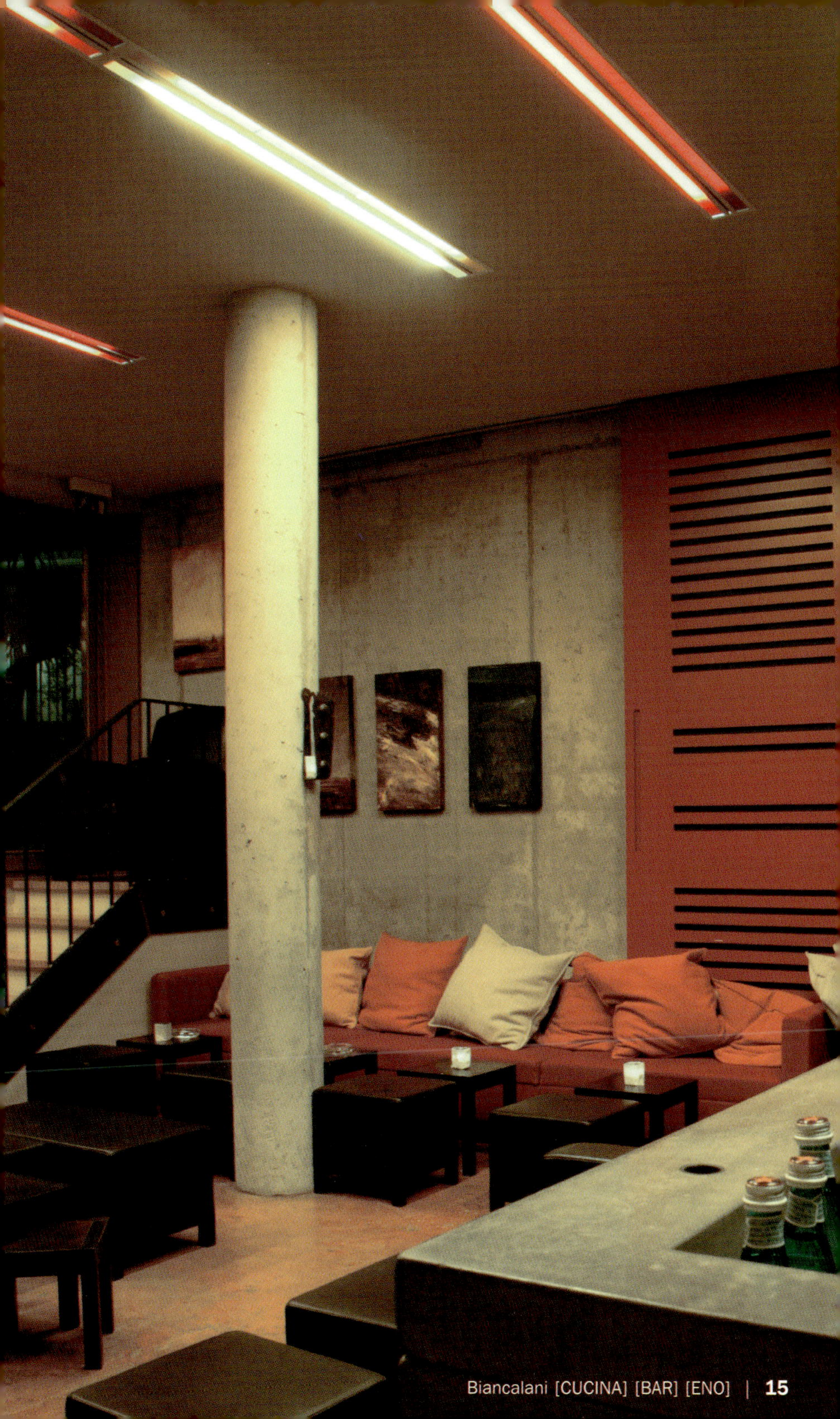
Biancalani [CUCINA] [BAR] [ENO]

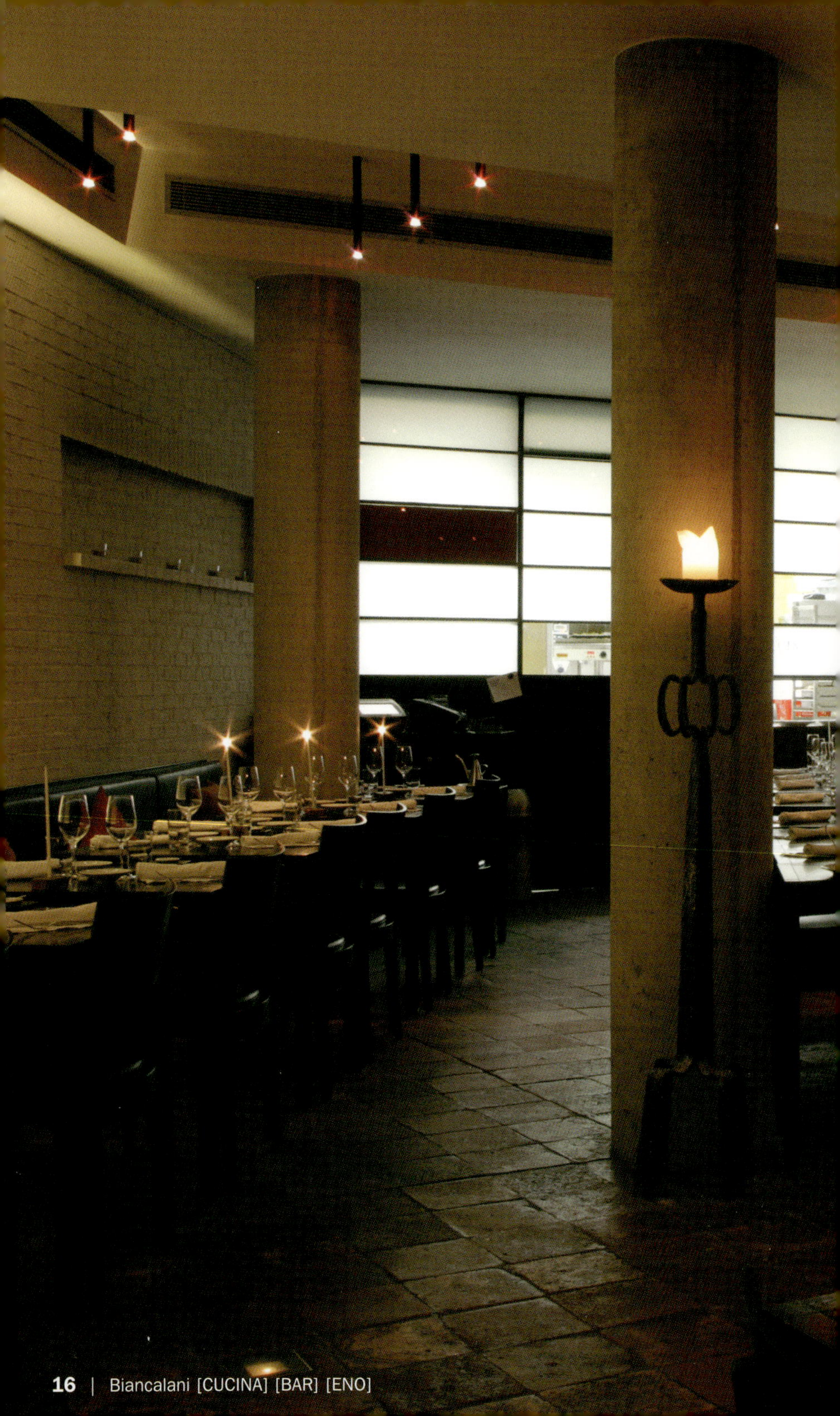

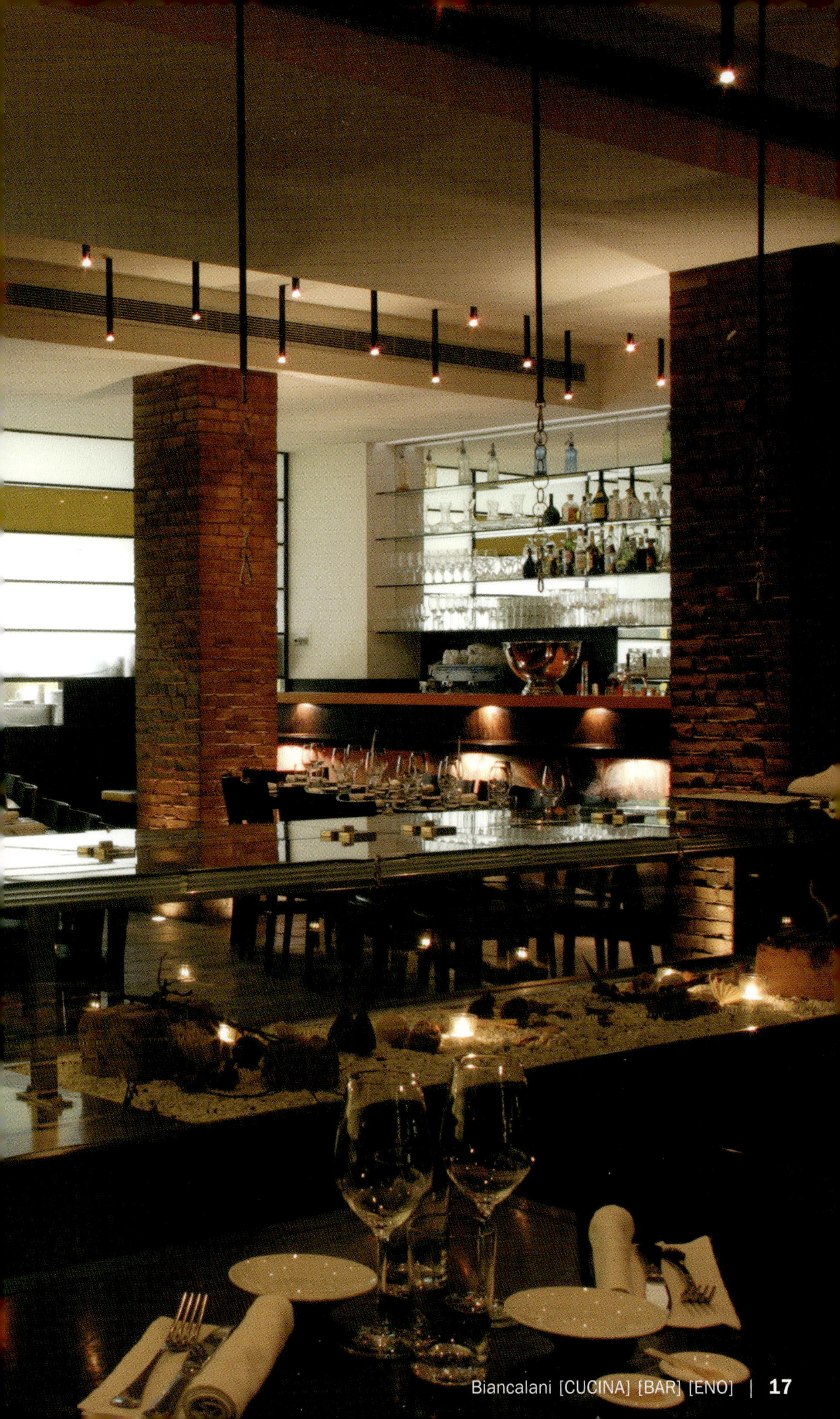

Parmesanmousse
mit Pesto-Tomaten

Parmesan Mousse with Pesto-Tomatoes

Mousse de parmesan sur lit de tomates au pesto

Mousse de parmesano con pesto y tomates

Mousse di parmigiano con pomodori al pesto

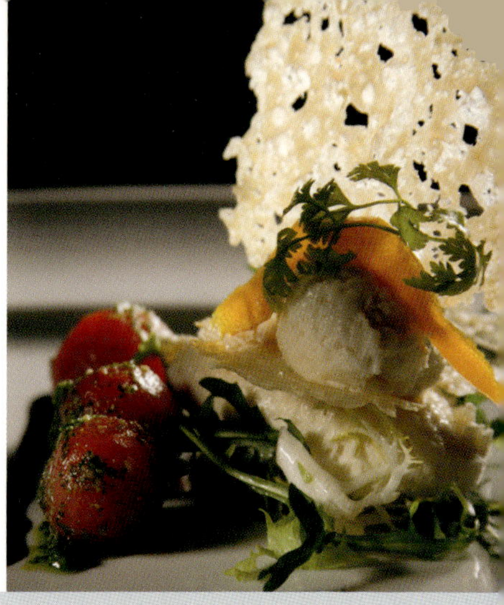

160 ml Milch
1 TL Olivenöl
½ Knoblauchzehe, gehackt
Salz, Pfeffer, Muskat, weißer Balsamico-Essig
160 g Parmesan
160 ml Sahne, geschlagen

Milch, Olivenöl und Knoblauch aufkochen und etwas abkühlen lassen. Mit Salz, Pfeffer, Muskat und Essig abschmecken und den Parmesan in der Milchmischung auflösen. Kaltstellen. Dann die geschlagene Sahne unterheben und mind. 2 Stunden kaltstellen.

1 Bund Basilikum, gewaschen und gehackt
½ Knoblauchzehe, gehackt
50 g Pinienkerne, geröstet und gehackt
50 g Parmesan, gerieben

Salz, Pfeffer, Zucker
1 TL Orangenschale, gehackt
Olivenöl

Alle festen Zutaten mischen und so lange Olivenöl zugeben, bis eine cremige Paste entsteht. Abschmecken.

12 Kirschtomaten, gehäutet
100 g Rucola
4 Parmesanchips
Dunkler Balsamico-Essig

Die Kirschtomaten mit dem Pesto mischen, mind. 1 Stunde marinieren lassen, pro Teller eine Nocke Mousse abstechen und mit den Tomaten und dem Rucola anrichten. Mit restlichem Pesto, Balsamico-Essig und Parmesanchips dekorieren.

160 ml milk
1 tsp olive oil
½ clove of garlic, chopped
Salt, pepper, nutmeg, white balsamic vinegar
5 ½ oz parmesan cheese
160 ml cream, whipped

Bring milk, olive oil and garlic to a boil and let it cool down. Season with salt, pepper, nutmeg and vinegar and dissolve the parmesan cheese in the milk mixture. Chill. Fold in the whipped cream and chill for another 2 hours.

1 bunch basil, washed and chopped
½ clove of garlic, chopped
2 oz pine nuts, toasted and chopped
2 oz parmesan cheese, grated

Salt, pepper, sugar
1 tsp orange zest, chopped
Olive oil

Combine all solid ingredients and add olive oil until it resembles a creamy paste. Season.

12 cherry tomatoes, peeled
3 ½ oz arugula
4 parmesan cheese slices
Dark balsamic vinegar

Combine cherry tomatoes with pesto and marinate for at least 1 hour, place one scoop of mousse on each plate and arrange with tomatoes and arugula. Decorate with leftover pesto, balsamic vinegar and parmesan cheese slices

160 ml de lait
1 c. à café d'huile d'olive
½ gousse d'ail, hachée
Sel, poivre, muscade, vinaigre balsamique blanc
160 g de parmesan
160 ml de crème liquide, battue

Faire bouillir le lait, l'huile d'olive et l'ail et laisser refroidir. Assaisonner avec le sel, le poivre, la muscade et le vinaigre et faire fondre le parmesan dans la préparation à base de lait. Mettre au frais. Ajouter ensuite la crème liquide battue et mettre au frais pendant au moins 2 heures.

1 bouquet de basilic, lavé et haché
½ gousse d'ail, hachée
50 g de pignons de pin, grillés et hachés
50 g de parmesan, râpé

Sel, poivre, sucre
1 c. à café d'écorce d'orange, hachée
Huile d'olive

Mélanger tous les ingrédients non liquides et ajouter de l'huile d'olive pour obtenir une pâte crémeuse. Saler et poivrer.

12 tomates cerises, sans peau
100 g de roquette
4 chips de parmesan
Vinaigre balsamique brun

Mélanger les tomates cerises au pesto, faire mariner pendant au moins 1 heure, former une quenelle de mousse sur chaque assiette et disposer avec les tomates et la roquette. Décorer avec le pesto restant, le vinaigre balsamique et les chips de parmesan.

160 ml de leche
1 cucharadita de aceite de oliva
½ diente de ajo, picado
Sal, pimienta, nuez moscada, vinagre balsámico blanco
160 g de queso parmesano
160 ml de nata, batida

Hierva la leche, el aceite de oliva y el ajo y déjelo enfriar un poco. Sazone con sal, pimienta, nuez moscada y vinagre e incorpore el queso parmesano a la mezcla. Póngala en el frigorífico. Añada después la nata batida y vuelva a dejar la mezcla en el frigorífico durante 2 horas como mínimo.

1 ramillete de albahaca, lavada y picada
½ de diente de ajo, picado
50 g de piñones, tostados y picados
50 g de queso parmesano, rallado

Sal, pimienta, azúcar
1 cucharadita de piel de naranja, picada
Aceite de oliva

Mezcle todos los ingredientes sólidos y añada aceite de oliva hasta conseguir una pasta cremosa. Sazone.

12 tomates cereza, pelados
100 g de rucola
4 laminillas de parmesano
Vinagre balsámico oscuro

Mezcle los tomates cereza con el pesto y deje que marinen durante 1 hora como mínimo. Ponga en cada plato un montoncito de mousse y los tomates con la rucola. Decore con el resto del pesto, el vinagre balsámico y las láminillas de parmesano.

160 ml di latte
1 cucchiaino di olio d'oliva
½ spicchio d'aglio tritato
Sale, pepe, noce moscata, aceto balsamico bianco
160 g di parmigiano
160 ml di panna montata

Bollire il latte, l'olio d'oliva e l'aglio e lasciarli raffreddare un poco. Assaggiare e condire con sale, pepe, noce moscata ed aceto. Sciogliere infine il parmigiano nel composto e mettere in frigorifero. Unire la panna montata e tenere in frigorifero per almeno 2 ore.

1 mazzetto di basilico lavato e tritato
½ spicchio d'aglio tritato
50 g di pinoli tostati e tritati
50 g di parmigiano grattugiato

Sale, pepe, zucchero
1 cucchiaino di buccia d'arancia tritata
Olio d'oliva q.b.

Mescolare tutti gli ingredienti solidi ed aggiungere olio d'oliva finché il composto sarà cremoso. Assaggiare e regolare il condimento.

12 pomodorini spellati
100 g di rucola
4 bocconcini di parmigiano
Aceto balsamico scuro

Mescolare i pomodorini ed il pesto e lasciar marinare per almeno 1 ora. Mettere in ogni piatto una noce di mousse e disporvi intorno i pomodori e la rucola. Guarnire con il pesto rimasto, l'aceto balsamico ed i bocconcini di parmigiano.

Bristol Bar

Design: Oana Rosen | Chef: Phatapong Sriwunglas
Owners: Micky Rosen, Alex Urseanu

Ludwigstraße 15 | 60327 Frankfurt | Gallusviertel
Phone: +49 69 24 23 90
www.bristol-hotel.de
Subway: Hauptbahnhof
Opening hours: 24 hours, food until 6 am
Average price: € 14
Cuisine: Mixed
Special features: Monthly club night

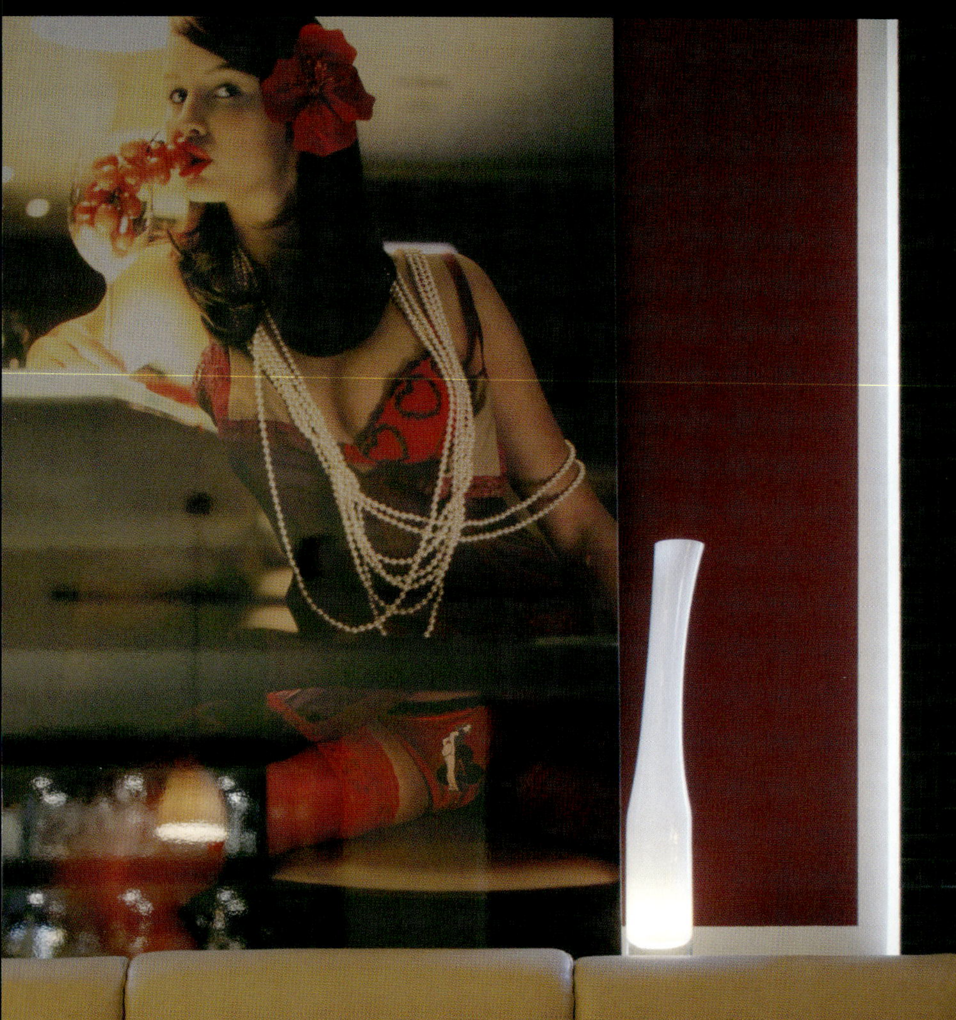

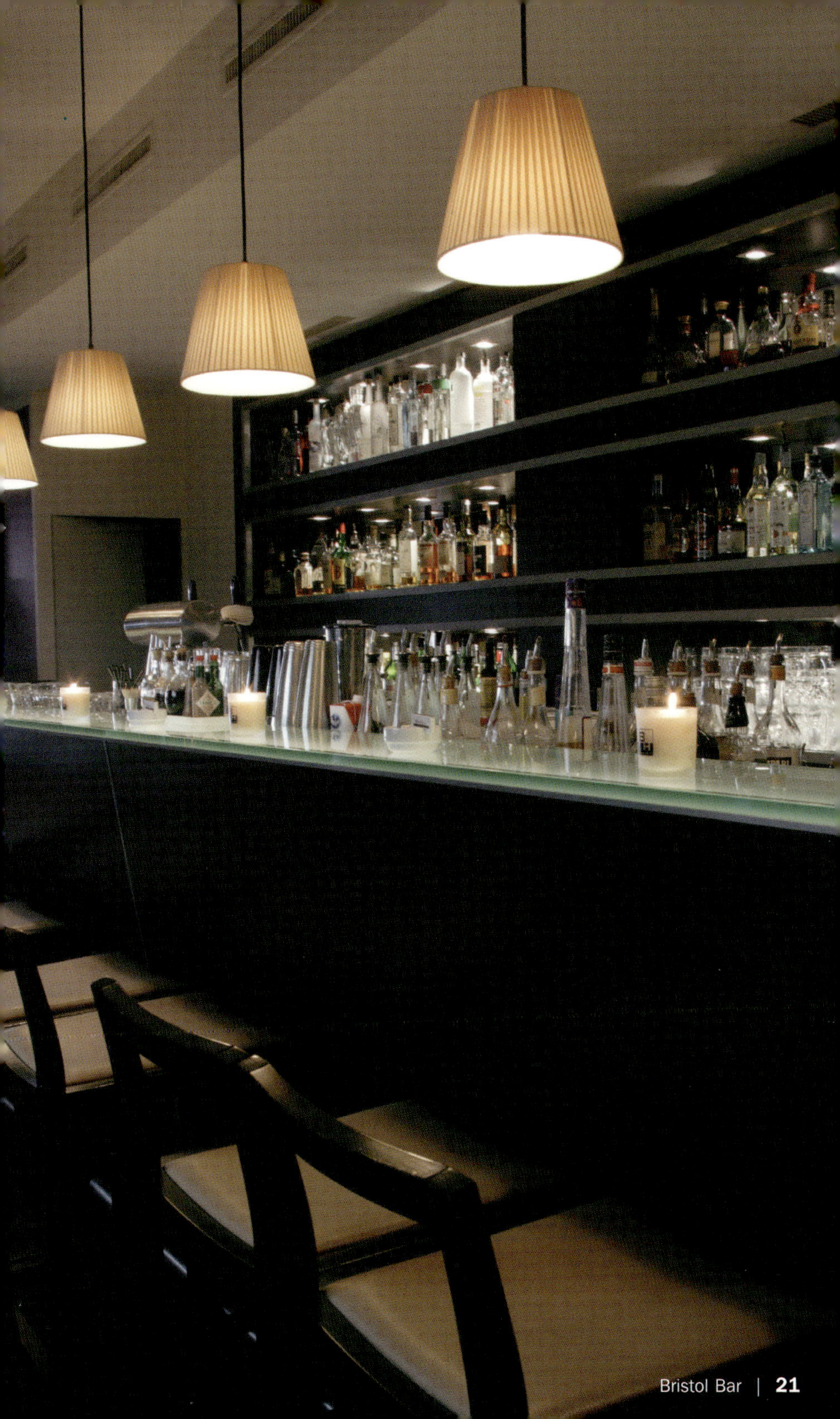

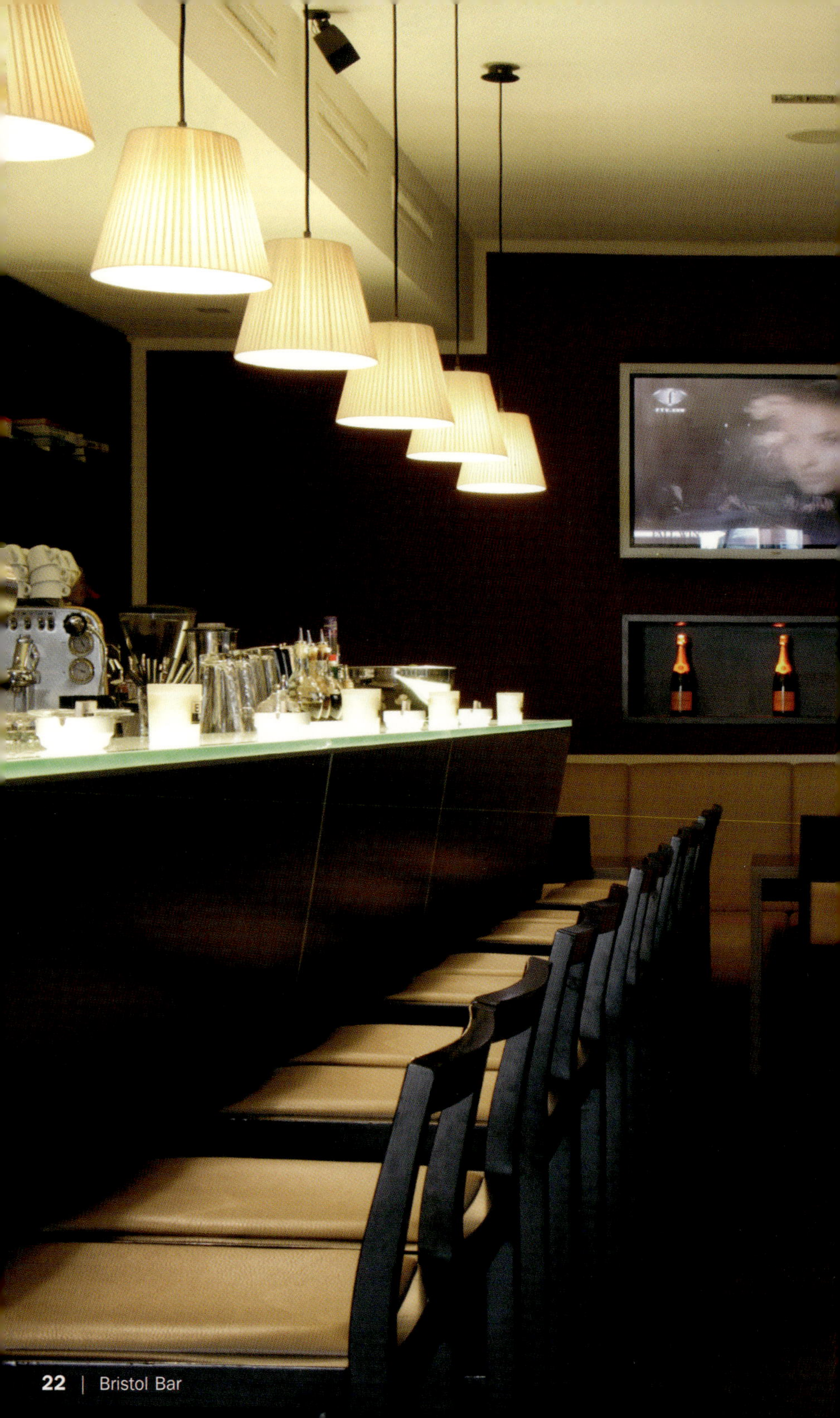

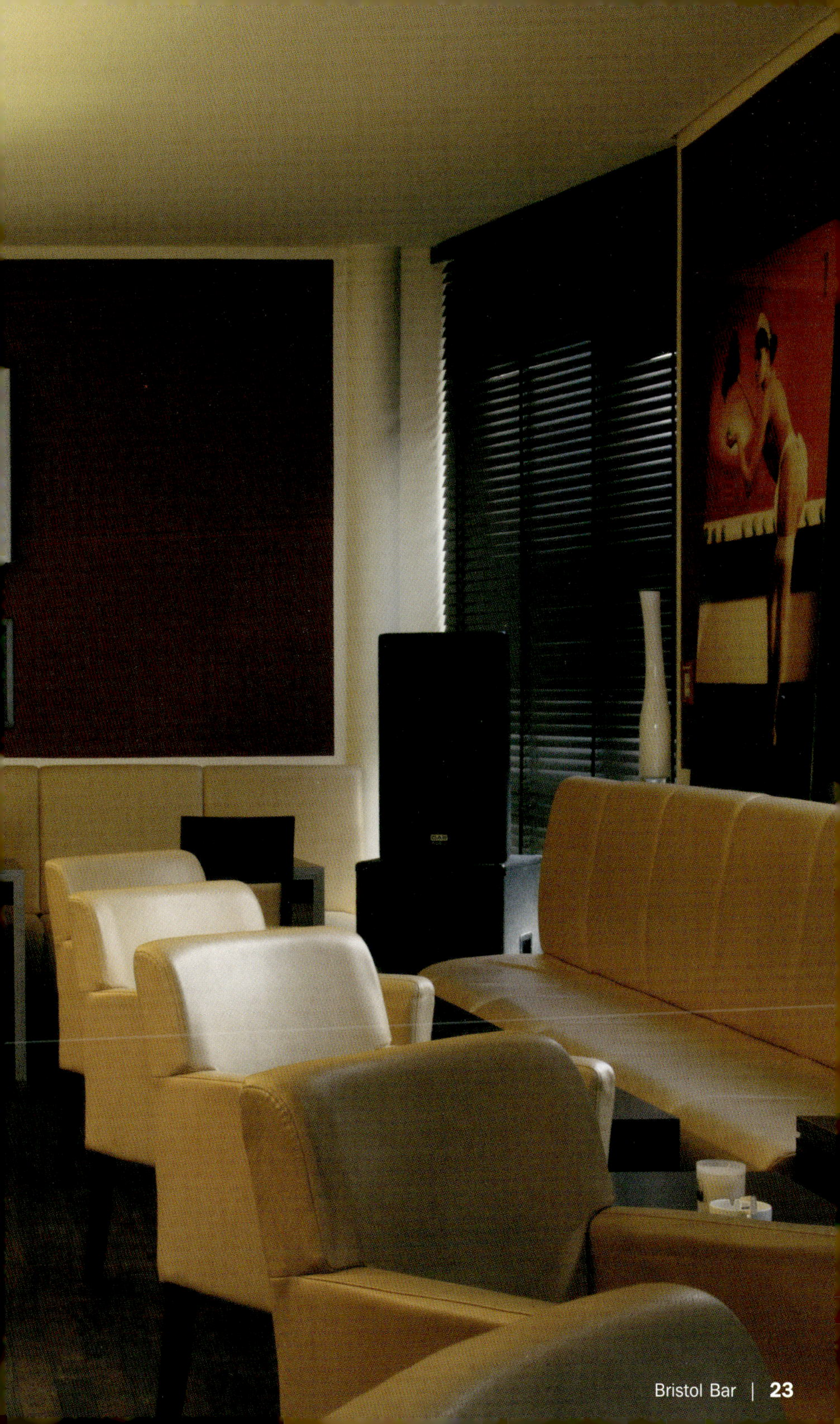

cesar's

Design: Linda Hillenbrand | Chef: Vito Tosto
Owner: Manfred Hillenbrand

Friedhofstraße 72 | 63263 Frankfurt | Neu-Isenburg
Phone: +49 61 02 37 77 11
www.cesars-restaurant.de
Subway: Am Trieb
Opening hours: Mon–Sun 11 am to midnight
Average price: € 15
Cuisine: Light, traditional Italian

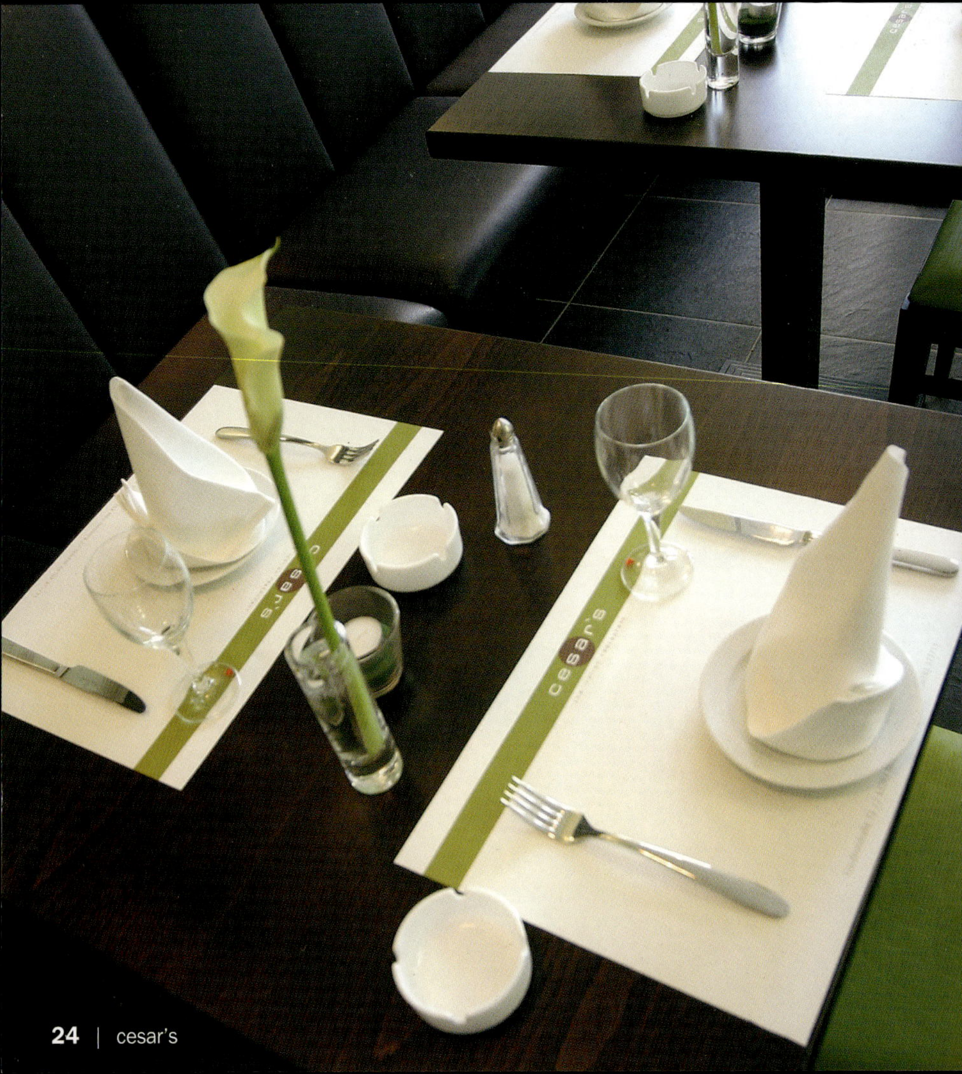

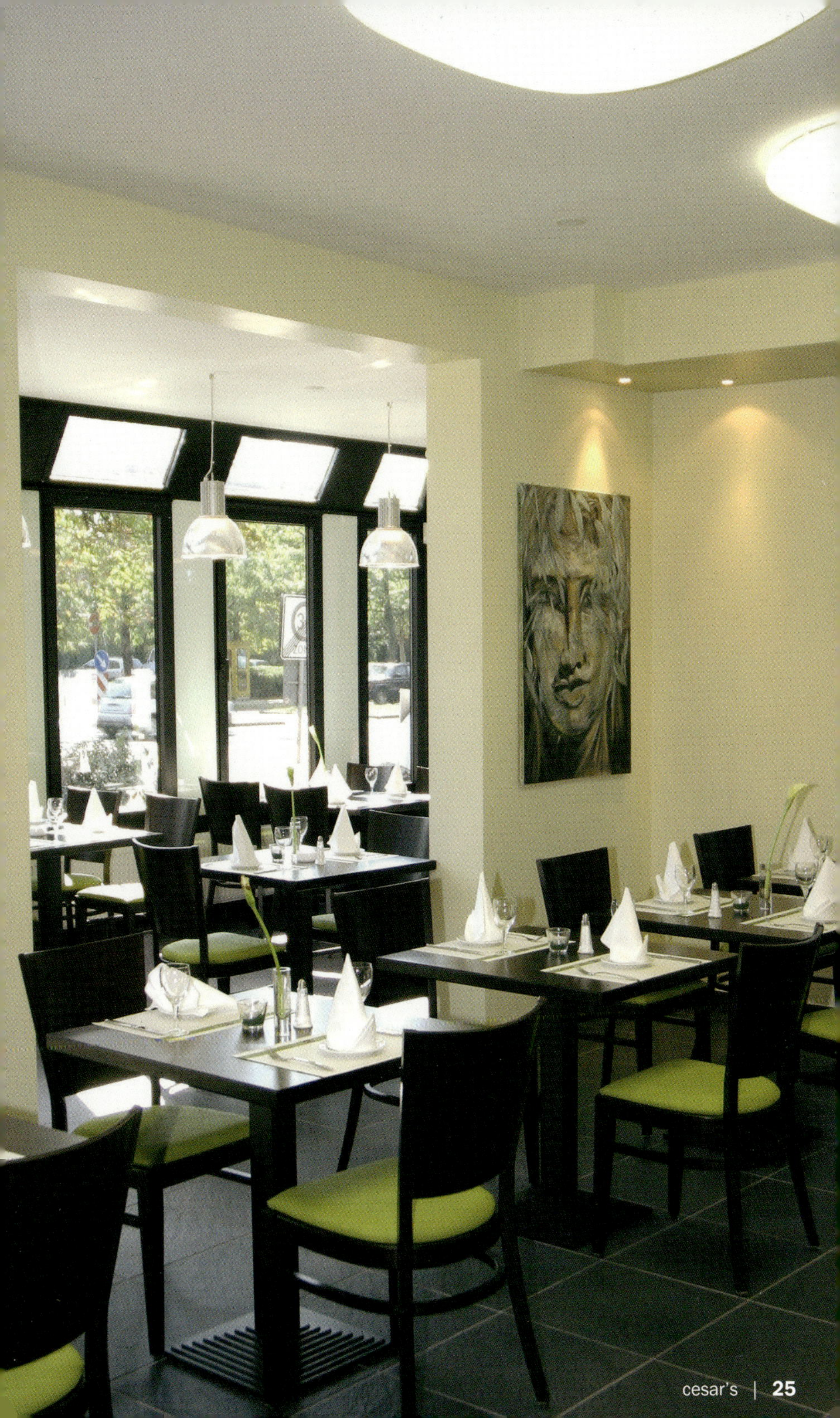

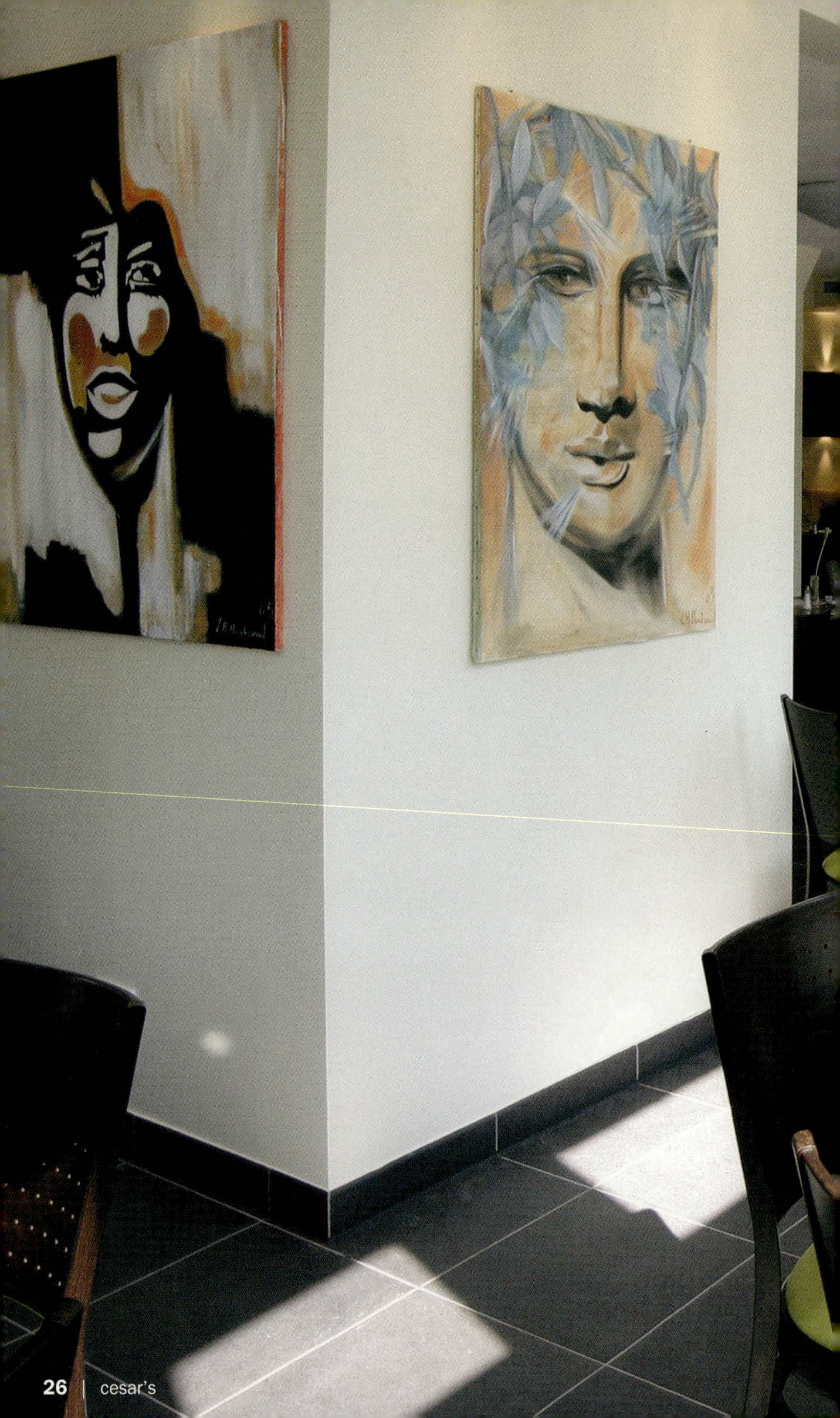

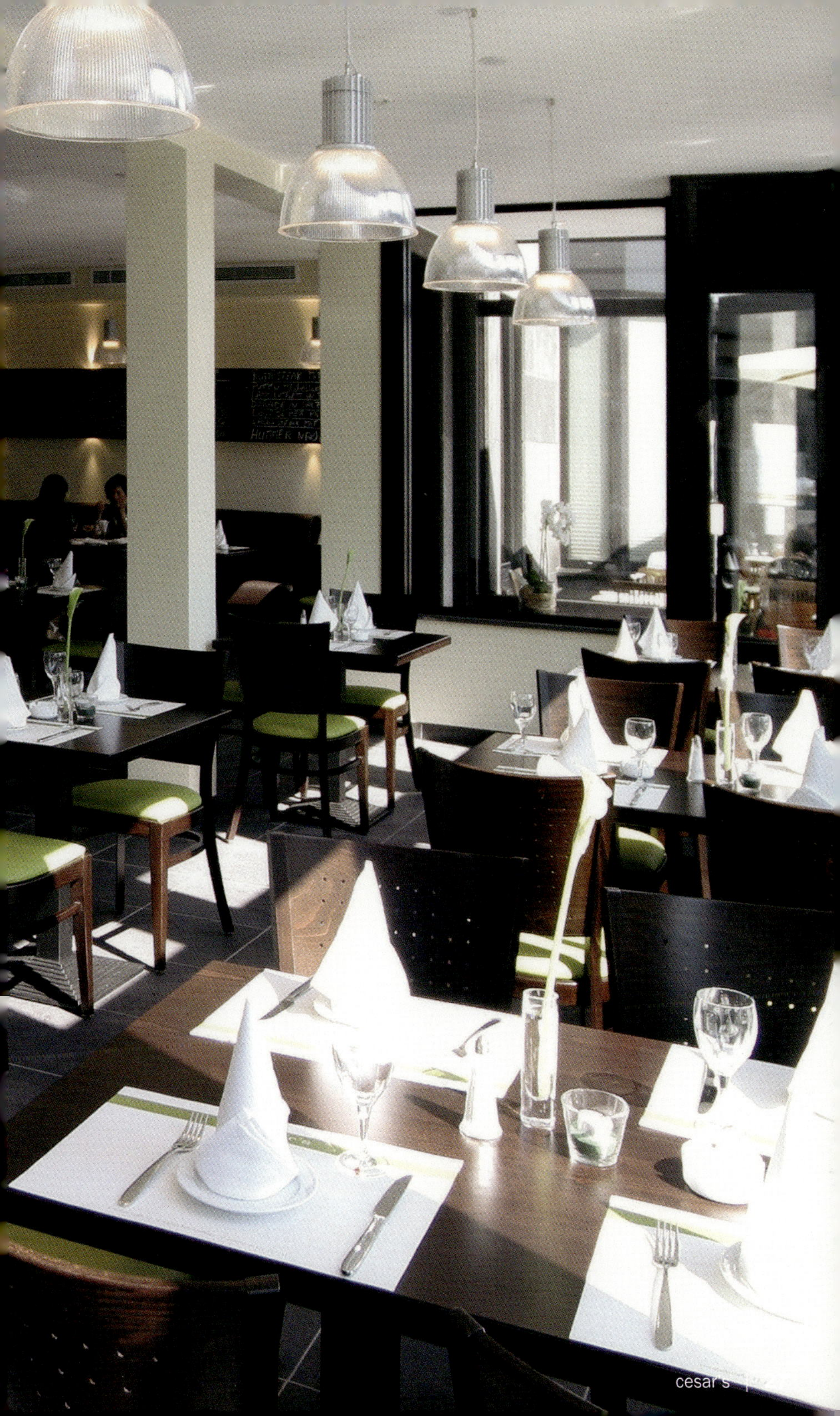

cesar's

Linguini
allo scoglio

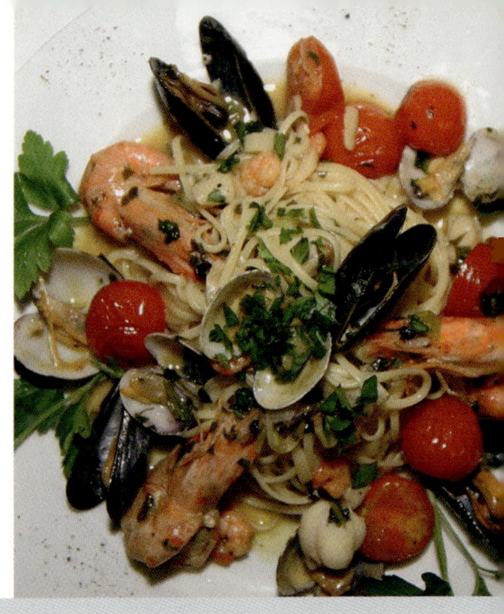

500 g Linguini, al dente
1 Knoblauchzehe, in feinen Scheiben
4 rote Chilischoten, schräg halbiert
16 Kirschtomaten, halbiert
200 g Seeteufel, gewürfelt
16 Venusmuscheln, gewaschen
16 Miesmuscheln, gewaschen
12 Scampi, gewaschen
200 ml Weißwein
3 EL Olivenöl
Salz, Pfeffer

Petersilie und Schnittlauch zur Dekoration

Die Knoblauchscheiben in Olivenöl anbraten, Chili und Kirschtomaten zugeben und kurz anschwitzen. Die Seeteufelwürfel, die Muscheln und die Scampi zugeben und 2 Minuten mitbraten. Mit Weißwein ablöschen und würzen. Die Linguini in die Pfanne geben und evtl. noch einmal würzen. Mit Petersilie und Schnittlauch dekorieren.

1 lb 2 oz linguini, al dente
1 clove of garlic, in thin slices
4 red chilies, cut in half diagonally
16 cherry tomatoes, halved
7 oz angler fish, diced
16 hard clams, cleaned
16 mussels, cleaned
12 scampi, cleaned
200 ml white wine
3 tbsp olive oil
Salt, pepper

Parsley and chives for decoration

Sear the garlic slices in olive oil, add chilies and cherry tomatoes and toss quickly. Add the angler fish, clams, mussels and scampi and sear for another 2 minutes. Deglaze with white wine and season. Place the linguini in the pan and season again if necessary. Decorate with parsley and chives.

500 g de linguinis, al dente
1 gousse d'ail, en fines tranches
4 piments rouges, coupés en deux et en biais
16 tomates cerises, coupées en deux
200 g de lotte, coupée en dés
16 praires, lavées
16 moules, lavées
12 scampi, lavées
200 ml vin blanc
3 c. à soupe d'huile d'olive
Sel, poivre

Persil et ciboulette pour décorer

Faire revenir les tranches d'ail dans l'huile d'olive, ajouter le piment et les tomates cerises et faire suer un court instant. Ajouter les dés de lotte, les moules, les praires et les scampi et faire revenir pendant 2 minutes. Ajouter le vin blanc et assaisonner. Mettre les linguistes dans la poêle et assaisonner de nouveau si nécessaire. Décorer avec le persil et la ciboulette.

500 g de *linguini, al dente*
1 diente de ajo, en finas láminas
4 guindillas rojas, en mitades diagonales
16 tomates cereza, en mitades
200 g de rape, en dados
16 almejas, lavadas
16 mejillones, lavados
12 gambas, lavadas
200 ml de vino blanco
3 cucharadas de aceite de oliva
Sal, pimienta

Perejil y cebollino para decorar

Sofría las láminas de ajo en aceite de oliva, incorpore la guindilla y los tomates cereza y rehóguelos brevemente. Añada los dados de rape, los moluscos y las gambas y sofríalos durante 2 minutos. Incorpore el vino blanco y sazone. Ponga los *linguini* en la sartén y vuelva a sazonar si fuera necesario. Decore con perejil y cebollino.

500 g di trenette cotte al dente
1 spicchio d'aglio tagliato a fettine sottili
4 peperoncini rossi tagliati diagonalmente
16 pomodorini tagliati a metà
200 g di rane pescatrice tagliata a pezzetti
16 vongole pulite
16 cozze pulite
12 scampi puliti
200 ml di vino bianco
3 cucchiai di olio d'oliva
Sale, pepe

Prezzemolo ed erba cipollina per decorare

Dorare le fettine d'aglio nell'olio d'oliva, unire il peperoncino ed i pomodorini e rosolare brevemente. Aggiungere i pezzetti di rane, le vongole, le cozze e gli scampi e cuocere il tutto per 2 minuti. Bagnare con il vino bianco e condire. Aggiungere in padella le trenette ed eventualmente regolare il condimento. Guarnire con prezzemolo ed erba cipollina.

Coconut Groove

Design: Volker Bender | Chef: Ahmed Imourig
Owner: M.K.A Gastronomie Betriebs-GmbH

Kaiserstraße 53 | 60329 Frankfurt | Bahnhofsviertel
Phone: +49 69 27 10 79 99
www.coconut-groove.de
Subway: Frankfurt Hauptbahnhof
Opening hours: Mon–Fri 10 am to 1 am, Sat noon to 2 am, Sun closed
Average price: € 12
Cuisine: Miami New World

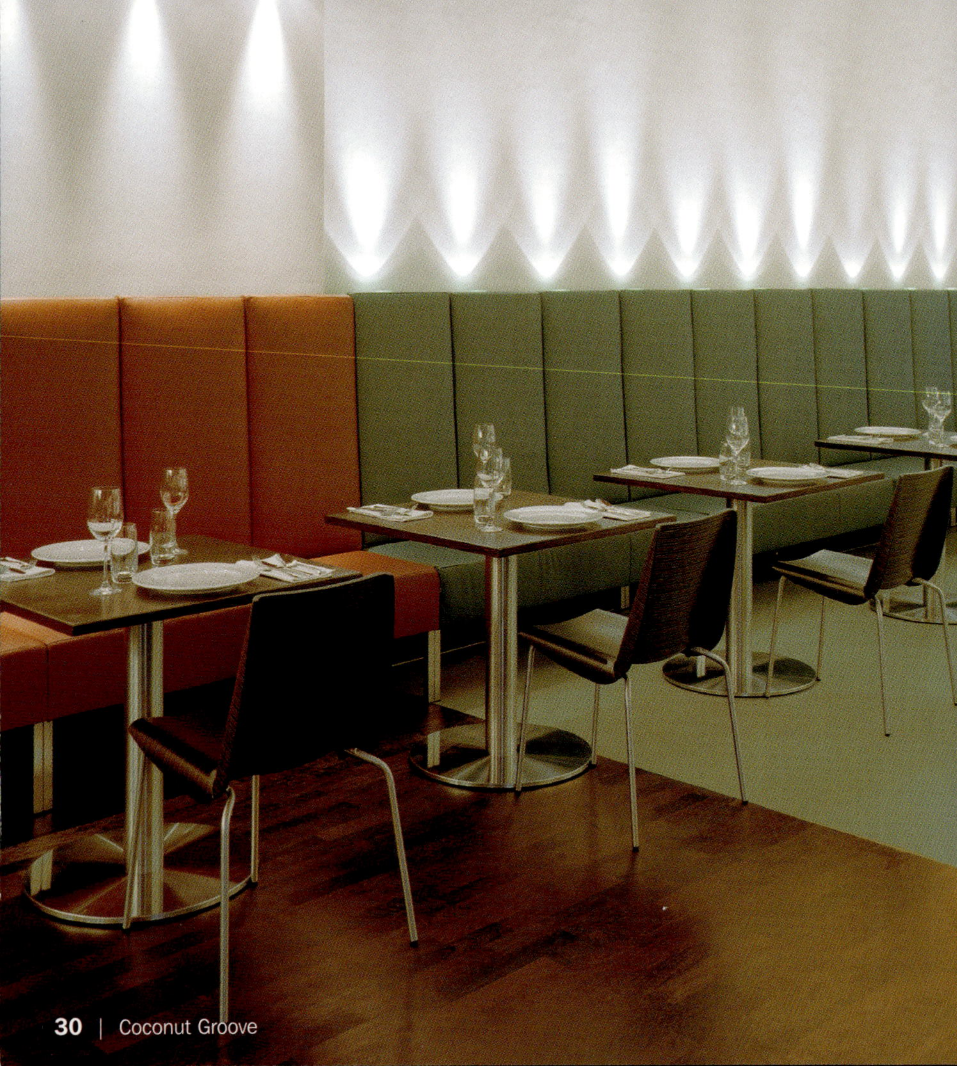

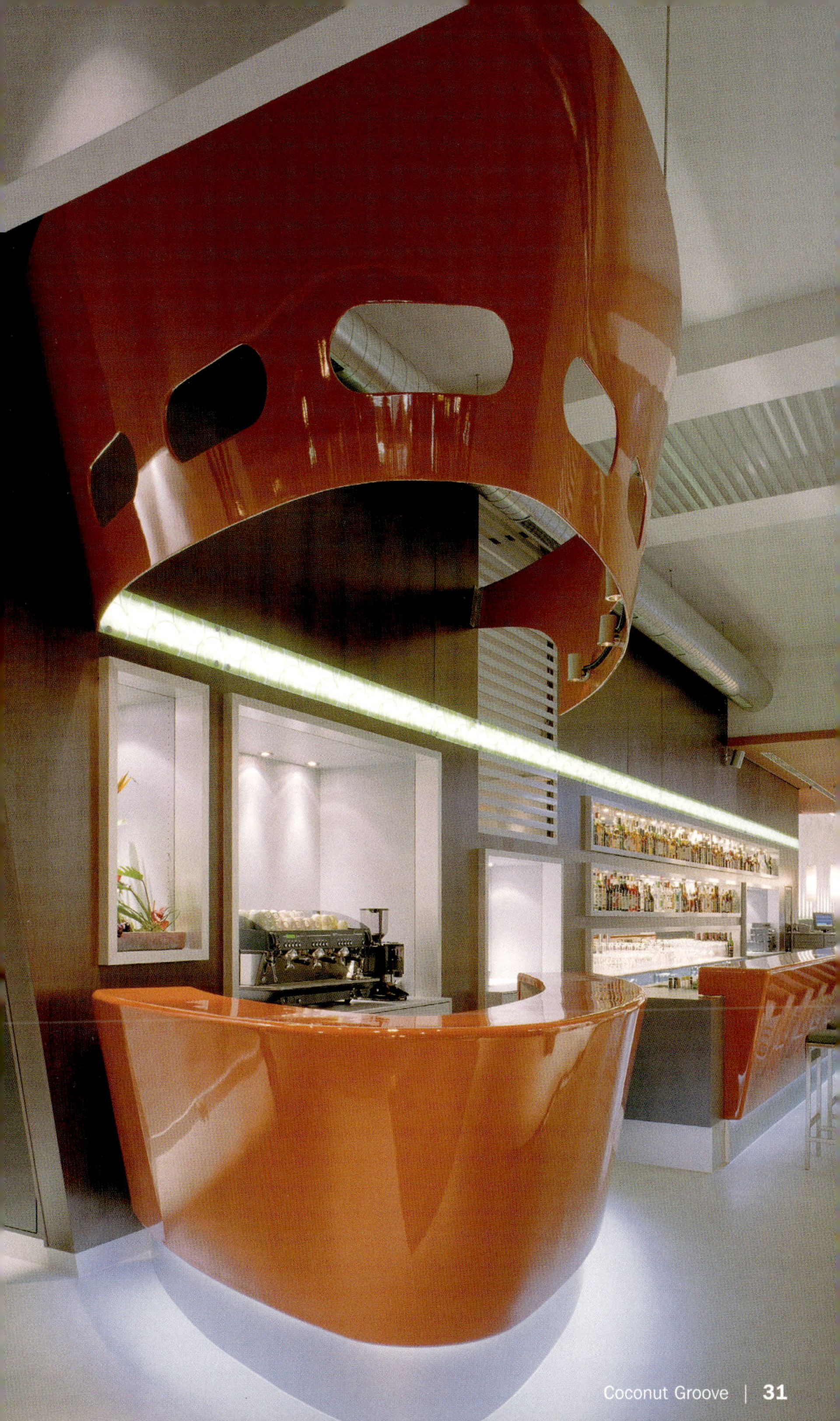

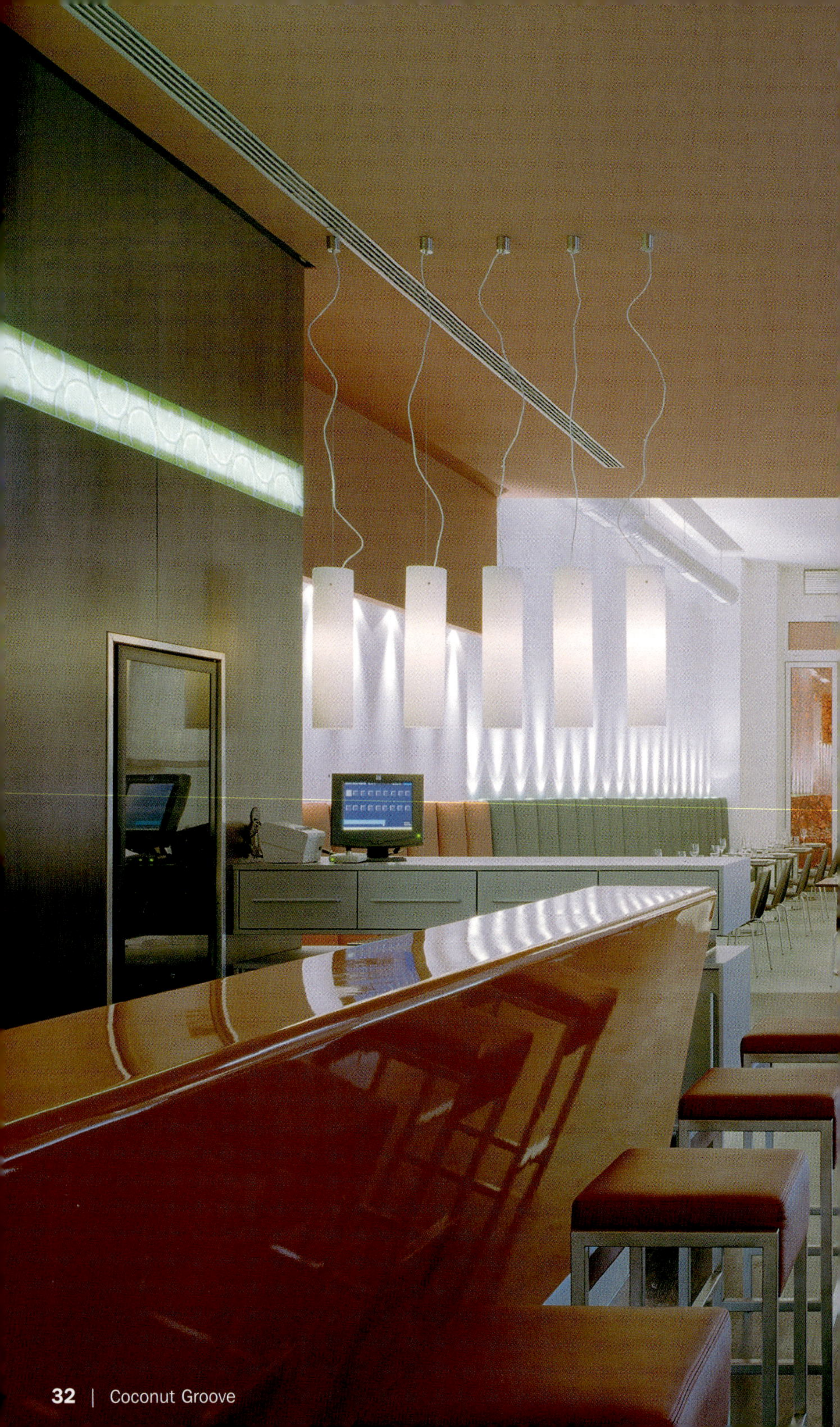

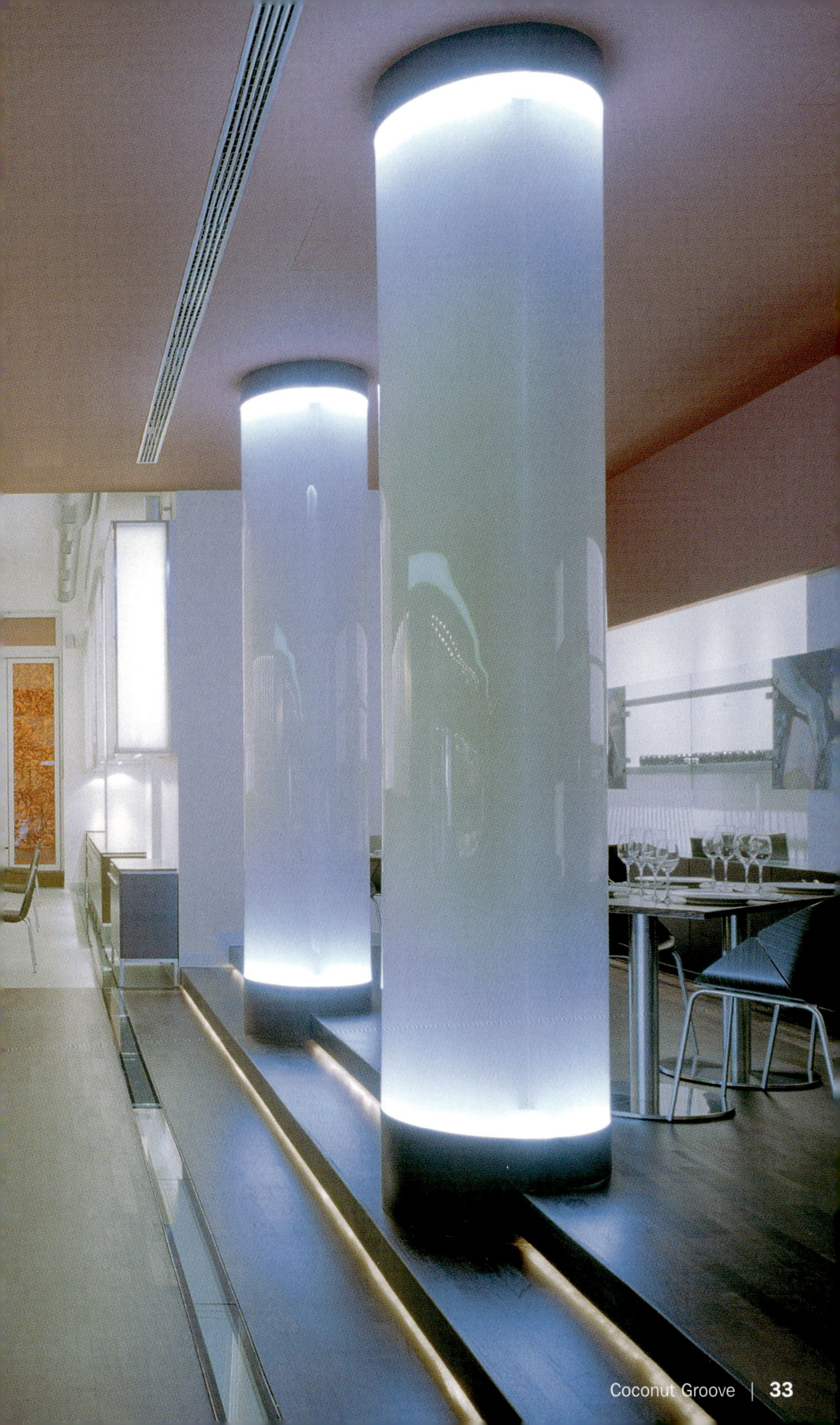

Das 21. Jahrhundert

Design: Oliver Uhlig | Chef: Steffen Wiesener
Owner: GbR Körner, Abbas, Rosenbaum

Oeder Weg 21 | 60313 Frankfurt | Nordend
Phone: +49 69 55 67 46
www.das-21-jahrhundert.de
Subway: Eschersheimerturm
Opening hours: Daily 10 am to open end
Average price: € 9
Cuisine: Crossover

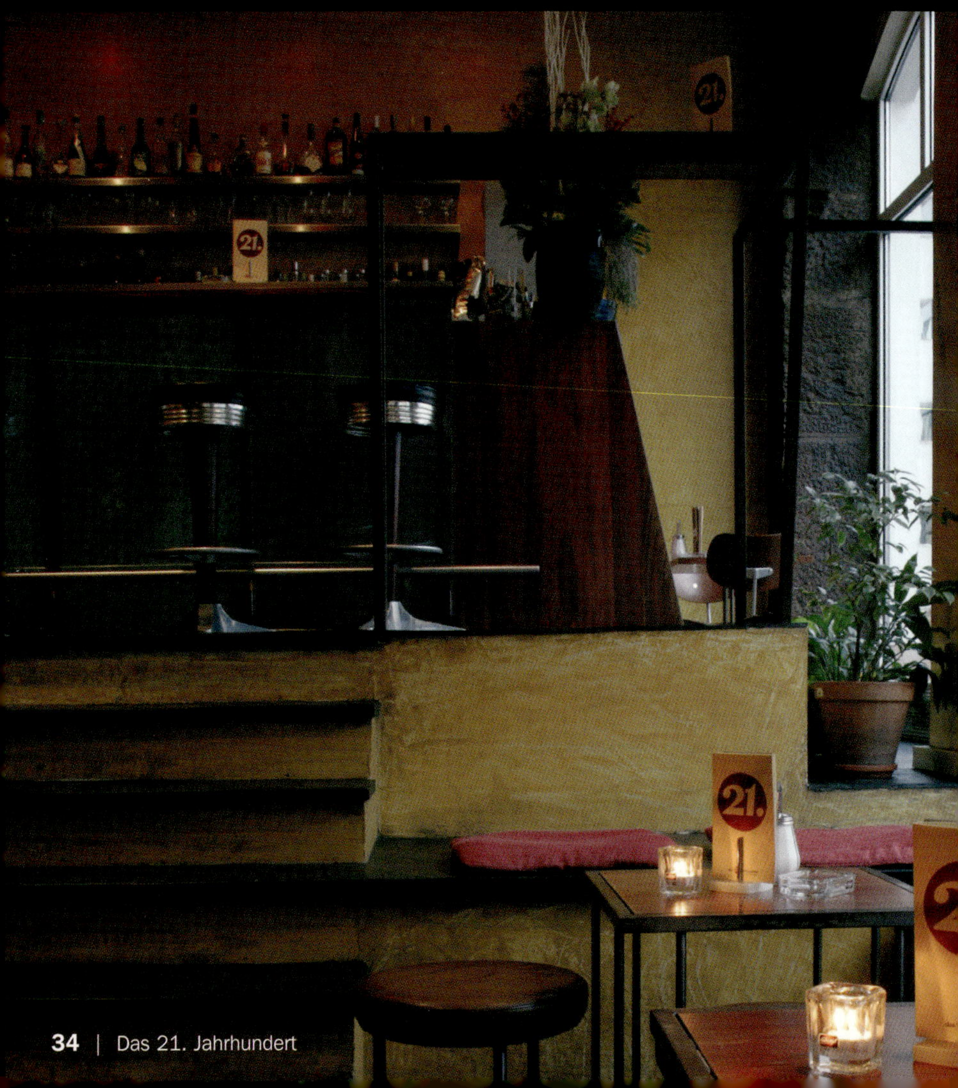

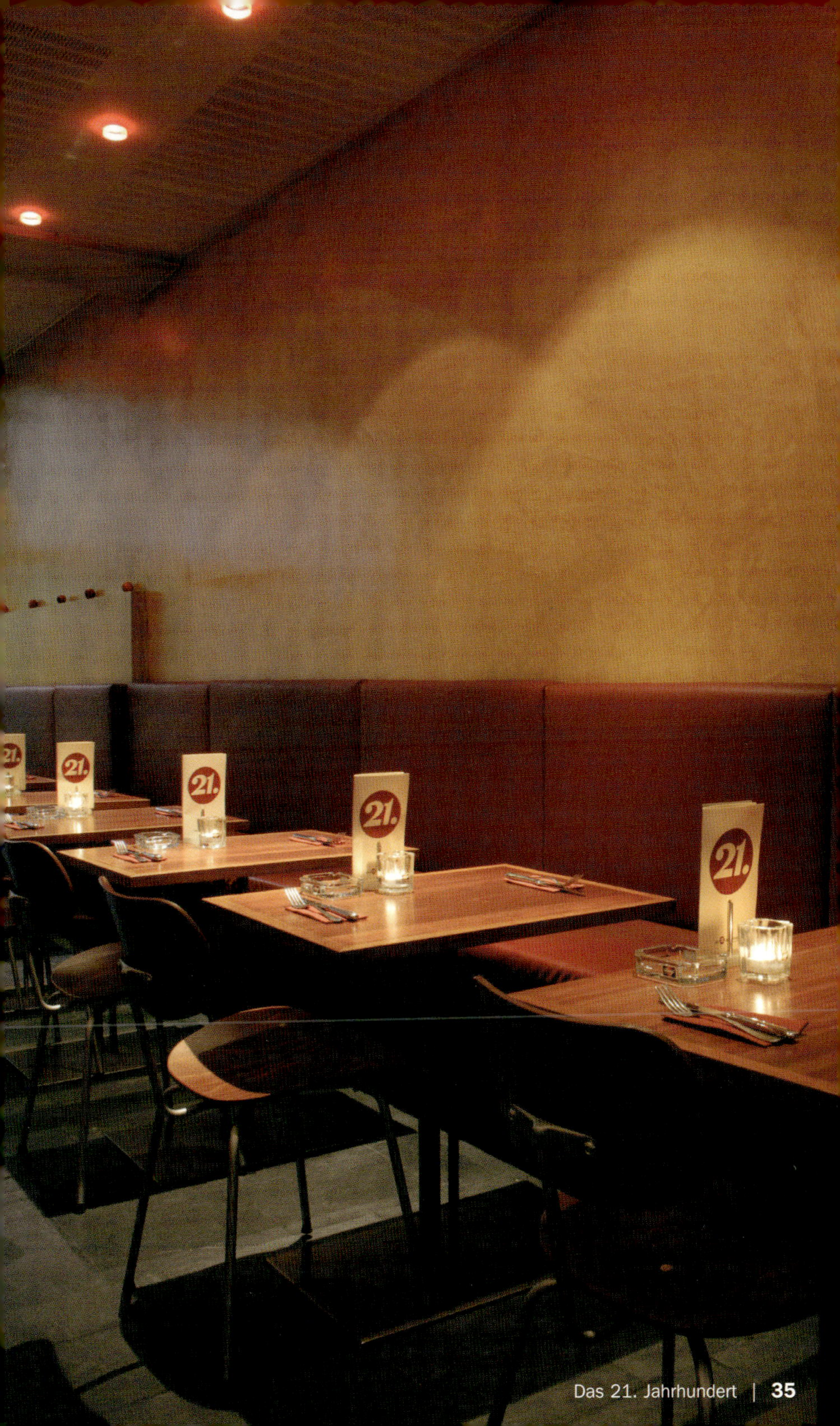

Destino

Design: Martin Willems | Chef: Konstantin Mezei
Owner: Goran Petreski

Habsburgerallee 9 | 60385 Frankfurt | Nordend
Phone: +49 69 24 24 08 88
www.destino-bar.de
Subway: Höhenstraße
Opening hours: Fri–Sat 6 pm to 2 am, Sun–Thu 6 pm to 1 am
Average price: € 5
Cuisine: Tapas, crossover
Special features: Seperate loft for events

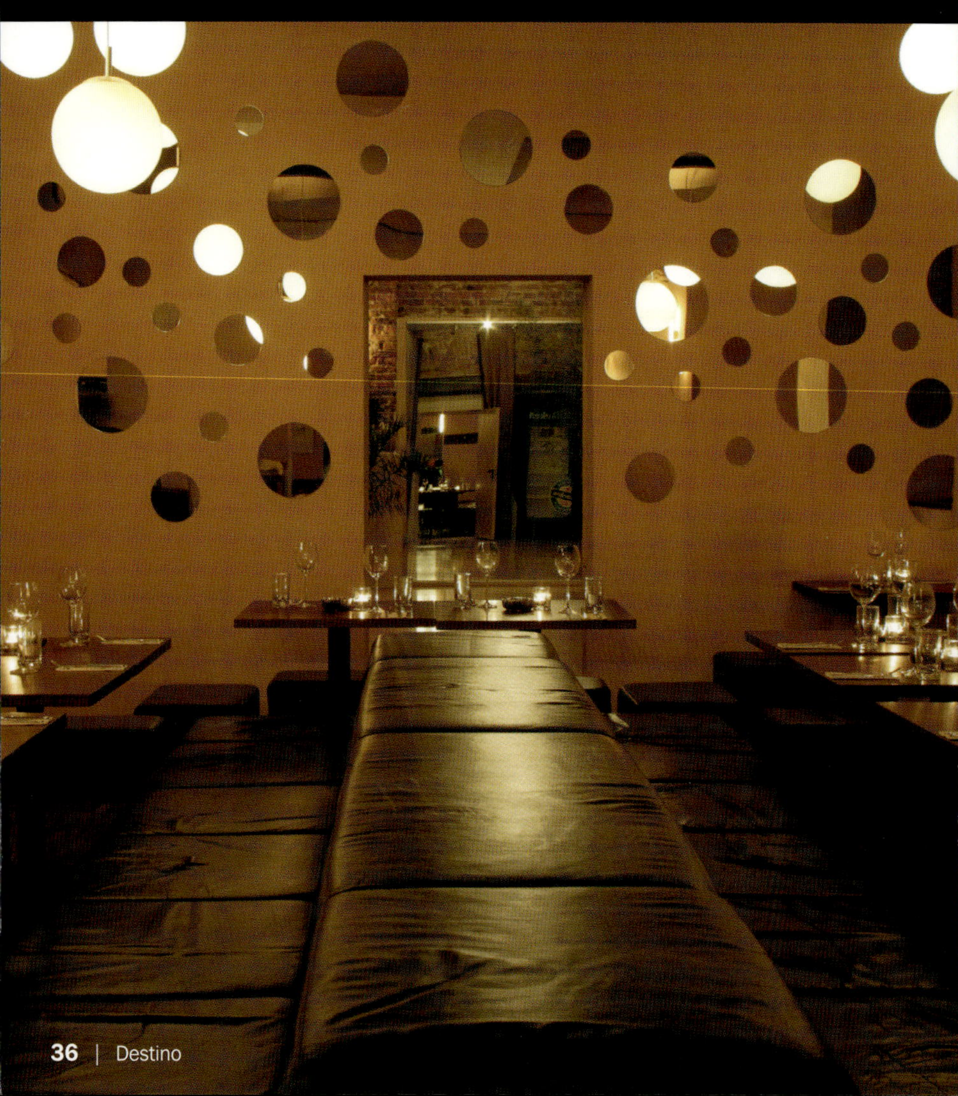

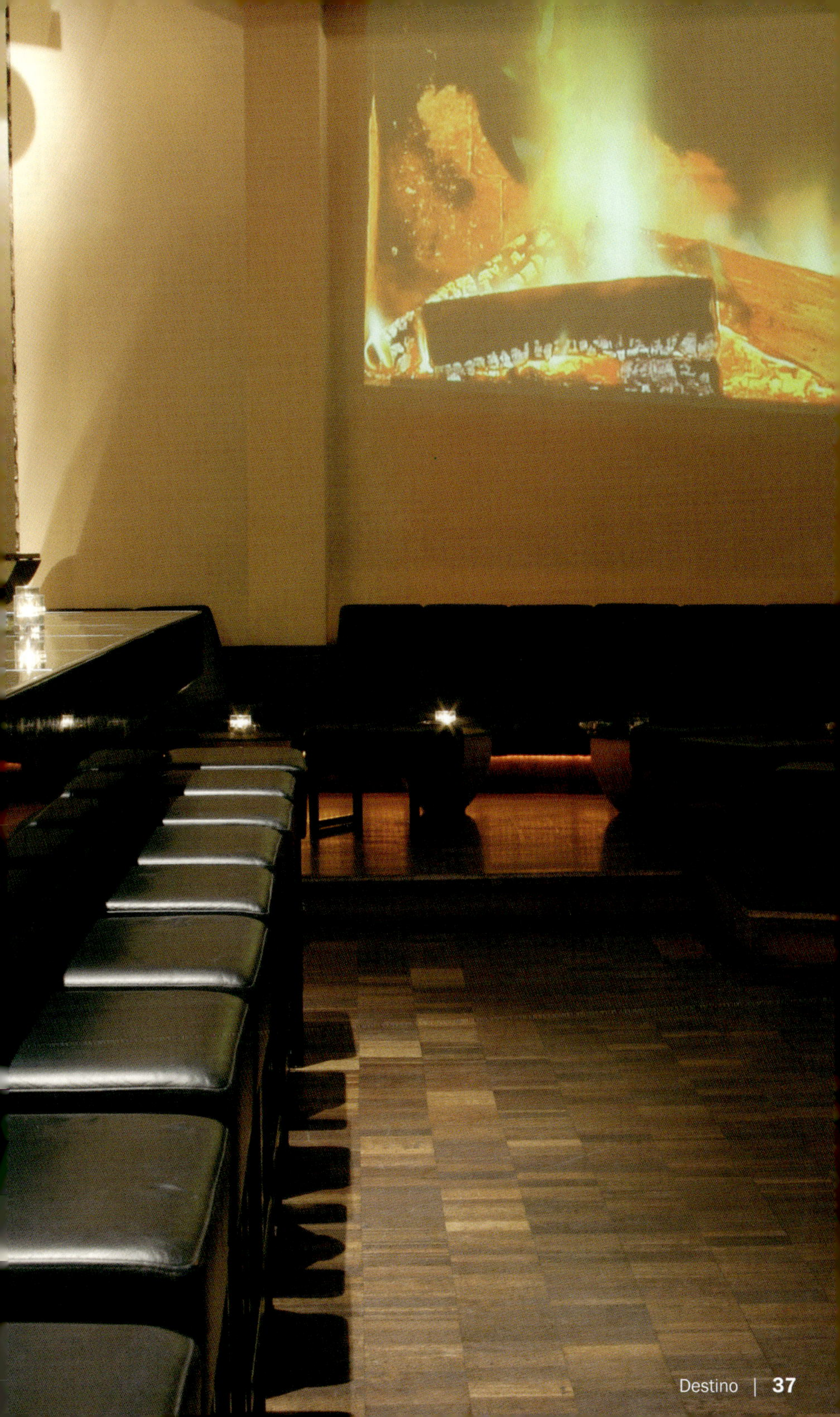

diamonds+pearls

Design: Vince Vega | Chef: Gregor Nowak
Owners: Dimitrios Chinitidis, Martin Peters

Carl-Theodor-Reiffenstein-Platz 6 | 60313 Frankfurt | Altstadt
Phone: +49 69 94 94 28 64
www.dp-frankfurt.de
Subway: Konstabler Wache, Hauptwache
Opening hours: Mon–Wed 11 am to 1 am, Thu–Sat 11 am to 2 am,
Sun 6 pm to 1 am
Average price: € 18
Cuisine: Regional and international

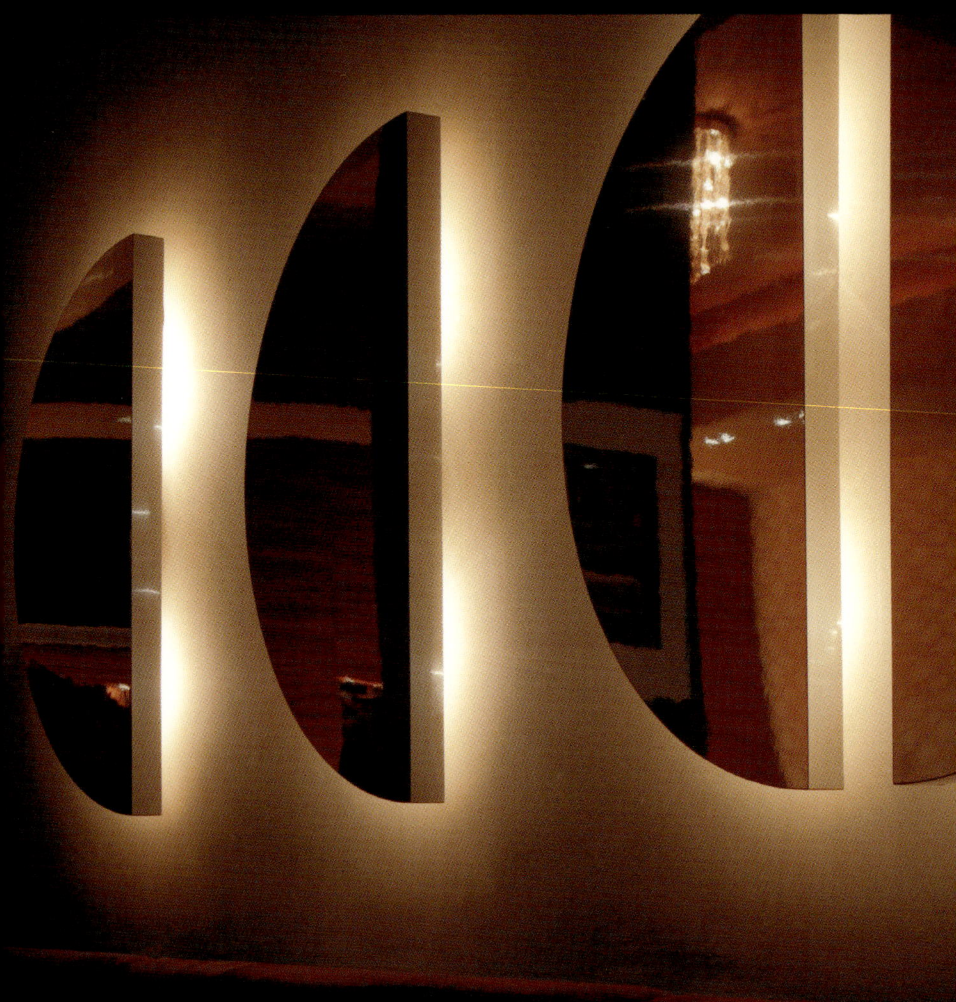

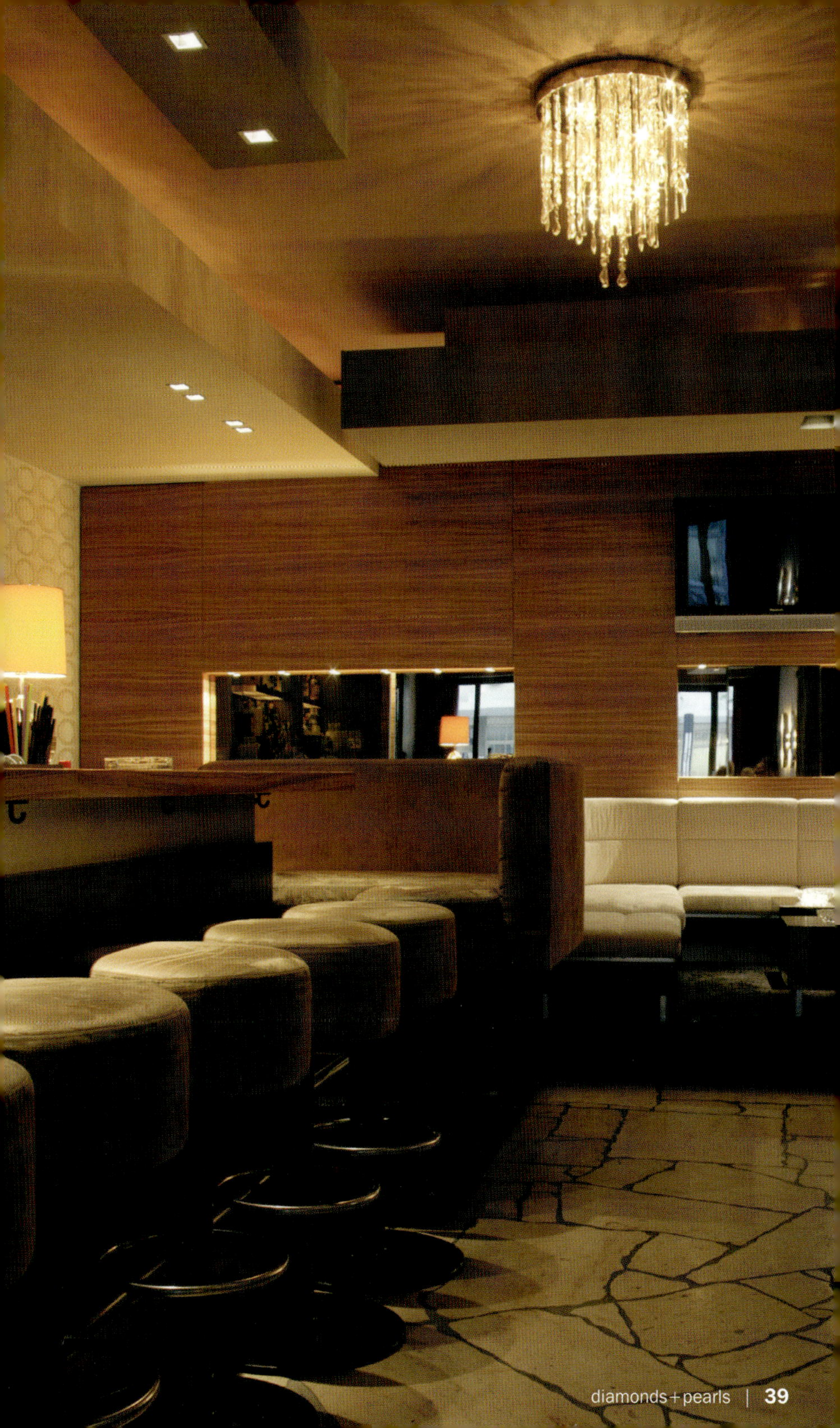

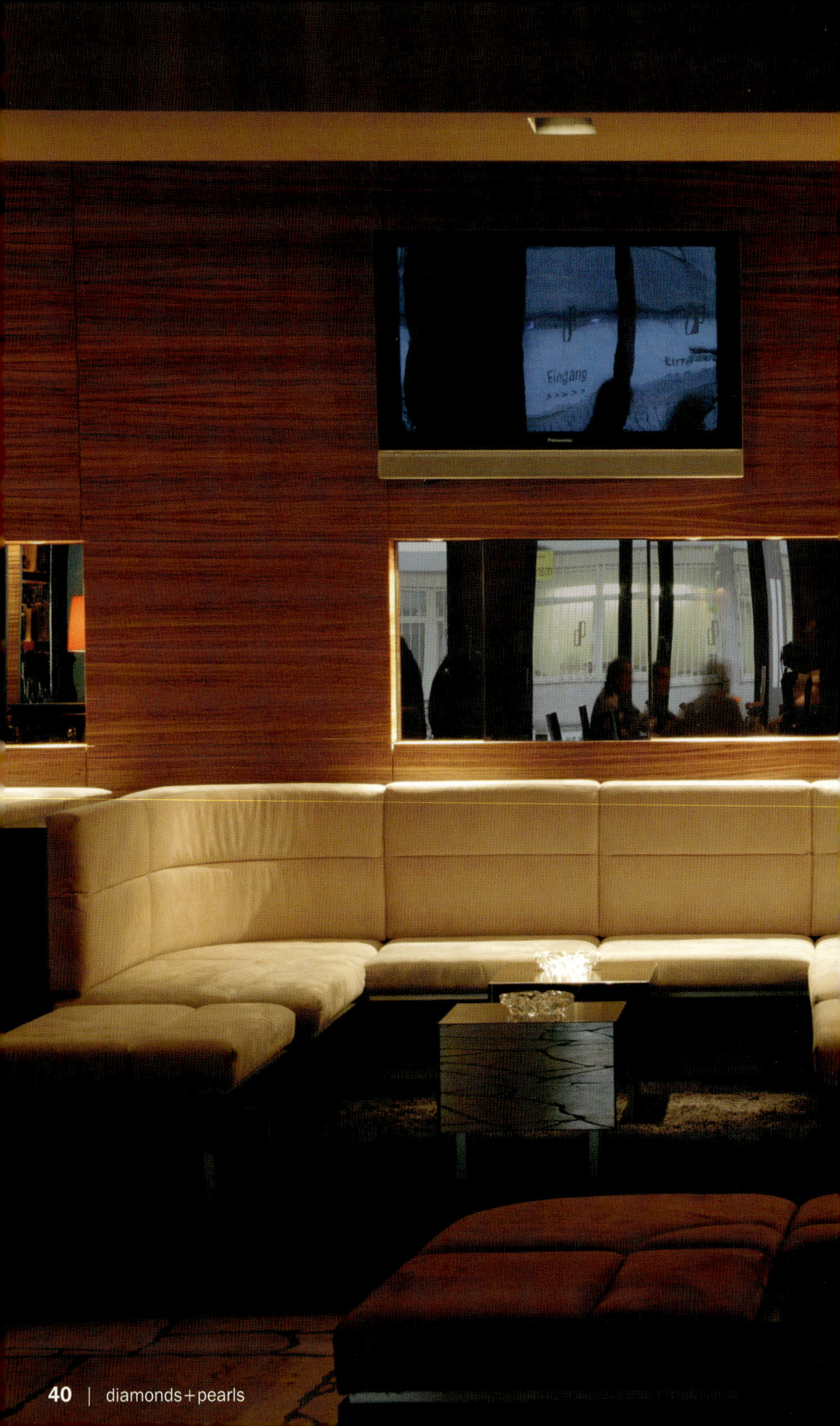

Eingang

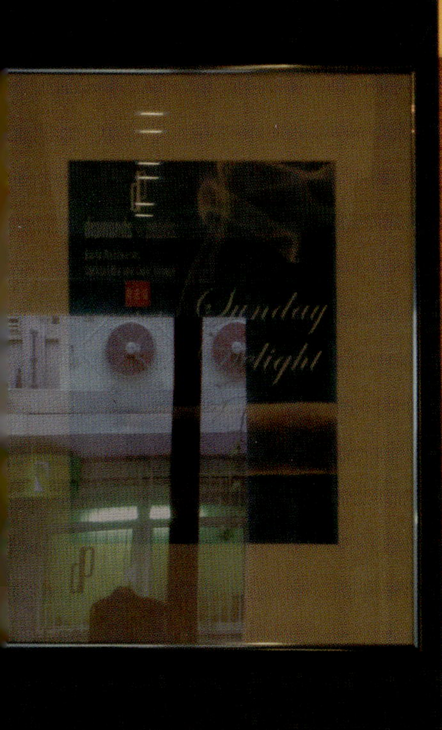

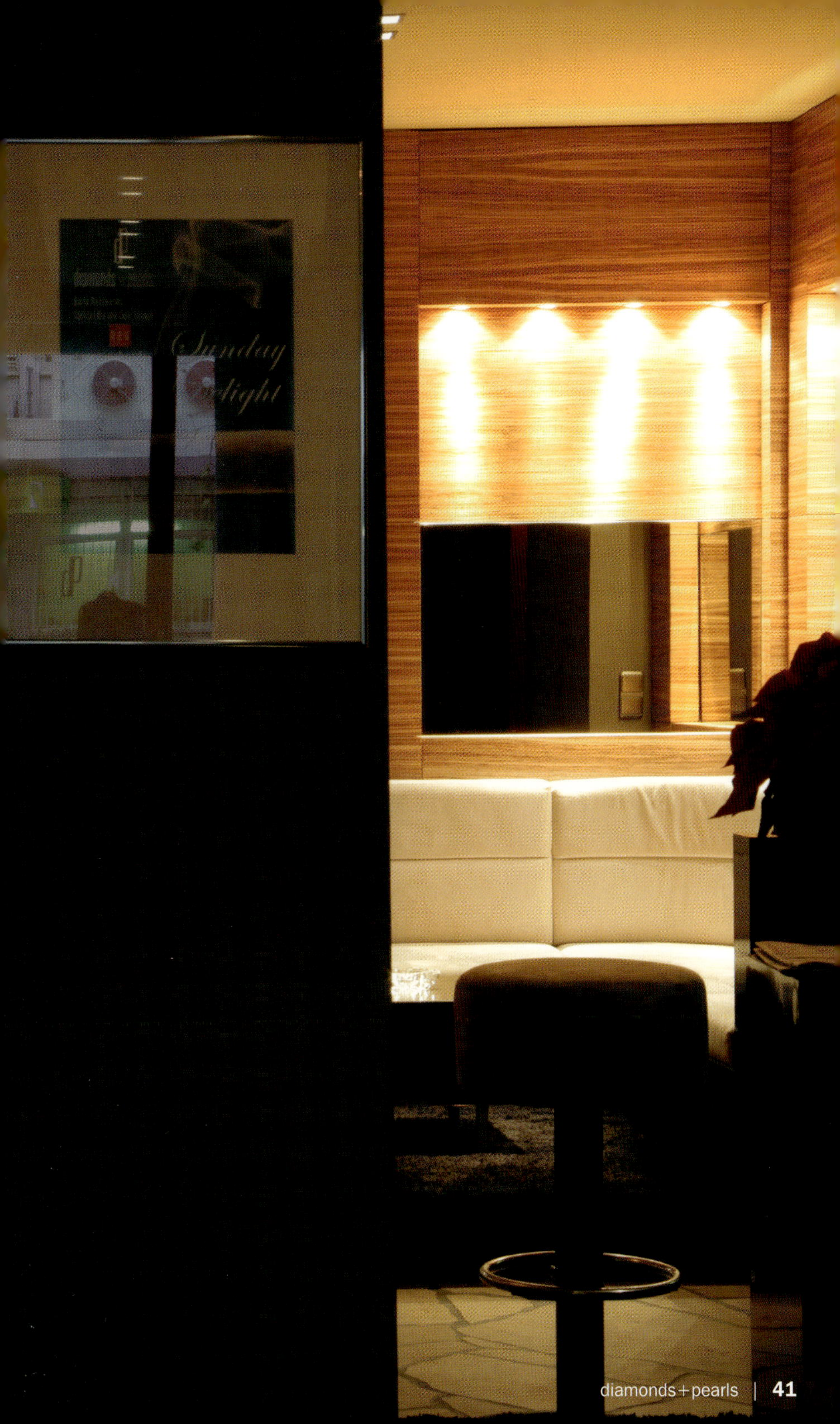

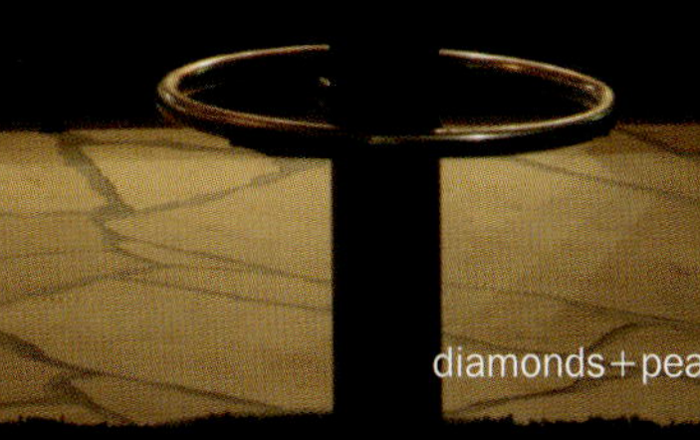

Hirschkalbssteak
mit Preiselbeer-Aprikosen-Jus

Venison Steak with Cranberry Apricot Jus

Steak de faon au jus d'airelles rouges et d'abricot

Filete de ciervo joven con zumo de arándanos rojo y albaricoque

Bistecca di cerbiatto con salsa di mirtilli e albicocche

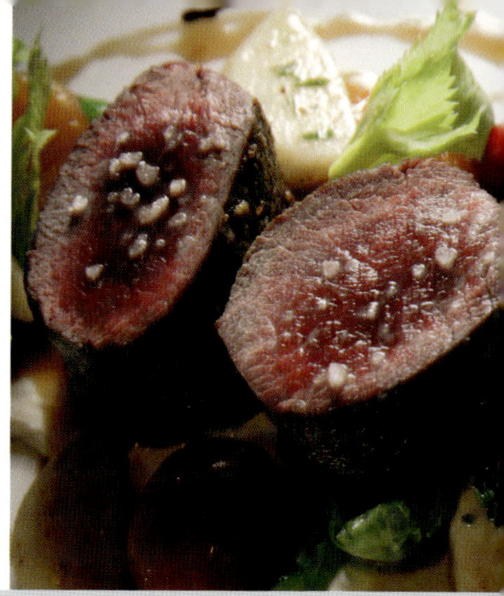

800 g Hirschkalbsfilet
Salz, Pfeffer
3 EL Pflanzenöl
4 EL Butter
500 g Hirschknochen und Abschnitte
3 EL Pflanzenöl
2 Karotten, gewürfelt
2 Zwiebeln, gewürfelt
1 Sellerieknolle, gewürfelt
2 EL Tomatenmark
200 ml Portwein, 500 ml Rotwein
1½ l Wildfond
1 EL Wildgewürz (Fertigprodukt)
Saft und Schale von 2 Orangen
2 Lorbeerblätter
2 Zweige Thymian
20 getrocknete Aprikosen
4 EL frische Preiselbeeren

Die Knochen und Abschnitte in Öl kräftig anrösten, aus dem Bräter nehmen und in demselben Bräter das Gemüse dunkelbraun braten. Die Knochen und Abschnitte wieder zugeben, das Tomatenmark einrühren und ca. 3 Minuten mitbraten lassen. Dann mit Portwein und Rotwein 5–6 Mal ablöschen und immer wieder einreduzieren lassen. Wildfond, Wildgewürz, Orangensaft und Orangenschale, Lorbeerblätter und Thymian zugeben und ca. 1 Stunde leise köcheln lassen. Zwischendurch immer wieder den Schaum abschöpfen. Die Sauce abpassieren, evtl. etwas andicken und abschmecken. Die getrockneten Aprikosen und die Preiselbeeren einrühren und warmstellen. Die Hirschkalbssteaks würzen, von beiden Seiten scharf anbraten und bei 160 °C 10–15 Minuten garen. Vor dem Servieren in heißer Butter schwenken.

1 lb 12 oz venison filet
Salt, pepper
3 tbsp vegetable oil
4 tbsp butter
1 lb venison bones and tendons
3 tbsp vegetable oil
2 carrots, diced
2 onions, diced
1 celery root, diced
2 tbsp tomato paste
200 ml port wine, 500 ml red wine
1 l venison fond
1 tbsp venison seasoning
Juice and zest from 2 oranges
2 bay leaves
2 twigs thyme
20 dried apricots
4 tbsp fresh cranberries

Roast the bones and tendons in oil, remove from the pan and sear the vegetables in the same pan until golden brown. Place the bones and tendons back in the pan, stir in the tomato paste and sear for another 3 minutes. Deglaze with port wine and red wine 5–6 times and let the liquid evaporate. Add venison fond, venison seasoning, orange juice and orange zest, bay leaves and thyme and let simmer for approx. 1 hour. Remove the foam from the fond every now and then. Strain the sauce, thicken, if necessary and season. Stir in the dried apricots and the cranberries and keep warm. Season the venison steaks, sear from both sides and bake at 320 °F for 10–15 minutes. Right before serving toss in hot butter.

800 g de filet de faon
Sel, poivre
3 c. à soupe d'huile végétale
4 c. à soupe de beurre
500 g d'os et de morceaux de cerf
3 c. à soupe d'huile végétale
2 carottes, coupées en dés
2 oignons, coupés en dés
1 bulbe de céleri, coupé en dés
2 c. à soupe de concentré de tomate
200 ml de Porto, 500 ml de vin rouge
1½ l de fond de gibier
1 c. à soupe d'épices de gibier (en sachet)
Le jus et l'écorce de 2 oranges
2 feuilles de laurier
2 branches de thym
20 abricots secs
4 c. à soupe d'airelles rouges fraîches

Faire revenir à feu vif les os et les morceaux dans de l'huile, les retirer de la sauteuse et y faire revenir les légumes jusqu'à ce qu'ils soient bien dorés. Ajouter de nouveau les os et les morceaux, y mélanger le concentré de tomate et laisser mijoter pendant env. 3 minutes. Verser ensuite le Porto et le vin rouge en 5–6 fois et faire réduire à chaque fois. Ajouter le fond de gibier, les épices de gibier, le jus et l'écorce d'orange, les feuilles de laurier et le thym et laisser mijoter à feu doux pendant env. 1 heure. Ecumer régulièrement. Filtrer la sauce, l'épaissir si nécessaire et rectifier l'assaisonnement. Ajouter les abricots secs et les airelles et conserver au chaud. Assaisonner les steaks de faon, les faire revenir à feu puissant des deux côtés et faire cuire à 160 °C pendant 10–15 minutes. Faire un allert retour dans le beurre chaud avant de servir.

800 g de filetes de ciervo joven
Sal, pimiento
3 cucharadas de aceite vegetal
4 cucharadas de mantequilla
500 g de huesos de ciervo y trozos de carne sobrante
3 cucharadas de aceite vegetal
2 zanahorias, en dados
2 cebollas, en dados
1 bulbo de apio, en dados
2 cucharadas de concentrado de tomate
200 ml de oporto, 500 ml de vino tinto
1½ l de caldo de caza
1 cucharada de especias para caza (producto preparado)
El zumo y la piel de 2 naranjas
2 hojas de laurel
2 ramitas de tomillo
20 albaricoques secos
4 cucharadas de arándanos rojos frescos

Fría a fuego fuerte los huesos y los trozos de carne sobrante, sáquelos después de la sartén y fría en ella la verdura hasta que esté marrón. Vuelva a introducir los huesos y los trozos de carne, incorpore el concentrado de tomate, remueva y sofría durante 3 minutos. Añada después en 5 o 6 veces el oporto y el vino tinto dejando que se reduzcan cada vez. Incorpore el fondo de caza, las especias, el zumo de naranja y la piel, las hojas de laurel y el tomillo y deje que hierva a fuego lento durante aprox. 1 hora. Retire de vez en cuando la espuma. Cuele la salsa, espésela ligeramente y sazone. Incorpore los albaricoques secos y los arándanos y reserve caliente. Sazone los filetes de ciervo, fríalos a fuego fuerte por ambos lados y áselos a 160 °C durante 10–15 minutos. Antes de servirlos saltéelos en mantequilla caliente.

800 g di filetto di cerbiatto
Sale, pepe
3 cucchiai di olio vegetale
4 cucchiai di burro
500 g di ossi e altri residui di cervo
3 cucchiai di olio vegetale
2 carote tagliate a dadini
2 cipolle tagliate a dadini
1 bulbo di sedano tagliato a dadini
2 cucchiai di concentrato di pomodoro
200 ml di vino Porto, 500 ml di vino rosso
1½ l di fondo di selvaggina
1 cucchiaio di spezie per selvaggina (acquistate pronte)
Il succo e la buccia di 2 arance
2 foglie di alloro
2 rami di timo
20 albicocche secche
4 cucchiai di mirtilli freschi

Rosolare a fuoco vivo nell'olio gli ossi e i residui di carne ed estrarli dalla casseruola. Abbrustolire quindi le verdure nello stesso recipiente. Unire gli ossi e i residui di carne, incorporare il concentrato di pomodoro e lasciar rosolare il tutto per circa 3 minuti. Bagnare quindi per 5–6 volte con il vino di Porto ed il vino rosso, lasciando restringere ogni volta. Aggiungere il fondo e le spezie per selvaggina, il succo e la buccia d'arancia, le foglie di alloro ed il timo. Lasciar cuocere a fuoco lento per circa 1 ora schiumando di tanto in tanto. Passare la salsa in un colino, eventualmente addensarla, assaggiarla e regolare il condimento. Incorporare le albicocche secche ed i mirtilli e tenere in caldo. Condire le bistecche di cerbiatto, rosolarle a fuoco vivo da entrambi i lati e cuocerle in forno a 160 °C per 10–15 minuti. Prima di servire, saltarle nel burro caldo.

edmw eatdrinkmanwoman

Design: Martin Willems | Chef: Prasat Raklee
Owner: EDMW Gastronomie GmbH

Jahnstraße 1 | 60318 Frankfurt | Nordend
Phone: +49 69 51 28 22
www.edmw.com
Subway: Musterschule
Opening hours: Mon–Thu & Sun 6 pm to 2 am, Fri–Sat 6 pm to 3 am
Average price: € 5
Cuisine: Neo-Asian
Special features: Aquariums, big cocktail selection

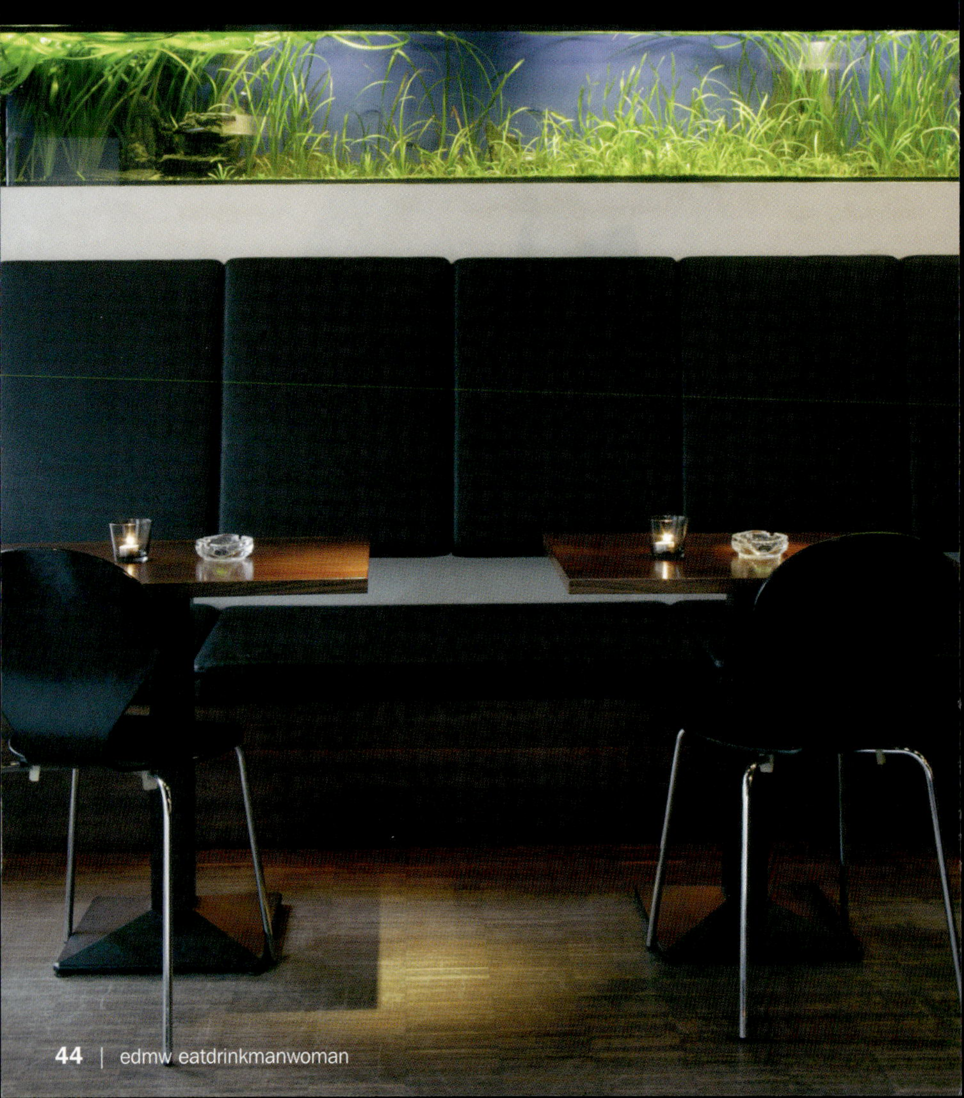

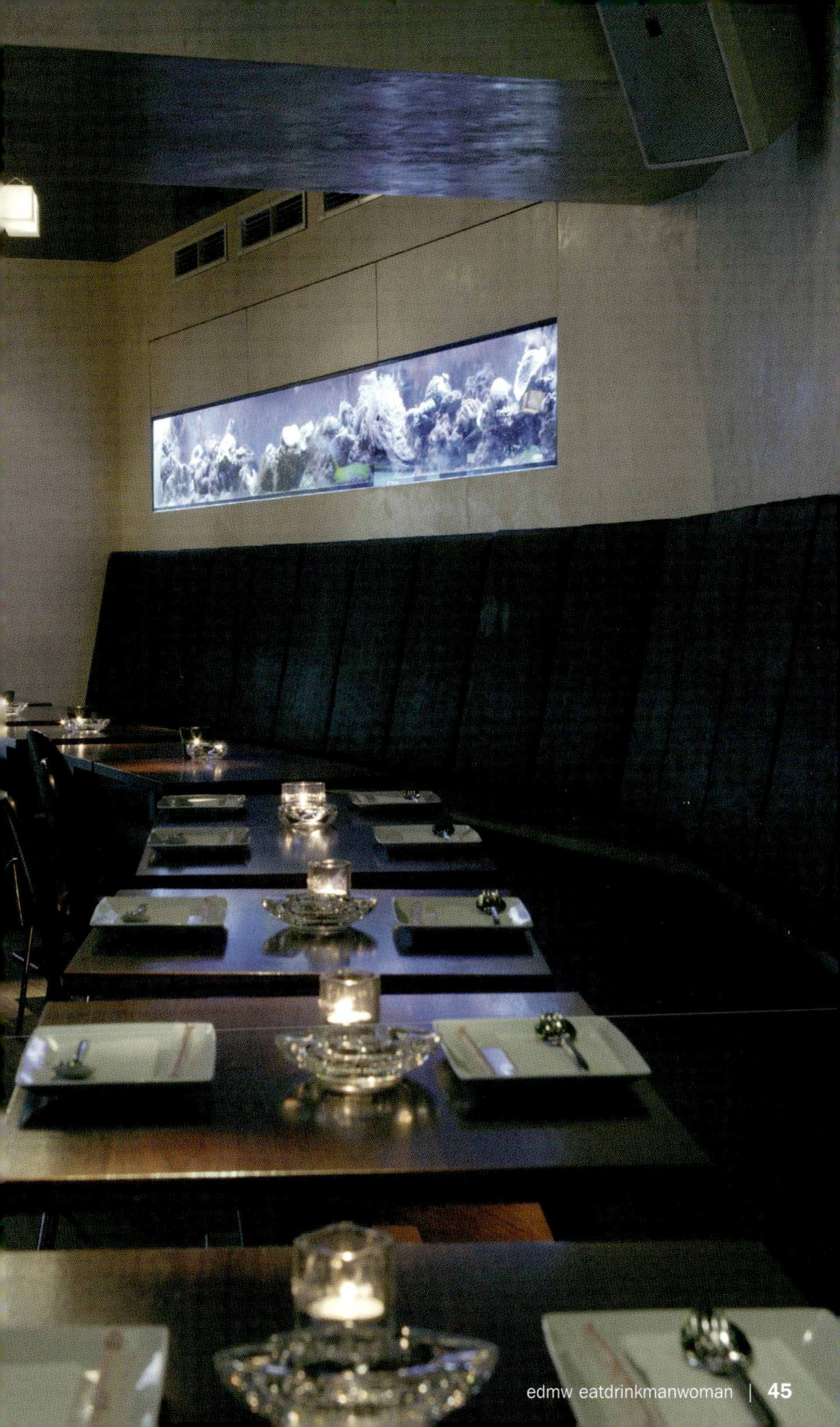

Embassy

Design: Michael Kleespieß | Chef: Massimilliano Naitana
Owner: Ewa & Maciej Urbanski

Zimmerweg 1 | 60325 Frankfurt | Westend
Phone: +49 69 74 09 08 44
www.embassy-frankfurt.de
Subway: Taunus-Anlage
Opening hours: Mon–Fri 9 am to 2 am, Sat 6 pm to 1 am, Sun closed
Average price: € 13
Cuisine: Italian and international
Special features: After work party every Wednesday from 6 pm

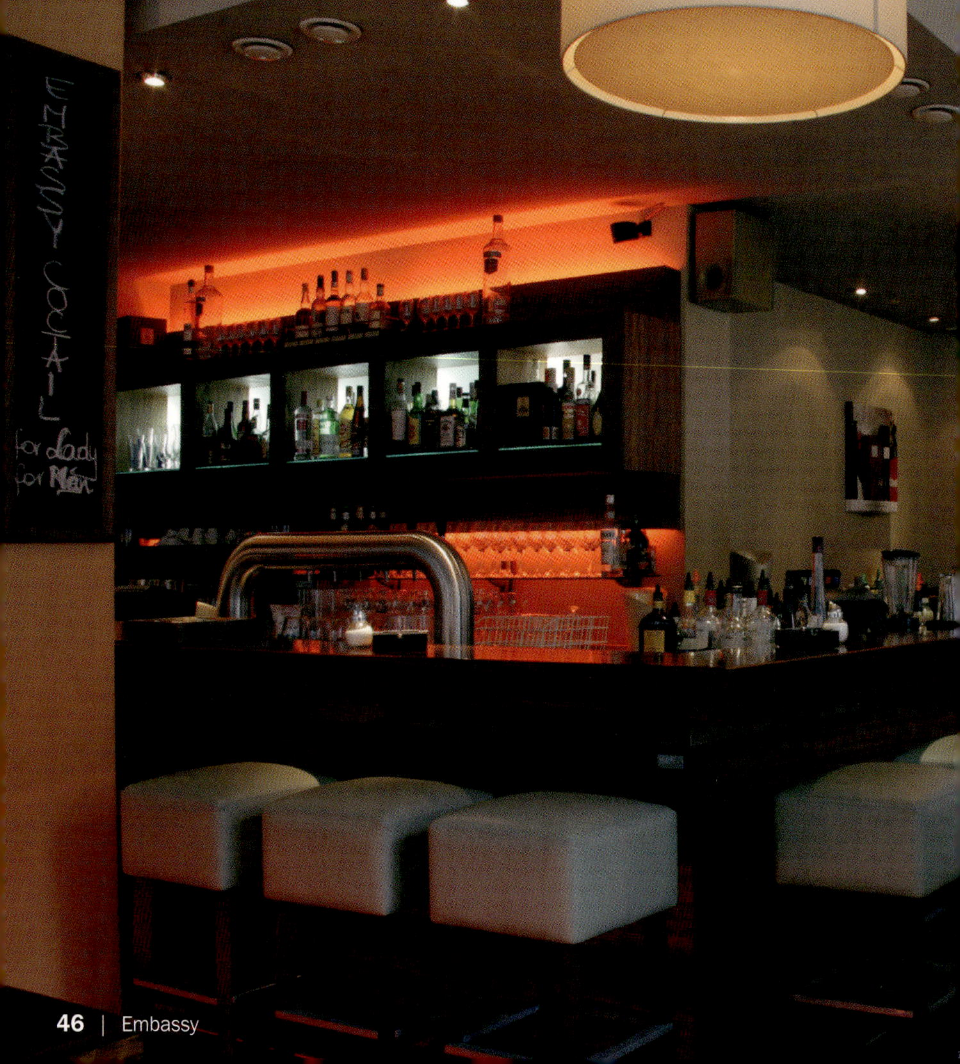

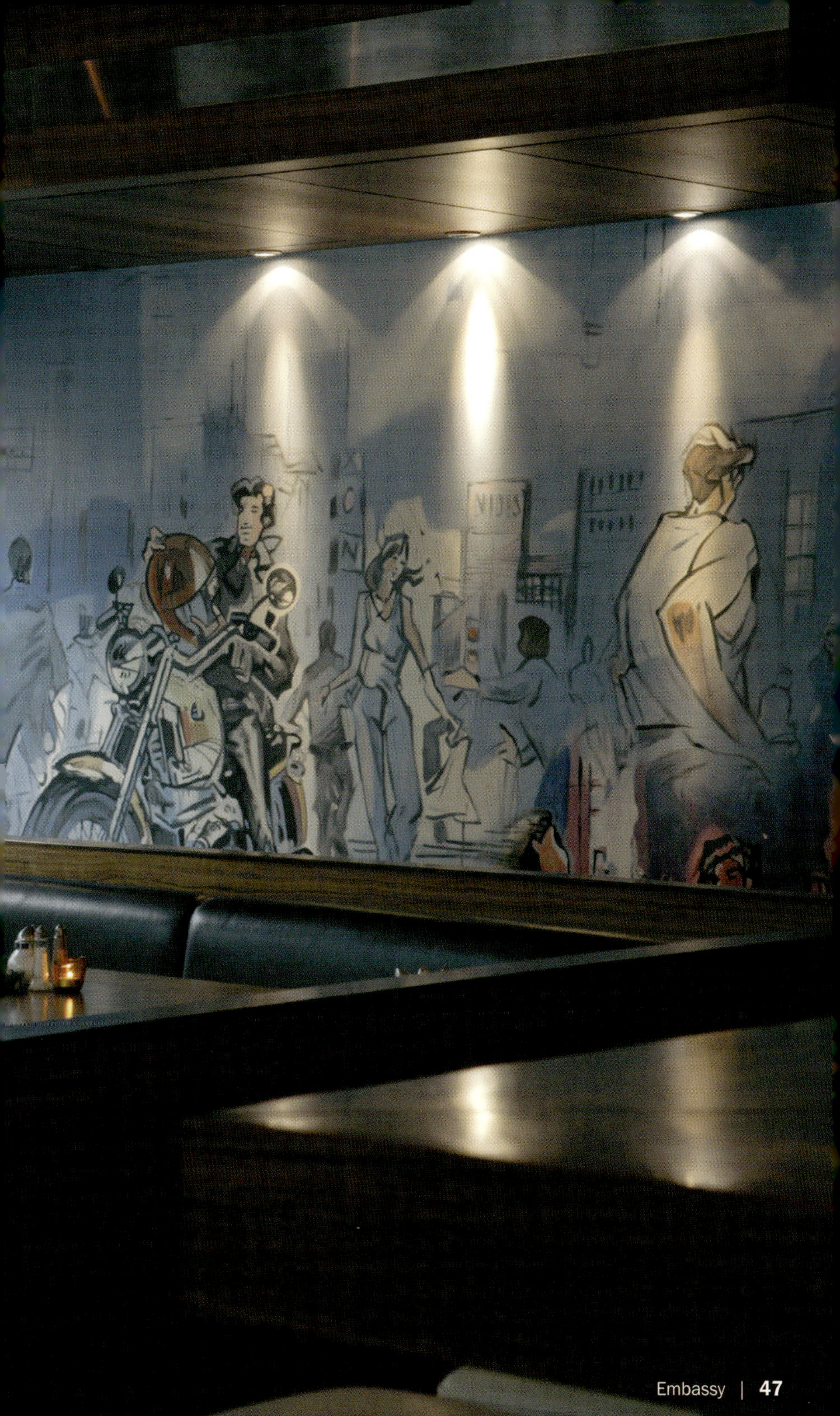

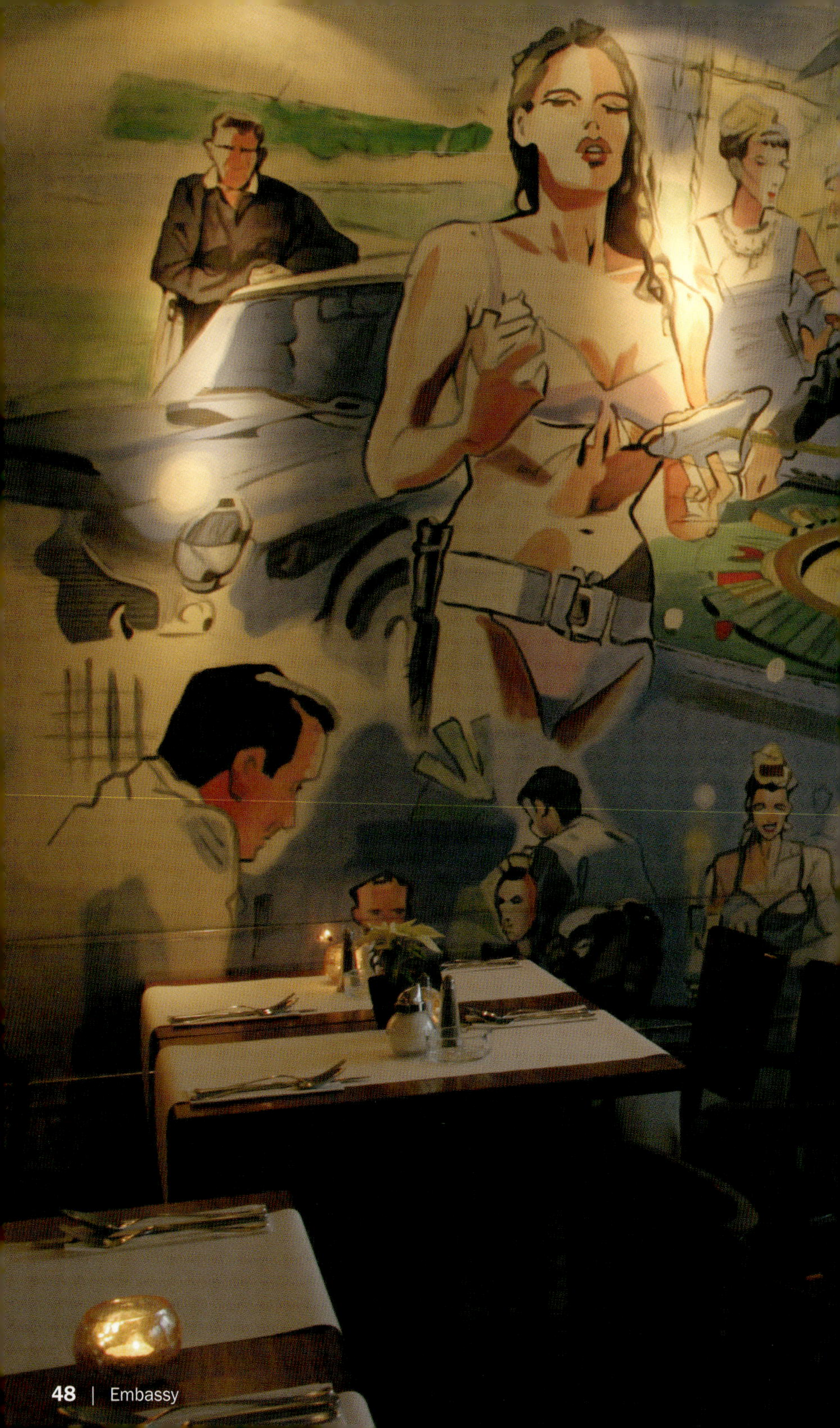

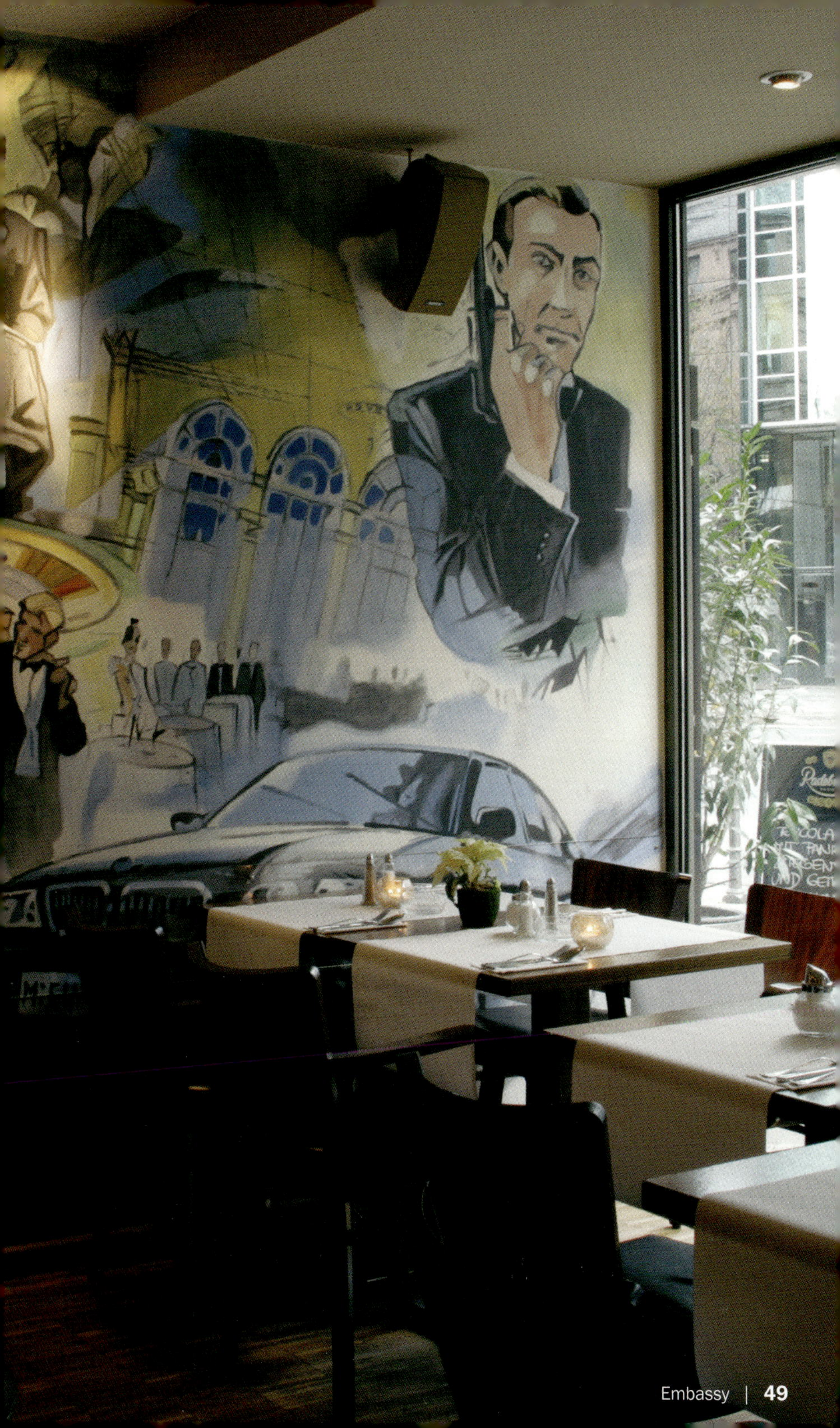

Opening hours: Tue–Sat noon to 2:30 pm and 6 pm to midnight,
Sun noon to 6 pm, Mon closed
Average price: € 50
Cuisine: Southwest German and French

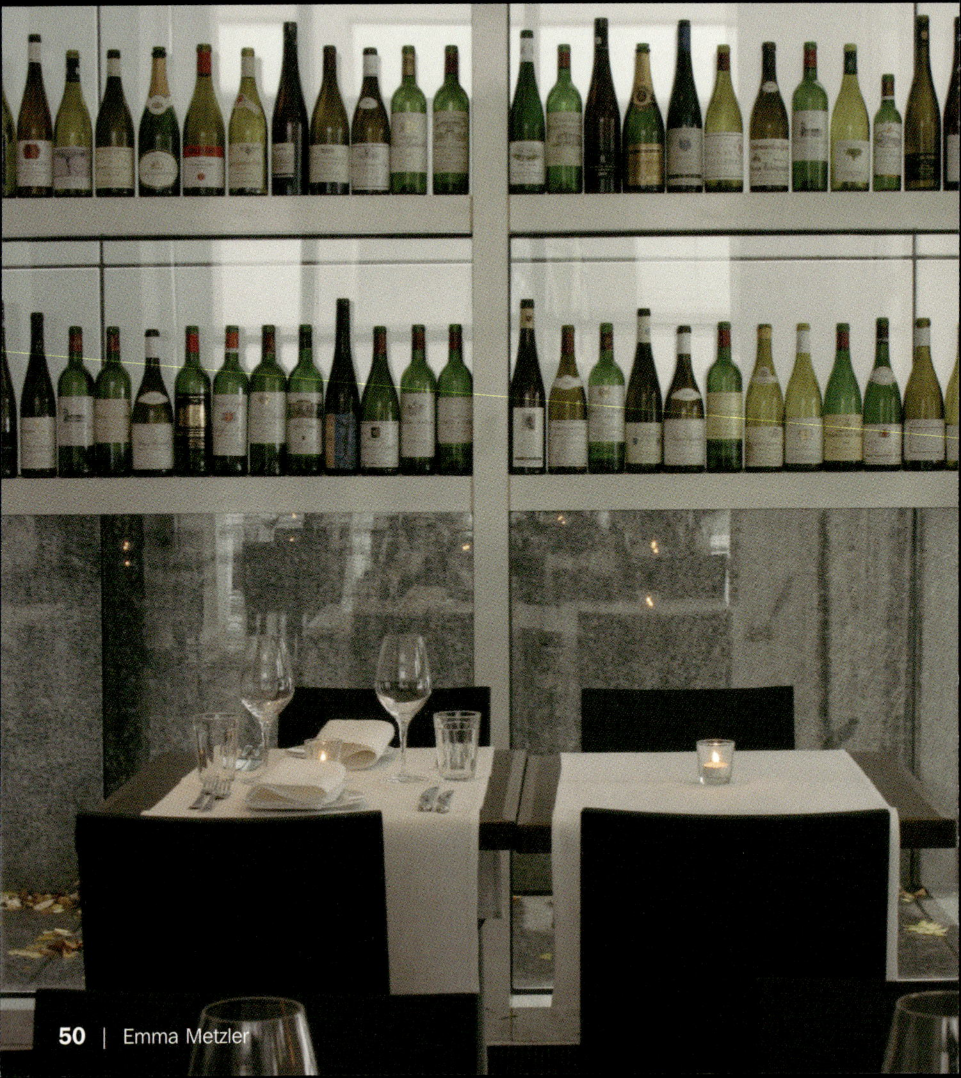

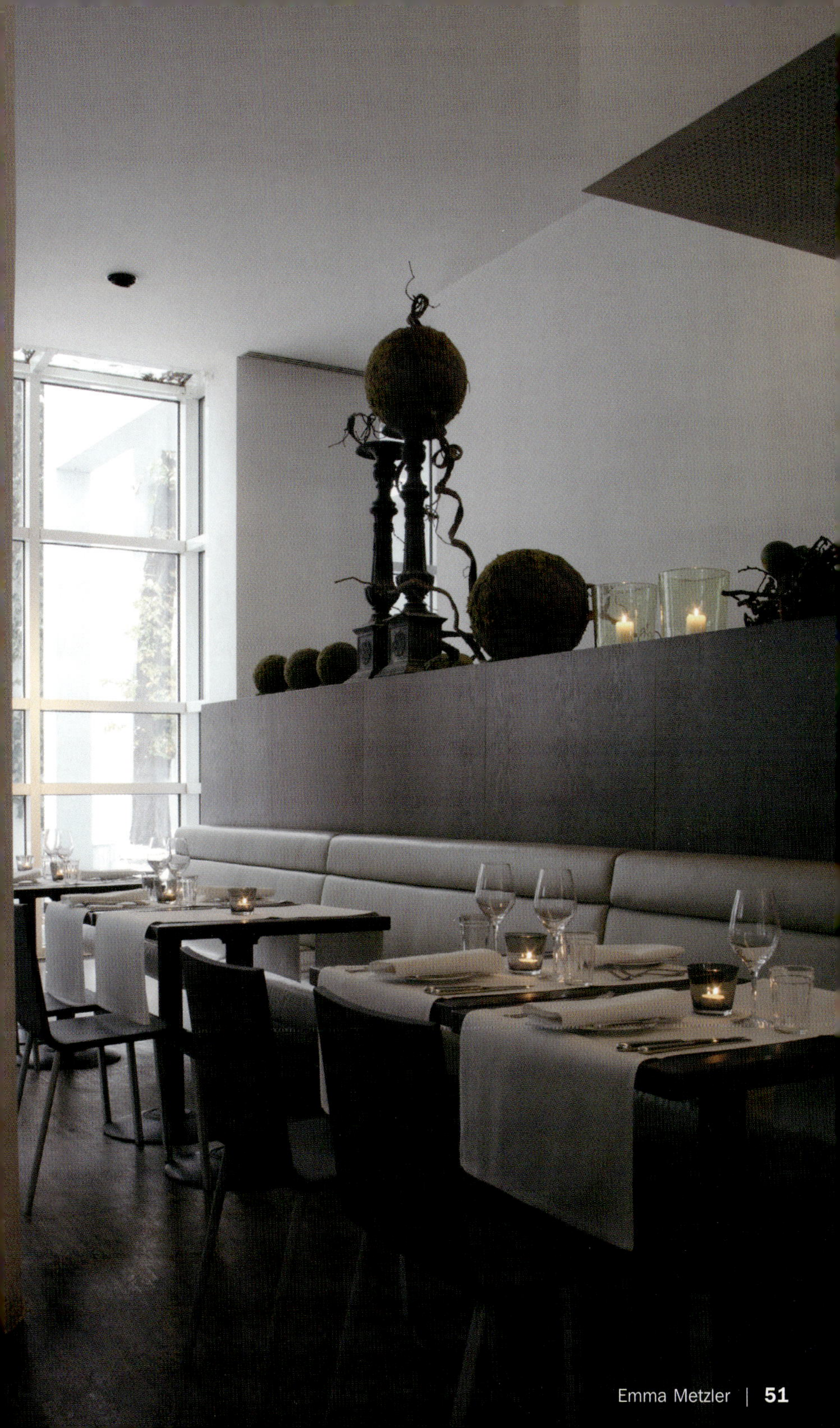

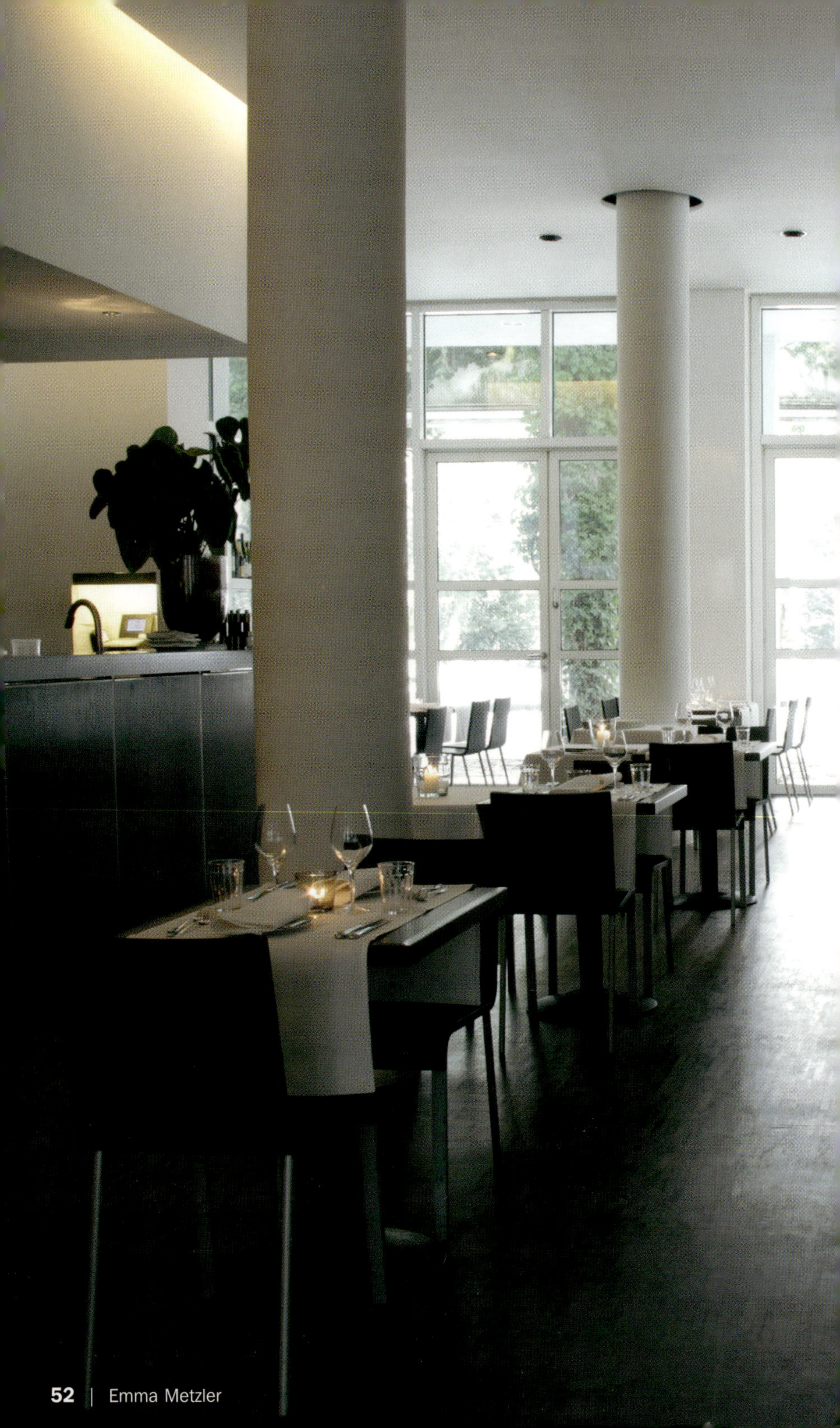

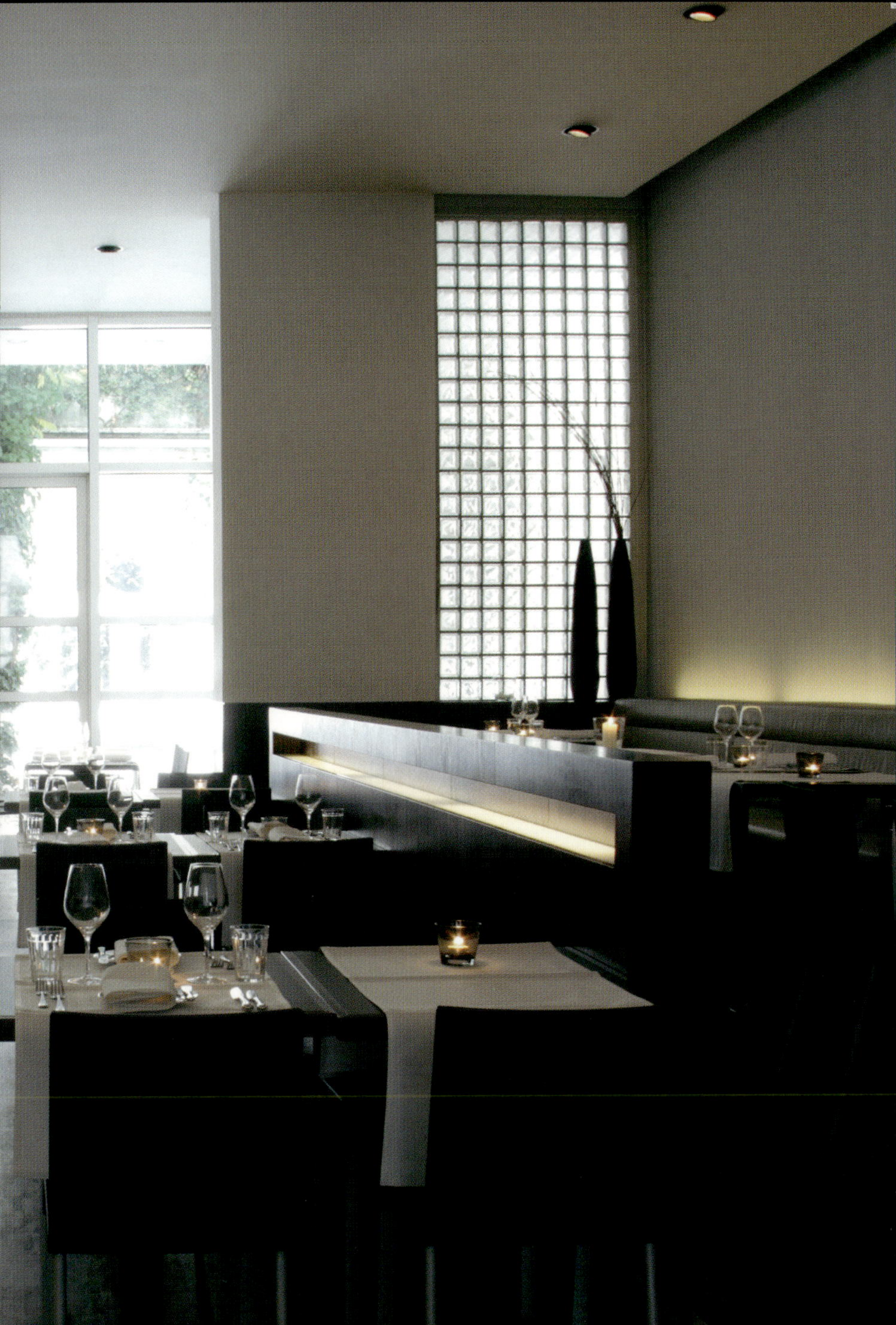

Gewürzcreme

mit Orangen und Brownie

Spice Cream with Oranges and Brownie

Crème d'épices aux oranges et au brownie

Crema especiada con naranjas y brownie

Crema speziata con arance e brownie

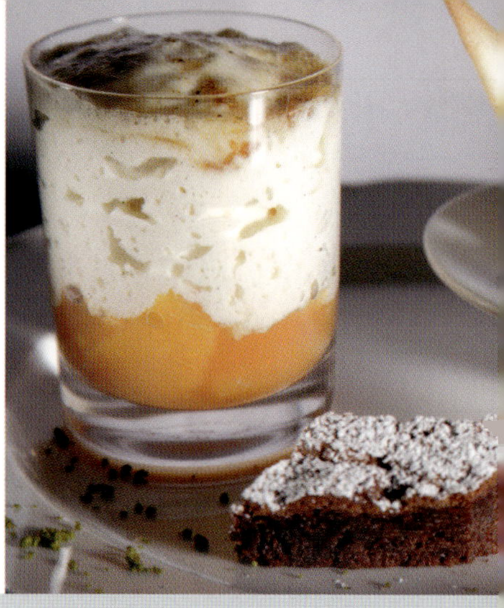

500 ml Sahne	25 g Vanillepudding-
150 ml Milch	pulver
1 TL Zimt	5 Eigelbe
1 TL Lebkuchengewürz	3 Blatt Gelatine,
50 g Zucker	eingeweicht

200 g dunkle Kuvertüre	1 TL Backpulver
80 g Butter	175 g Mehl
130 g Zucker	75 g Schokoladen-
2 Eier	raspel
1 Prise Salz	Filets von 2 Orangen,
	abgetropft

Sahne, Milch, Gewürze und Zucker aufkochen, das Puddingpulver in ca. 4 EL zurückbehaltener Sahne auflösen und in die kochende Flüssigkeit geben. 1 Minute aufkochen und beiseite stellen. Eigelbe und Gelatine in die Puddingmasse rühren und in einen Espumaspender füllen. Kaltstellen. Alternativ die Masse kaltstellen und kurz vor dem Servieren mit einem Handrührgerät kräftig aufschlagen.

Die Schokolade mit der Butter im Wasserbad auflösen, die Eier mit Zucker und Salz cremig schlagen, die Butter-Schokoladenmischung unterrühren und Backpulver, Mehl und Schokoladenraspel unterheben. Bei 180°C ca. 20 Minuten backen. Etwas abkühlen lassen und in Rauten schneiden. Die Orangenfilets auf vier Gläser verteilen, die Gewürzcreme in die Gläser spritzen und mit den Brownies und frischen Beeren garnieren.

500 ml cream	1 oz vanilla pudding
150 ml milk	powder
1 tsp cinnamon	5 egg yolks
1 tsp gingerbread spice	3 leaves gelatin,
2 oz sugar	soaked

7 oz dark chocolate	1 tsp baking soda
2 ½ oz butter	6 oz flour
4 ½ oz sugar	2 ½ oz grated chocolate
2 eggs	Filets of 2 oranges,
1 pinch salt	drained

Bring cream, milk, spices and sugar to a boil, dissolve the pudding powder in approx. 4 tbsp reserved cream and stir into the boiling liquid. Boil for 1 minute and set aside. Stir egg yolks and gelatin into the pudding mixture and fill into foam machine. Chill.
Alternatively, chill the mixture and just before serving beat with a hand holder mixer until stiff.

Melt the chocolate with the butter in a double boiler, whisk the eggs with sugar and salt until creamy, stir in the butter-chocolate mixture and fold in the baking soda, flour and grated chocolate. Bake at 360°F for approx. 20 minutes. Let cool down and cut into squares. Divide the orange filets amongst four glasses, scoop the spice cream on top and garnish with brownies and fresh berries.

500 ml de crème liquide
150 ml de lait
1 c. à café de cannelle
1 c. à café d'épices de pain d'épice
50 g sucre
25 g de poudre de crème à la vanille
5 jaunes d'œufs
3 feuilles de gélatine, ramollies

200 g de chocolat noir de couverture
80 g de beurre
130 g sucre
2 œufs
1 pincée de sel
1 c. à café de levure chimique
175 g de farine
75 g de chocolat râpé
Filets de 2 oranges, égouttés

Amener à ébullition la crème liquide, le lait, les épices et le sucre, diluer la poudre de crème à la vanille dans env. 4 c. à soupe de crème chantilly que vous aurez réservée et verser dans la préparation qui en train de bouillir. Faire bouillir pendant 1 minute et réserver. Mélanger les jaunes d'œufs et la gélatine dans la crème et remplir dans un siphon à espuma. Mettre au frais.
Variante : mettre la crème au frais et la battre vigoureusement au mixeur avant de la servir.

Faire fondre au bain-marie le chocolat et le beurre, battre les œufs avec le sucre et le sel pour obtenir un mélange crémeux, ajouter la préparation à base de beurre et de chocolat et la levure chimique, puis la farine et le chocolat râpé. Faire cuire à 180 °C pendant env. 20 minutes. Laisser un peu refroidir et couper en losanges. Disposer les filets d'oranges dans quatre verres, répartir la crème d'épices dans les verres à l'aide du siphon à espuma et garnir avec les brownies et les baies fraîches.

500 ml de nata
150 ml de leche
1 cucharadita de canela
1 cucharadita de especias para pan de especias
50 g de azúcar
25 g de pudin de vainilla en polvo
5 yemas
3 láminas de gelatina, reblandecidas

200 g de cobertura oscura
80 g de mantequilla
130 g de azúcar
2 huevos
1 pizca de sal
1 cucharadita de levadura en polvo
175 g de harina
75 g de ralladura de chocolate
Filetes de 2 naranjas, escurridos

Hierva la nata, la leche, las especias y el azúcar, disuelva el pudin en polvo en aprox. 4 cucharadas de nata reservada e introduzca la mezcla en el líquido hirviendo. Deje que siga cociendo durante 1 minuto y reserve. Añada las yemas y la gelatina y vierta la mezcla en un espumador. Reserve en el frigorífico.
Alternativamente puede reservar la mezcla en el frigorífico y batirla antes de servir con una batidora.

Derrita los chocolates y la mantequilla al baño maría, bata los huevos con el azúcar y la sal hasta obtener una masa cremosa y añada la mezcla del chocolate con mantequilla. Incorpore la levadura en polvo, la harina y la ralladura de chocolate y remueva. Hornee durante aprox. 20 minutos a 180 °C. Deje que se enfríe un poco y corte en el brownie en rombos. Reparta los filetes de naranjas en cuatro vasos, añada la crema especiada y decore con los rombos de brownie y los frutos frescos.

500 ml di panna
150 ml di latte
1 cucchiaino di cannella
1 cucchiaino di aromi per "Lebkuchen" (biscotti speziati, n.d.t.)
50 g di zucchero
25 g di polvere per budino alla vaniglia
5 tuorli d'uovo
3 fogli di gelatina ammorbiditi

200 g di glassa scura
80 g di burro
130 g di zucchero
2 uova
1 cucchiaino di lievito per dolci
1 presa di sale
175 g di farina
75 g di scagliette di cioccolato
Filetti sgocciolati di 2 arance

Portare a cottura la panna, il latte, gli aromi e lo zucchero, sciogliere la polvere per budino in circa 4 cucchiai di panna ed unirla al liquido durante la cottura. Cuocere per 1 minuto e mettere da parte. Incorporare al budino i tuorli d'uovo e la gelatina e versare il composto in uno schiumatore. Mettere in frigorifero.
Alternativamente, tenere in frigorifero il composto e, al momento di servirlo, sbatterlo energicamente con uno sbattitore.

Sciogliere a bagnomaria il cioccolato ed il burro, sbattere le uova, lo zucchero e il sale fino ad ottenere un composto cremoso, incorporarvi il cioccolato sciolto con il burro ed aggiungere il lievito, la farina e le scagliette di cioccolato. Cuocere in forno a 180 °C per circa 20 minuti, lasciar raffreddare un poco e tagliare a pezzetti romboidali. Ripartire i filetti d'arance in quattro bicchieri, versarvi la crema speziata e guarnire con i brownie e i frutti di bosco freschi.

Frankfurter Botschaft

Design: Komfort Bureau, Carsten Hitter | Chef: Tacmen Tonguc
Owner: AZAK Gastronomie GmbH

Westhafenplatz 6 | 60327 Frankfurt | Westhafen
Phone: +49 69 24 00 48 99
www.frankfurterbotschaft.de
Subway: Baseler Platz
Opening hours: Daily 10 am to open end
Average price: € 11
Cuisine: Inspired from all over the world

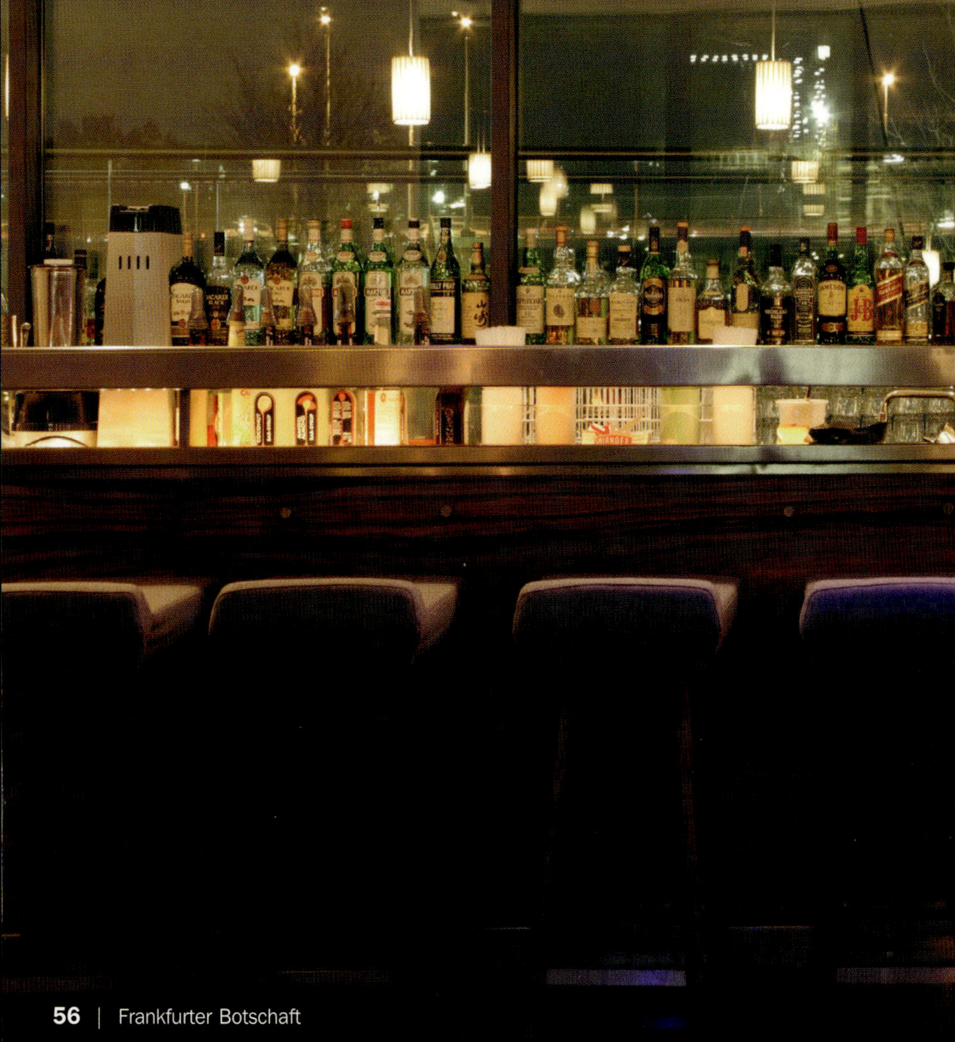

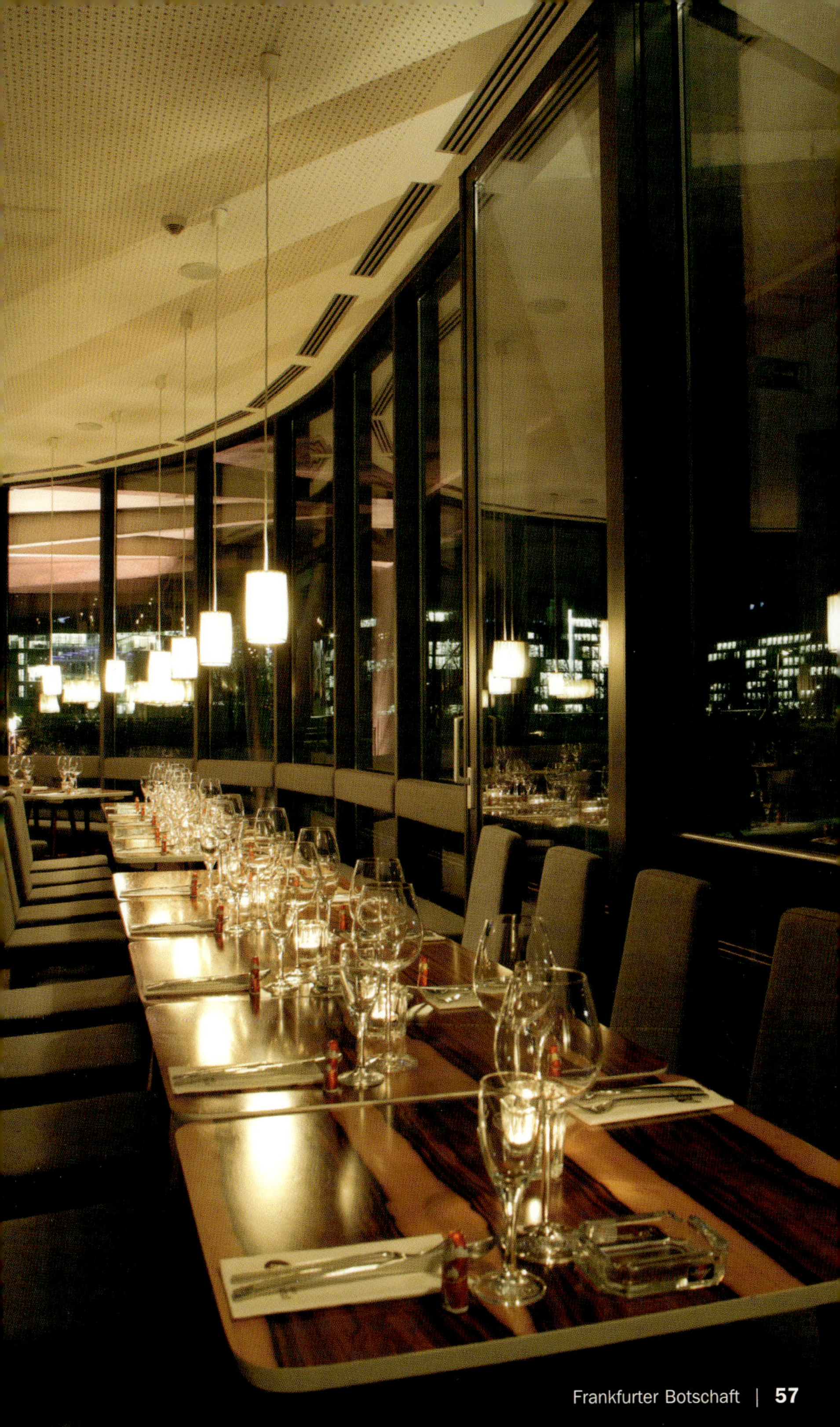

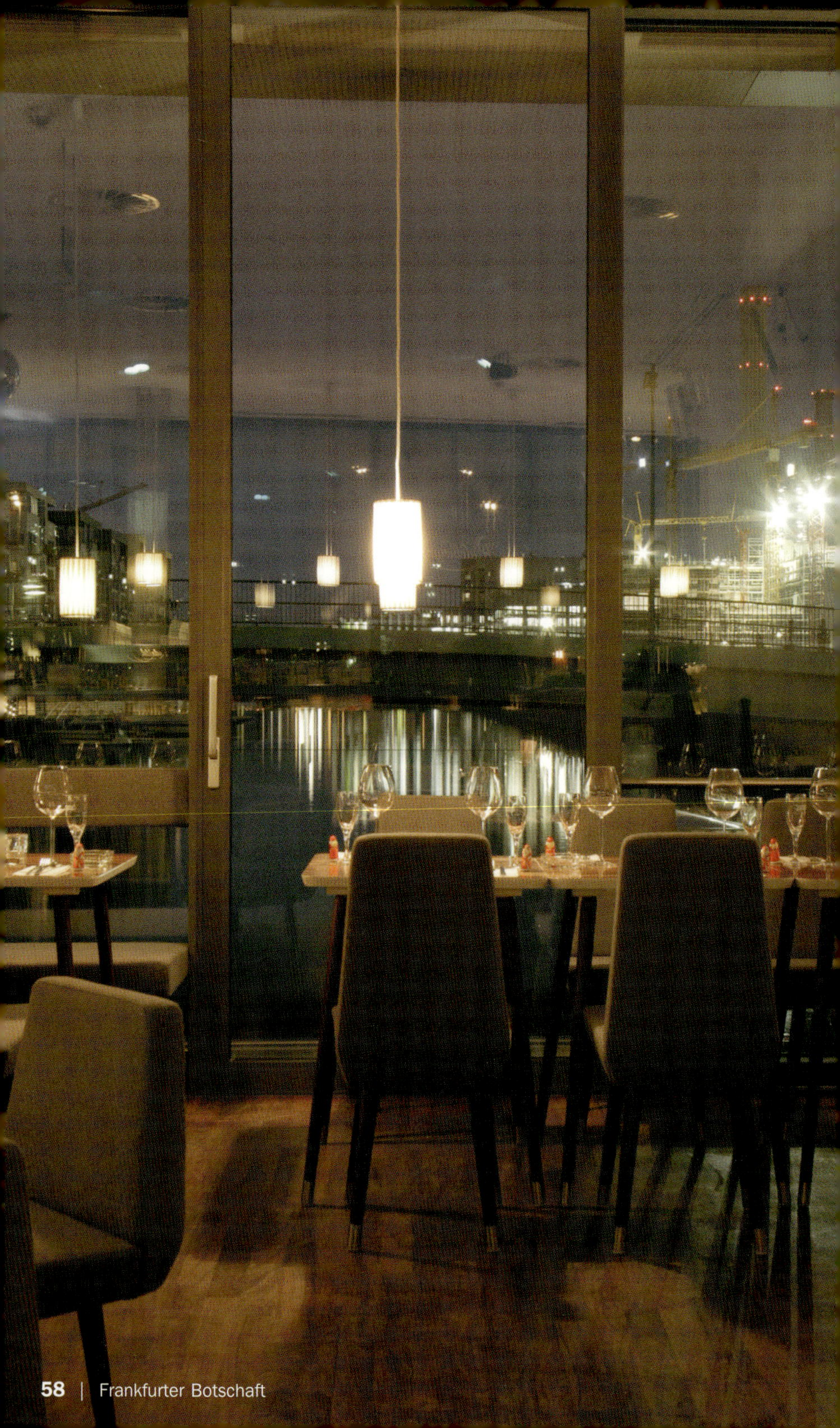

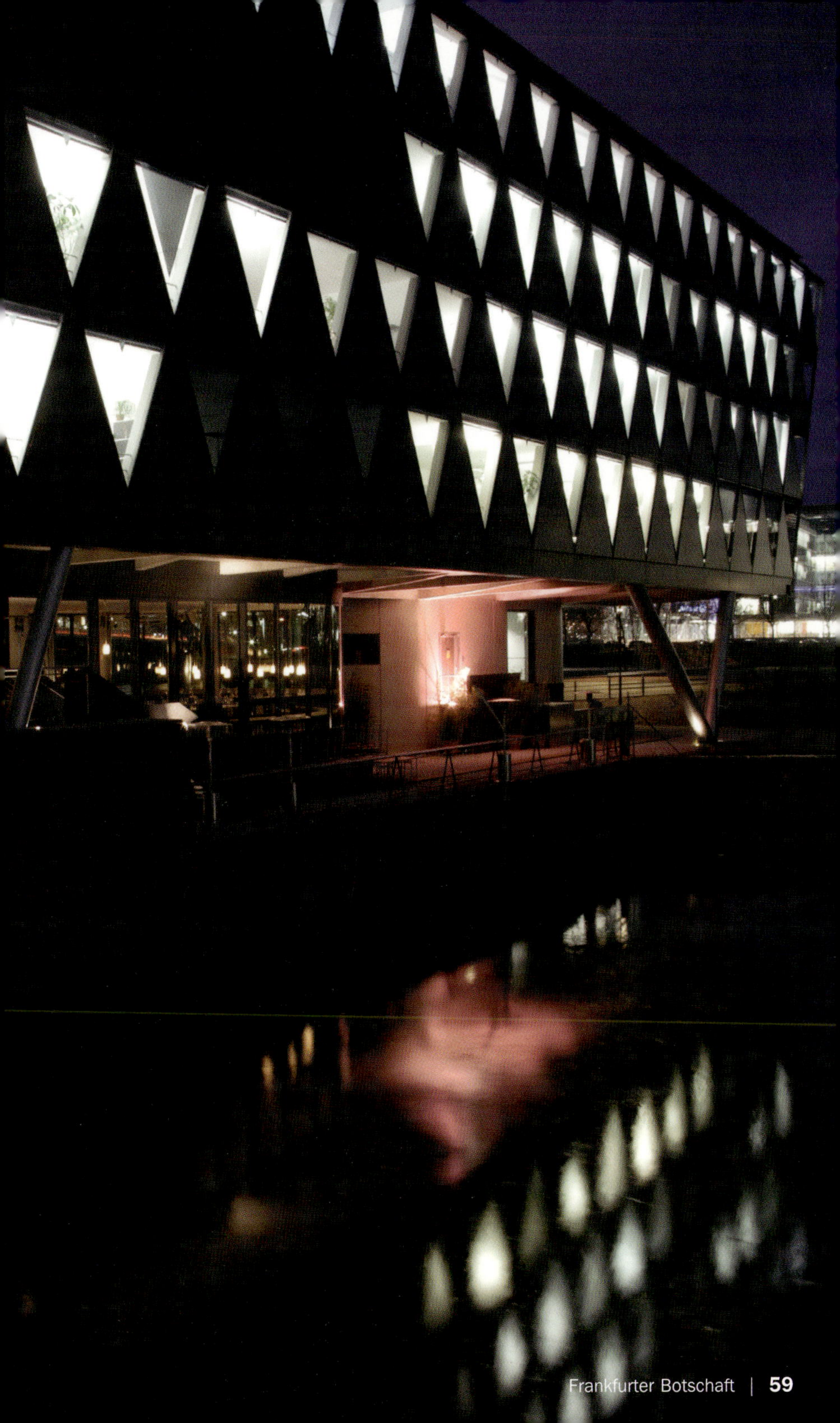

Garibaldi

Design & Owner: Eduardo Gregorelli | Chef: Jorno Oswaldo

Kleine Hochstraße 4 | 60131 Frankfurt | Innenstadt
Phone: +49 69 21 99 76 44
Subway: Alte Oper
Opening hours: Mon–Sat 11:30 am to 11:30 pm, Sun closed
Average price: € 13
Cuisine: Italian

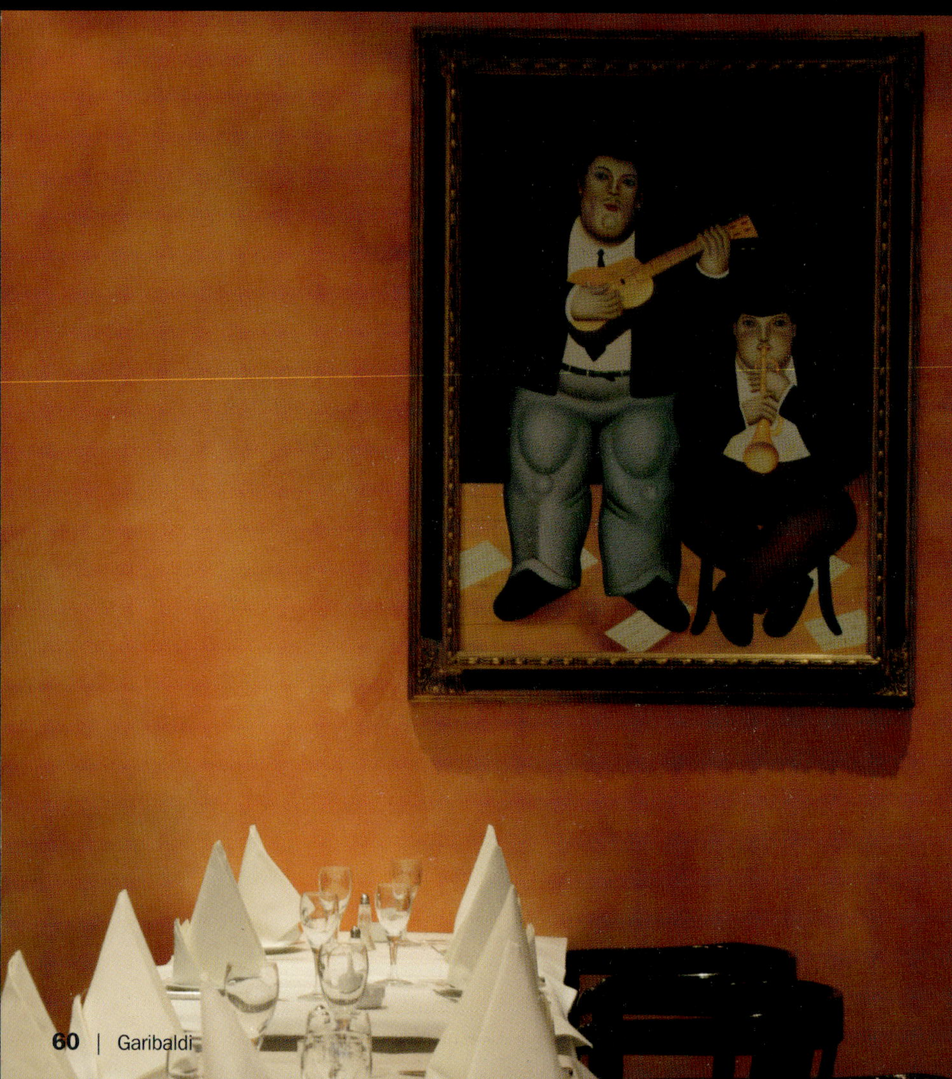

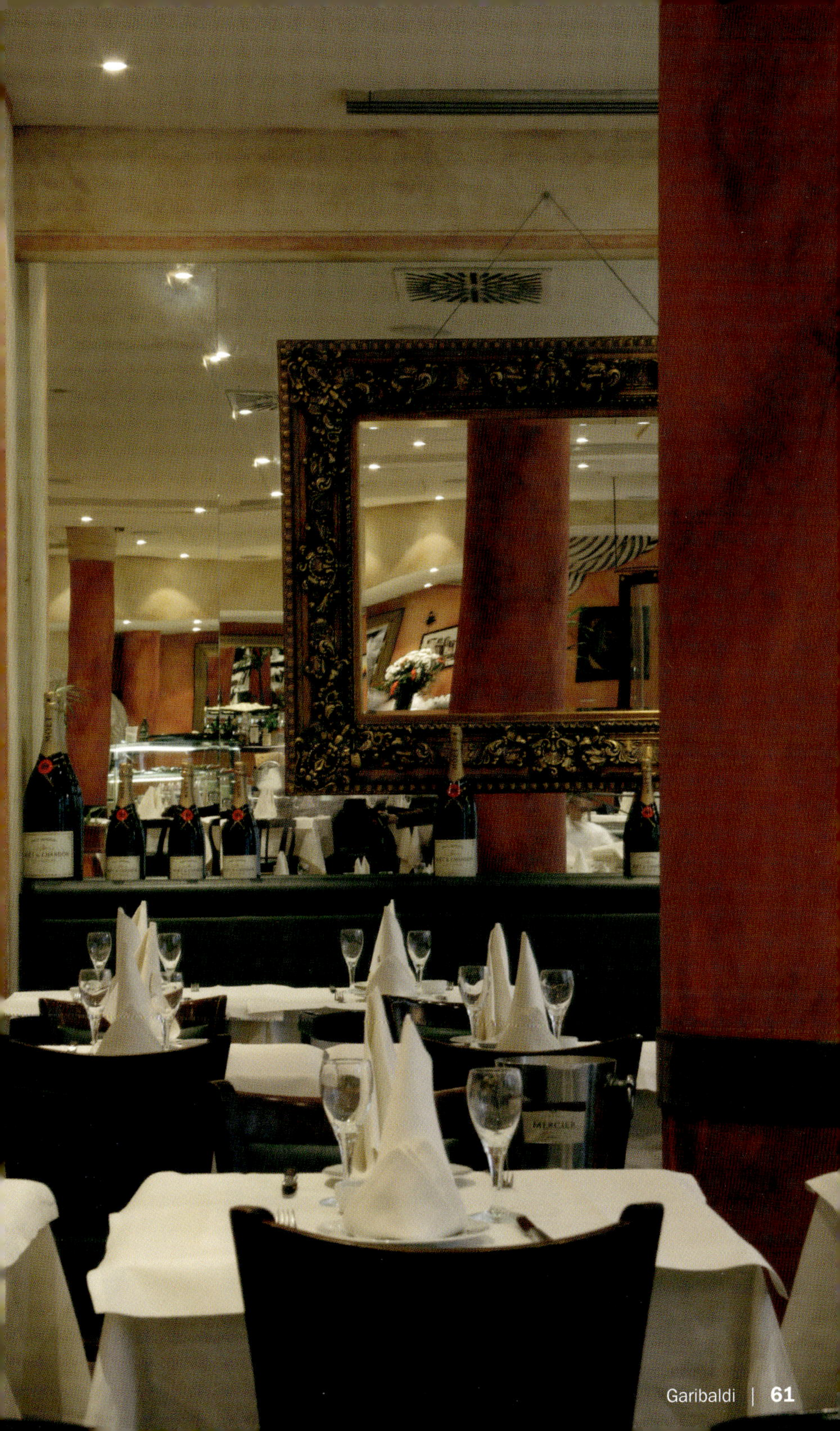

Ginkgo

Design: Harald Reeg | Chef: Holger Brinkmann, Dieter Emmel,
Monika Pflüger-Findeis | Owners: Klaus & Alexandra Knopp

Berger Straße 81 | 60316 Frankfurt | Nordend
Phone: +49 69 49 12 02
www.ginkgo-frankfurt.de
Subway: Merianplatz, Höhenstraße
Opening hours: Mon–Tue & Sun 9 am to 1 am, Fri–Sat 9 am to 2 am
Average price: € 10
Cuisine: Seasonal change
Special features: Live music once a month

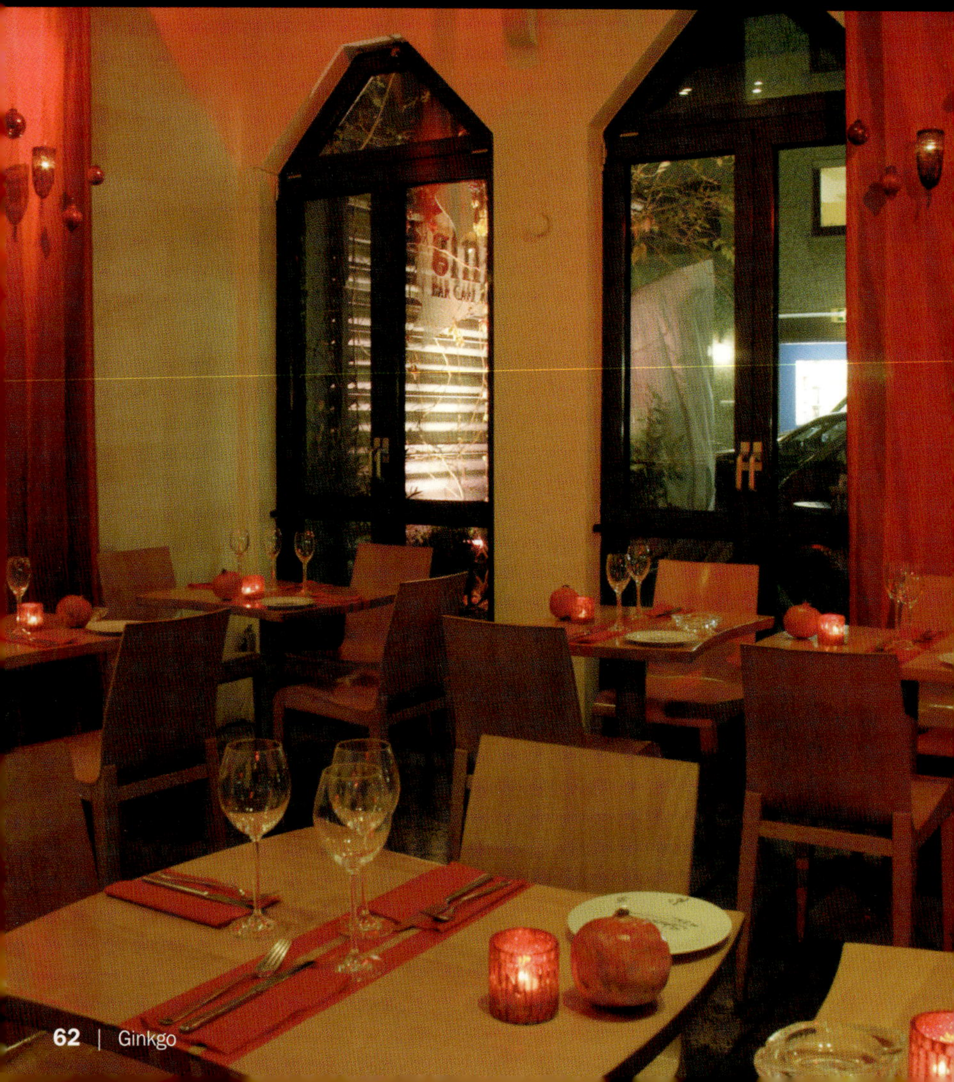

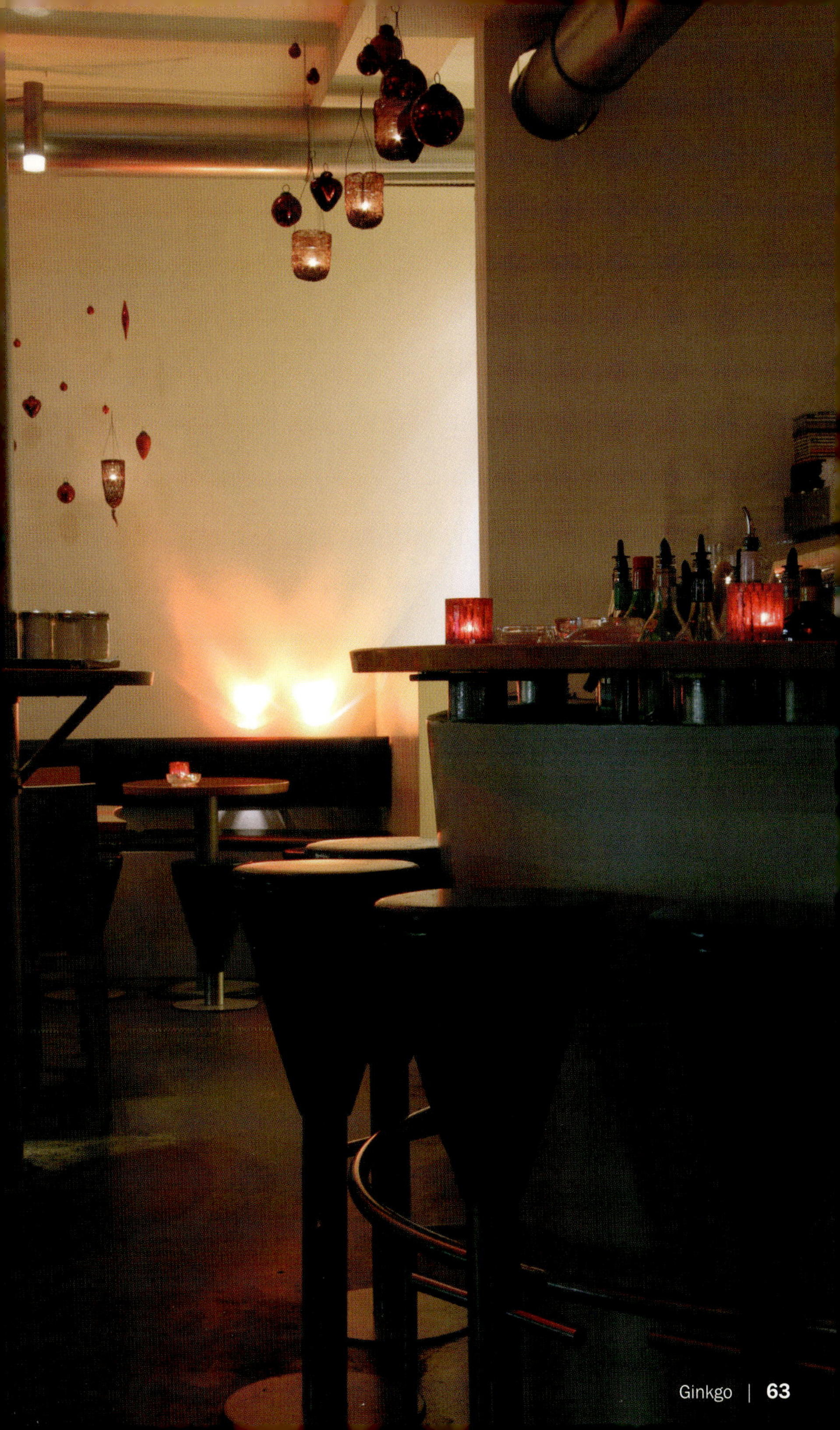

Zitronen-Chili-Huhn

Lemon-Chili-Chicken

Poulet au citron et au piment

Pollo con limón y guindilla

Pollo al limone e peperoncino

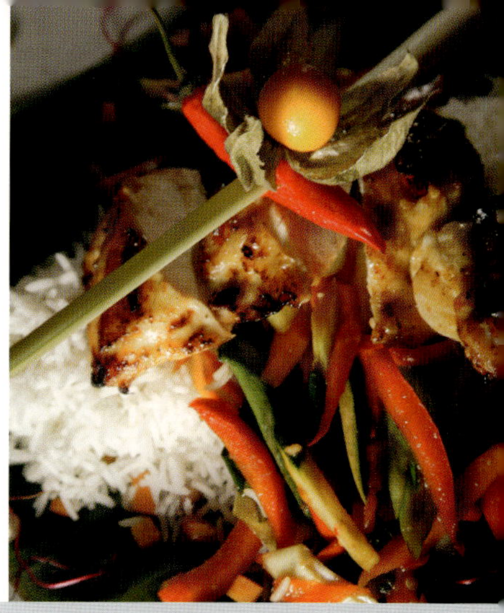

4 Maispoulardenbrüste, à 200 g
1 Chili, gehackt
Schale und Saft einer Zitrone
1 Knoblauchzehe, gehackt
5 EL Olivenöl

Alle Zutaten mischen und über Nacht im Kühlschrank marinieren lassen.
Die Brüste aus der Marinade nehmen, etwas abtupfen und auf beiden Seiten scharf anbraten. Bei 160°C ca. 10 Minuten fertig garen. Mit Salz und Pfeffer würzen.

400 g Basmatireis, gegart
600 g gemischtes Gemüse (z. B. Bok Choy, rote Paprika, Karotten)

Das Gemüse im Wok bissfest garen und würzen.

Poulardenbrüste auf Reis und Wokgemüse servieren.

4 chicken breasts, 7 oz each
1 chili, chopped
Zest and juice of 1 lemon
1 clove of garlic, chopped
5 tbsp olive oil

Combine all ingredients and marinate overnight in the refrigerator. Remove the breasts from the marinade, pat dry and sear on both sides. Bake at 320°F for approx. 10 minutes. Season with salt and pepper.

14 oz basmati rice, cooked
1 lb 5 oz mixed vegetables (e.g. bok choy, red bell pepper, carrots)

Sauté the vegetables in a wok until al dente and season.

Serve the chicken breasts on rice and wok vegetables.

4 blancs de poularde nourrie au maïs, de 200 g
chacune
1 piment, haché
Le jus et l'écorce d'un citron
1 gousse d'ail, hachée
5 c. à soupe d'huile d'olive

Mélanger tous les ingrédients et laisser mariner
pendant une nuit au réfrigérateur.
Retirer les blancs de la marinade, les tamponner
un peu et les saisir des deux côtés à feu puissant.
Finir la cuisson à 160 °C pendant env. 10 minutes. Saler et poivrer.

400 g de riz Basmati, cuit
600 g de mélange de légumes (par ex. chou de
Chine, poivron rouge, carottes)

Cuire les légumes dans le wok en veillant à ce
qu'ils restent fermes et assaisonner.

Servir les blancs de poularde sur le riz et les légumes cuits dans le wok.

4 pechugas de pularda, de 200 g cada una
1 guindilla, picada
La piel y el zumo de un limón
1 diente de ajo, picado
5 cucharadas de aceite de oliva

Mezcle todos los ingredientes y deje que marinen
durante la noche.
Saque las pechugas de pularda de la marinada,
séquelas un poco con papel de cocina y fríalas
a fuego fuerte por ambos lados. Áselas a 160 °C
durante aprox. 10 minutos hasta que estén
hechas. Salpimiente.

400 g de arroz basmati, cocido
600 g de mezcla de verduras (p.ej. *bok choy*,
pimiento rojo, zanahorias)

Saltee las verduras en el wok hasta que estén
crujientes.

Sirva la pularda son la verdura sobre un lecho
de arroz.

4 petti di pollastri di 200 g ciascuno
1 peperoncino tritato
La buccia e il succo di un limone
1 spicchio d'aglio tritato
5 cucchiai di olio d'oliva

Mescolare tutti gli ingredienti e lasciarli marinare
in frigorifero per una notte.
Estrarre i petti dalla marinata, tamponarli delica-
tamente e rosolarli a fuoco vivo da entrambi i lati.
Terminare la cottura in forno a 160 °C per circa
10 minuti. Salare e pepare.

400 g di riso Basmati bollito
600 g di verdure miste (ad es. bok choy, peperoni
rossi, carote)

Cuocere le verdure al dente nel wok e condirle.

Servire i petti di pollo con il riso e le verdure.

Halle der Helden

Design: Karim Teufel, Andreas Lucas, Harry Dehnhardt
Chef: Didier Birhartz | Owner: DeLuca Entertainment GmbH

Hanauer Landstraße 196, Union Gelände | 60314 Frankfurt | Ostend
Phone: +49 69 48 00 26 60
www.hallederhelden.de
Subway: Hanauer Landstraße
Opening hours: Mon–Fri noon to 3 pm, Mon–Wed 6 pm to 1 am,
Thu–Sat 7 pm to open end, Sun closed
Average Price: € 12
Cuisine: International

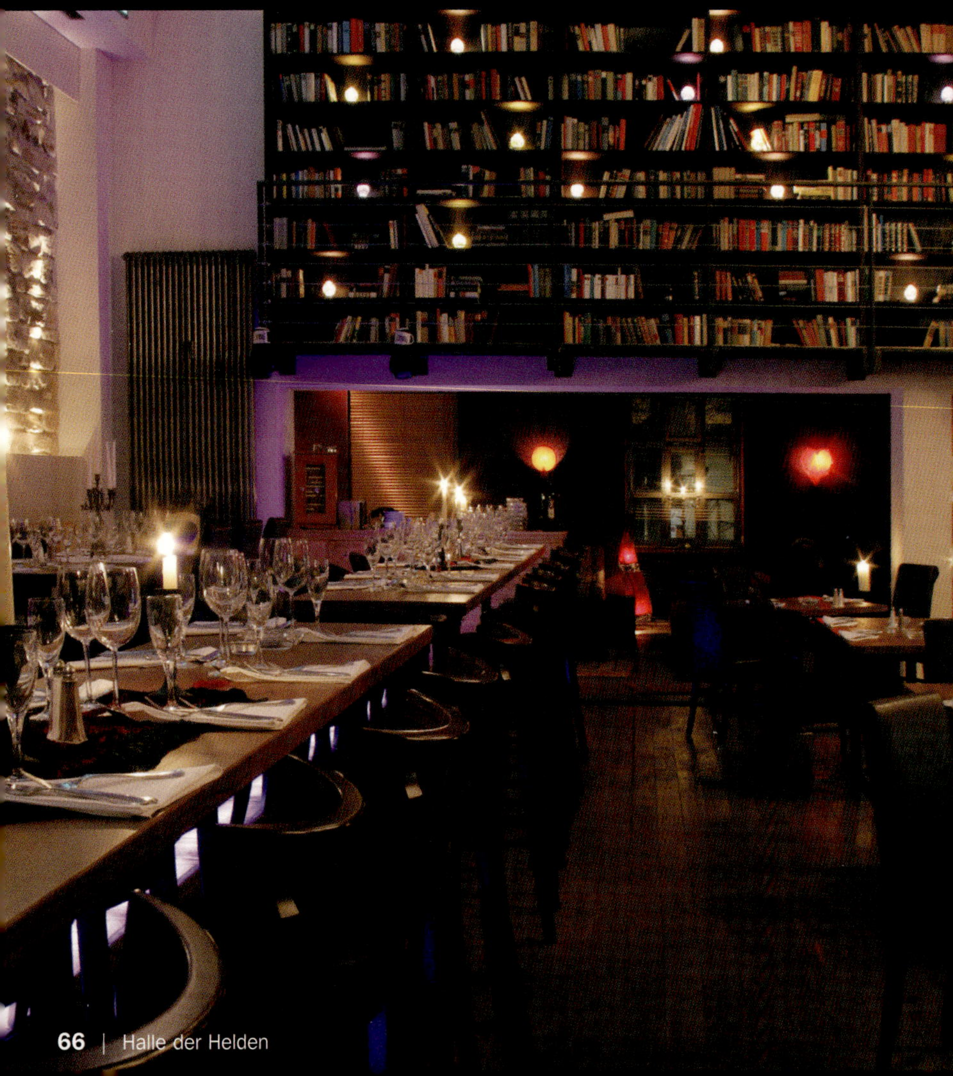

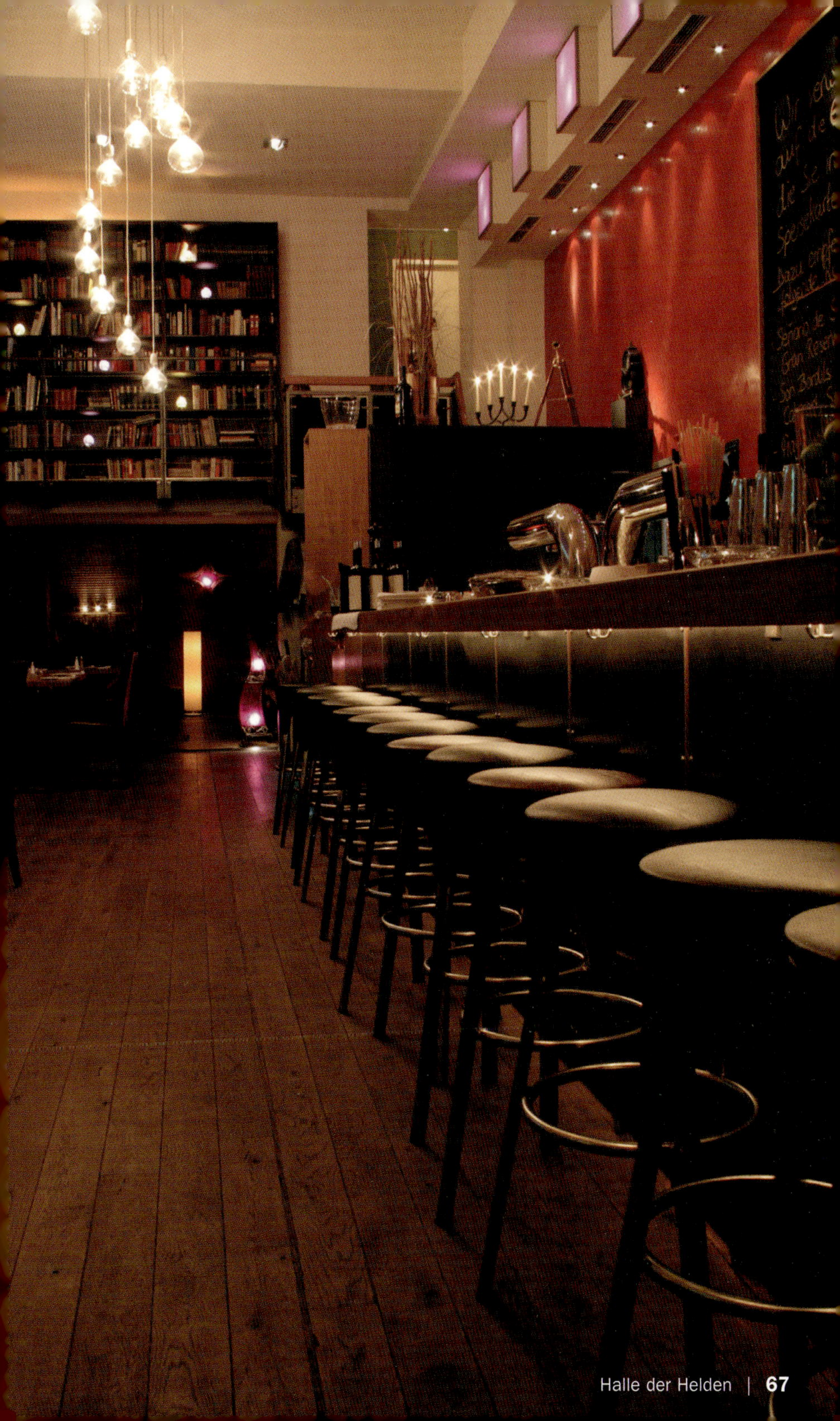

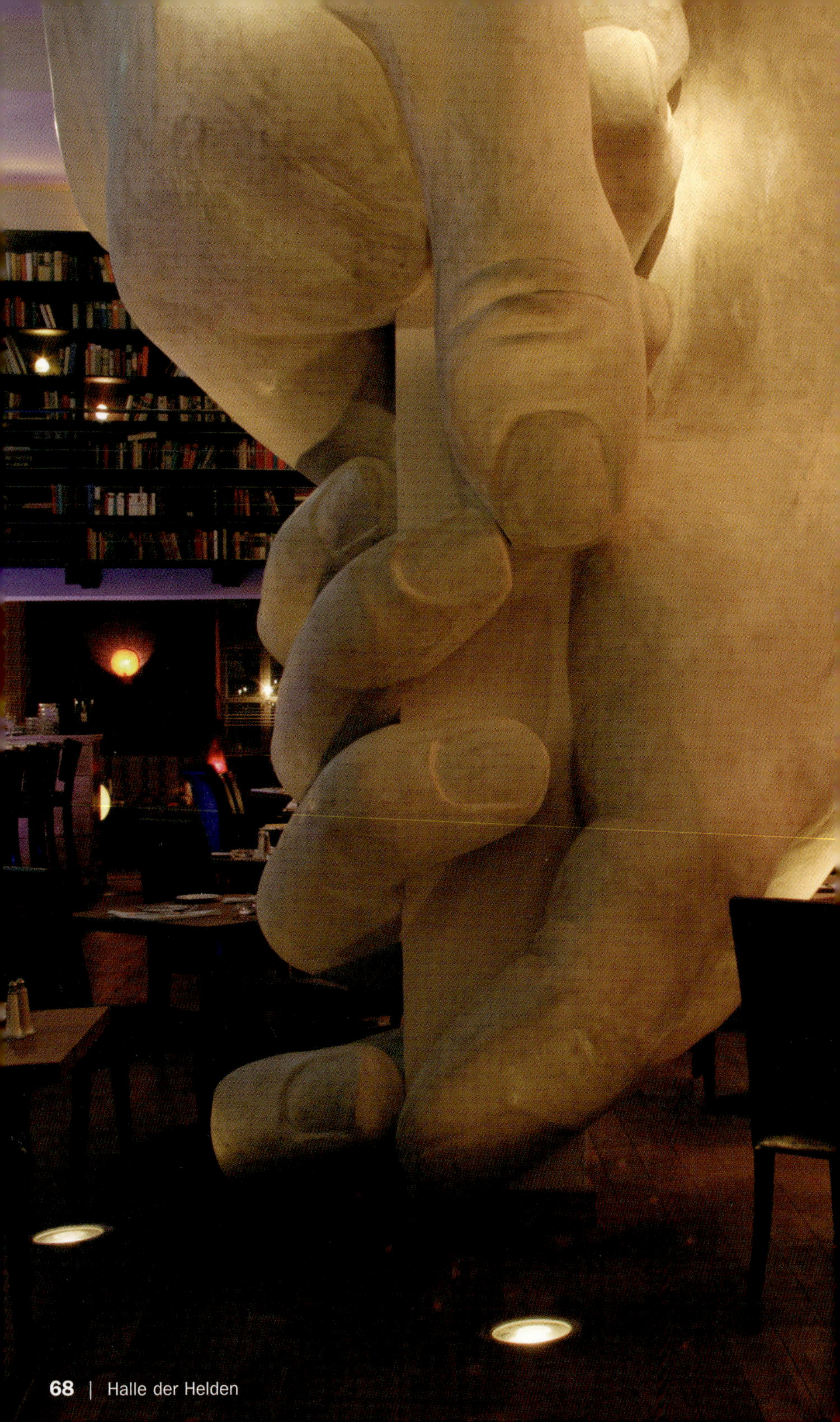

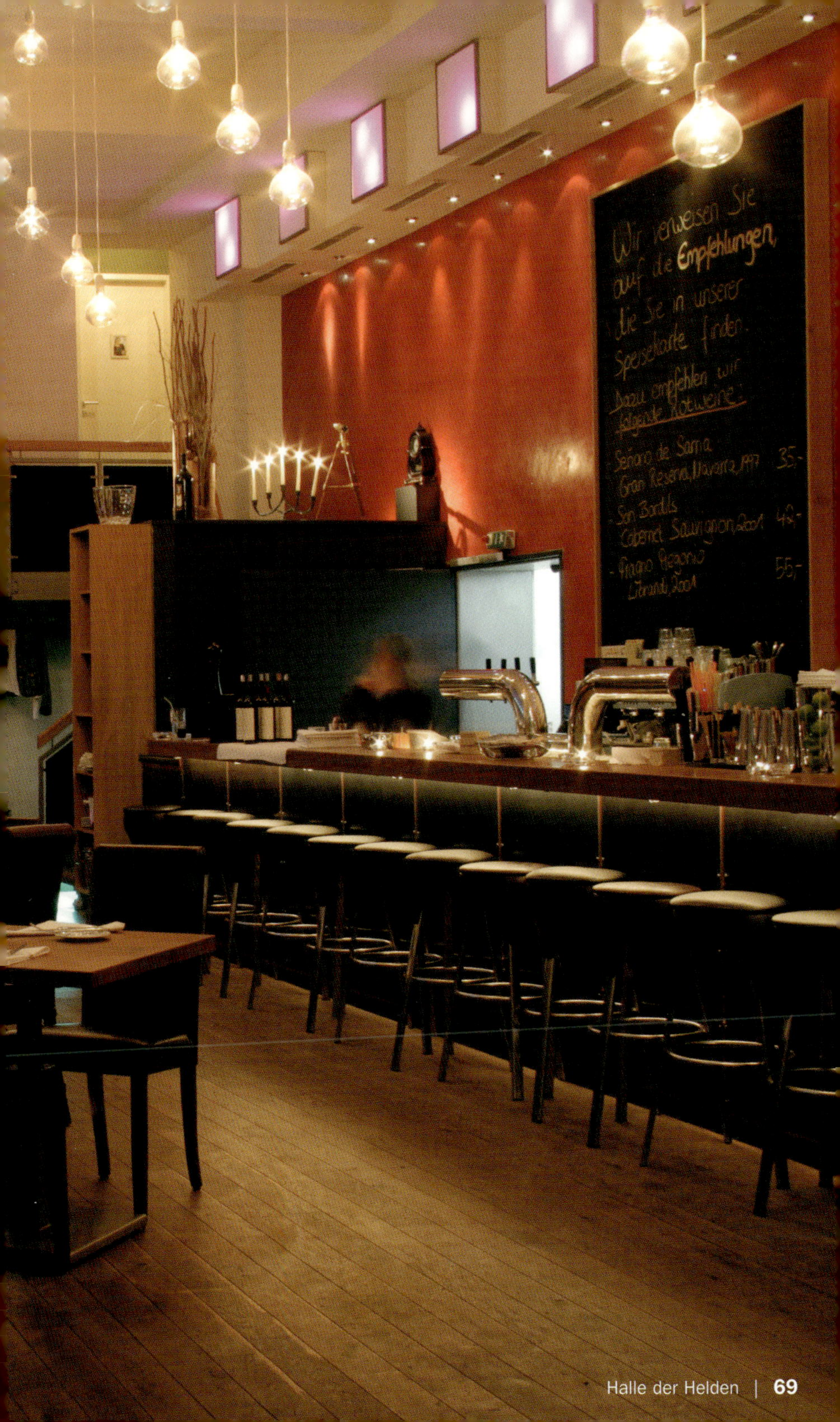

Wir verweisen Sie
auf die Empfehlungen,
die Sie in unserer
Speisekarte finden.
Dazu empfehlen wir
folgende Rotweine:

Señorío de Sarría
Gran Reserva Navarra 1997   35,-

San Bordils
Cabernet Sauvignon 2001   42,-

Pagno Regano
Z?brandi 2001   55,-

Holbein's

Design: Prof. Jochem Jourdan | Chef: Jo Ballmann
Owner: Gregor Meyer

Holbeinstraße 1 | 60596 Frankfurt | Sachsenhausen
Phone: +49 69 66 05 66 66
www.meyer-frankfurt.de
Subway: Schweizer Platz
Opening hours: Tue–Sun 10 am to midnight, Mon closed
Average price: € 22
Cuisine: Regional kitchen with mediterranean influences, crossover
Special features: Catering service, public banquet rooms for up to 300 persons

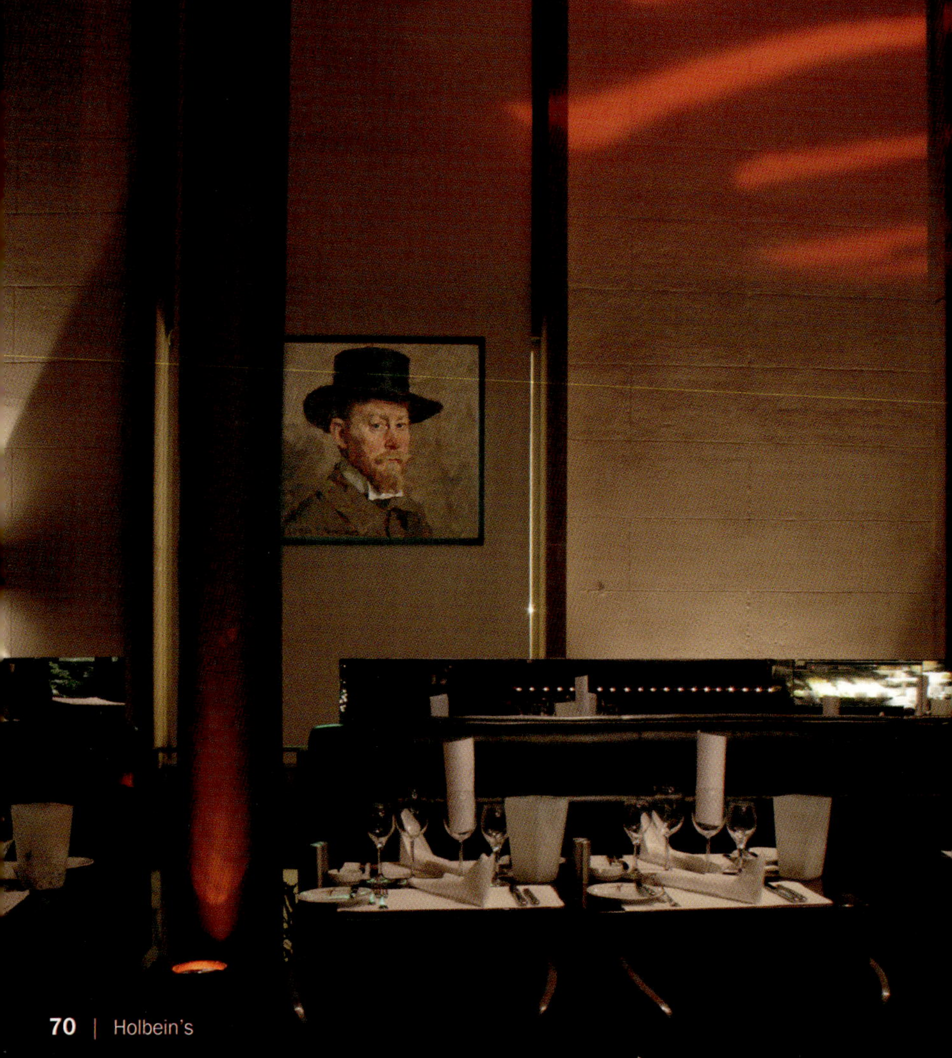

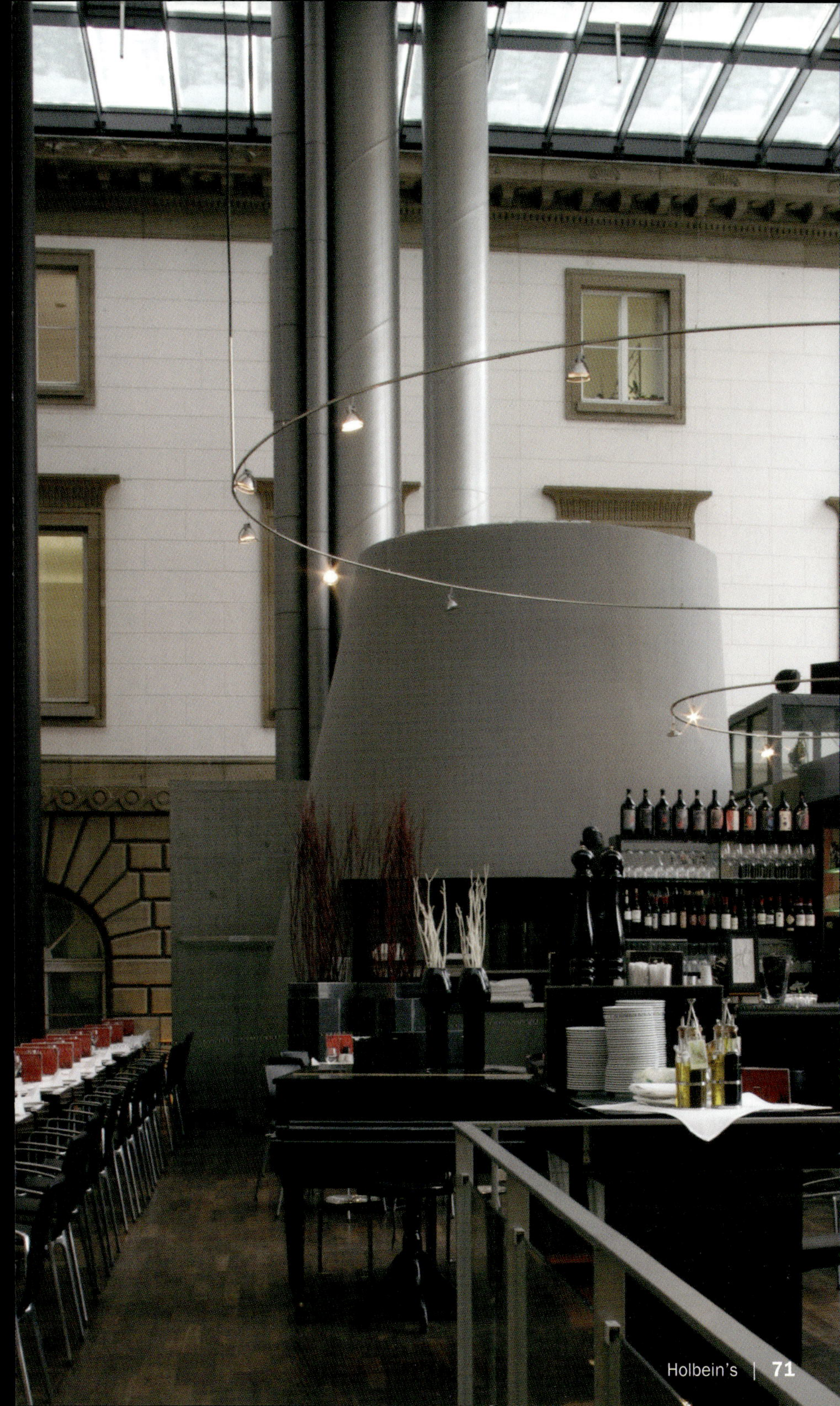

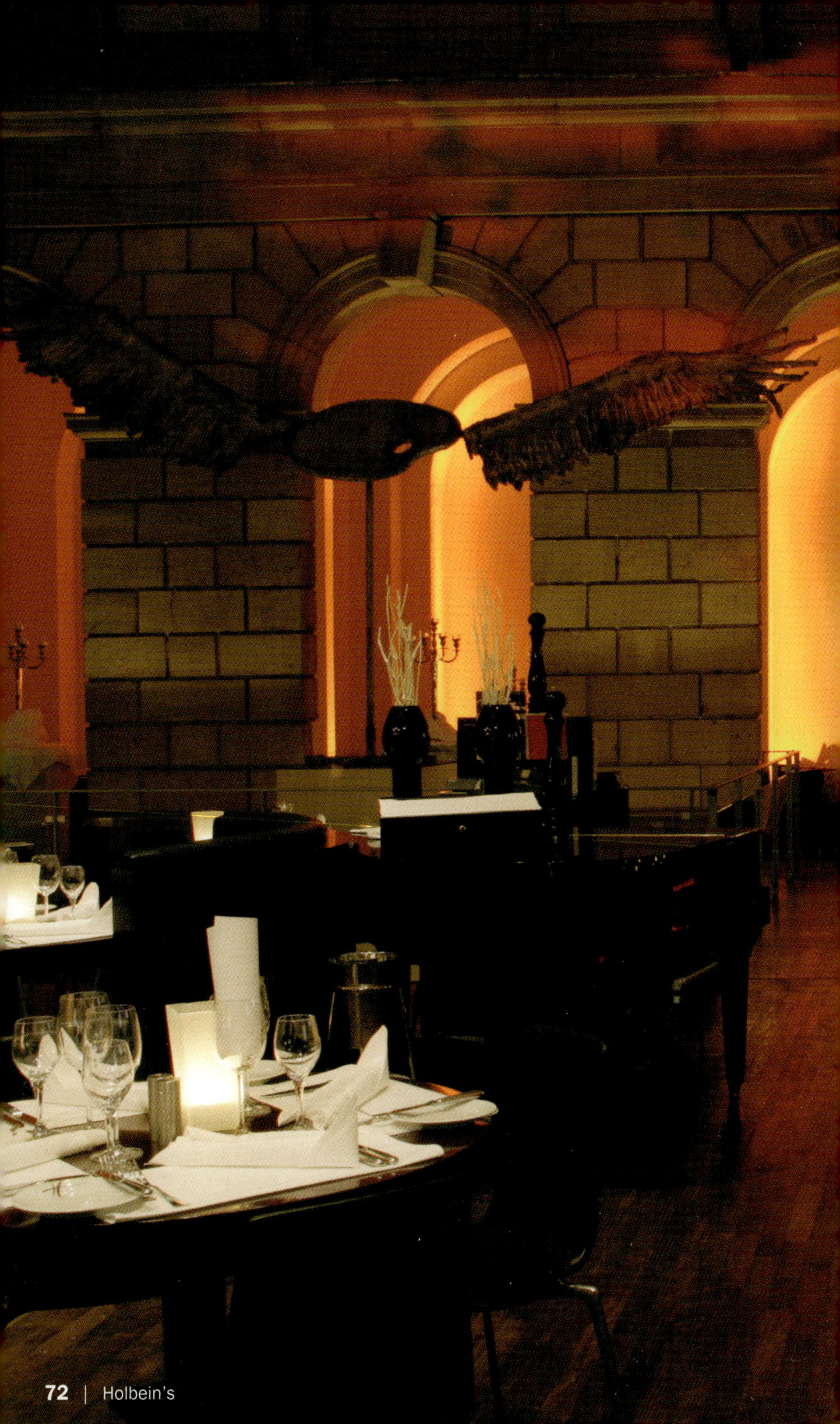

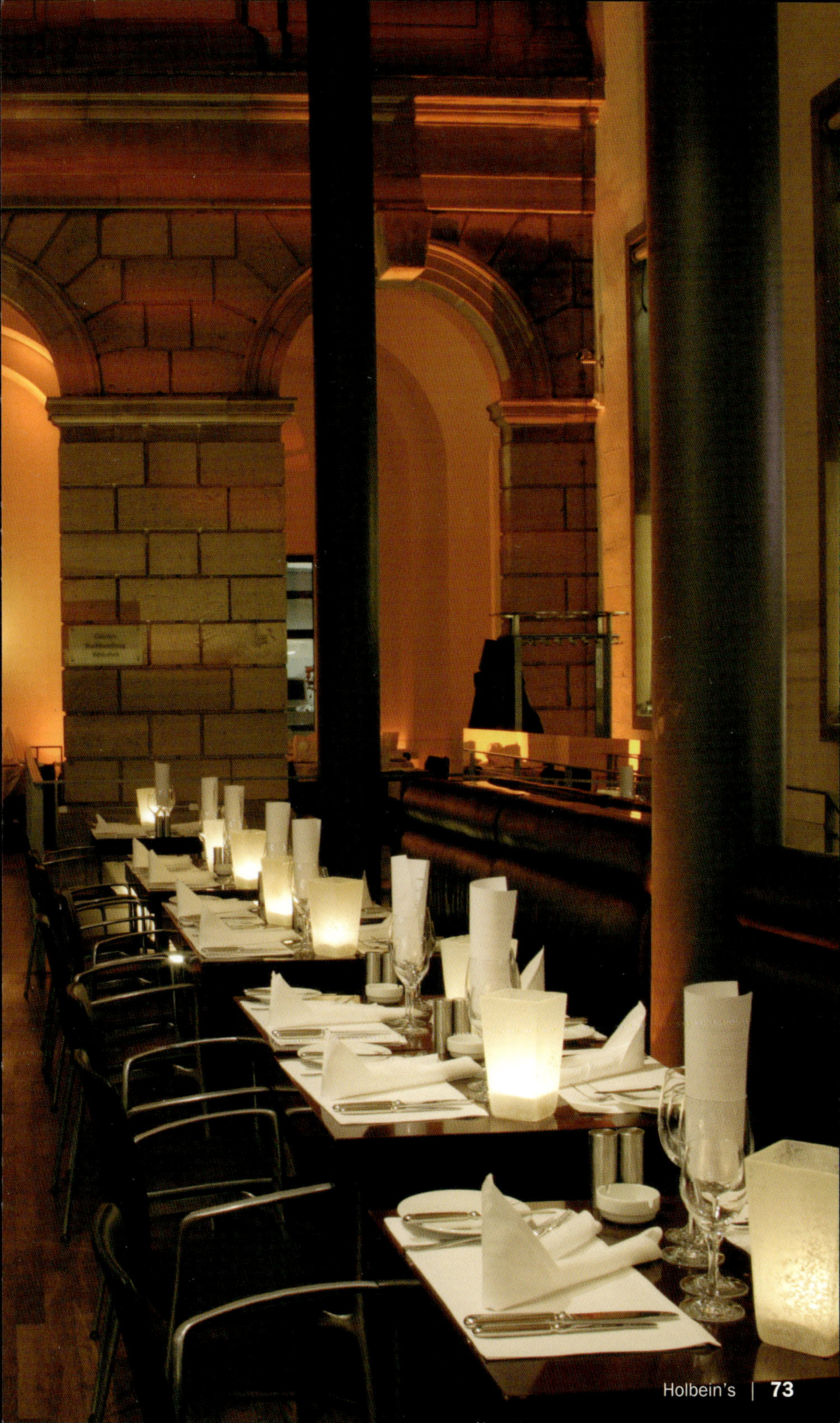

Haxe
und Rücken vom Lamm

Shank and Filet of Lamb

Jarret et selle d'agneau

Codillo y lomo de cordero

Stinco e schiena d'agnello

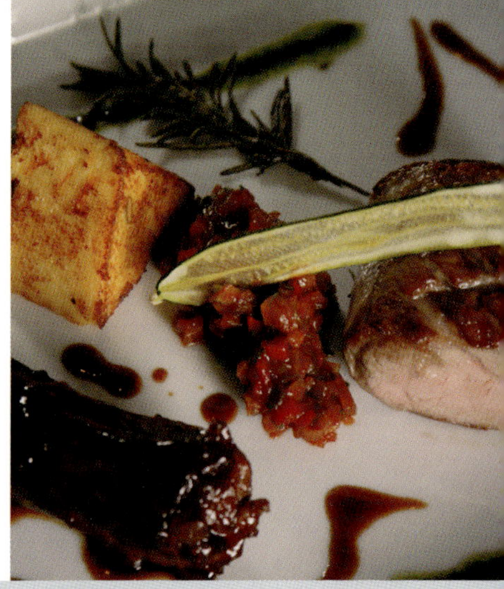

2 Lammhaxen
Salz, Pfeffer
3 EL Pflanzenöl
1 kleine Karotte, gewürfelt
½ Sellerieknolle, gewürfelt
1 Zwiebel, gewürfelt
1 Knoblauchzehe, halbiert
2 Zweige Rosmarin
250 ml Rotwein

Lammhaxen würzen und scharf anbraten. Das Fleisch aus der Pfanne nehmen und das Gemüse in derselben Pfanne anbraten. Knoblauch und Rosmarin zugeben und mit Rotwein ablöschen. Das Fleisch mit dem Gemüse in eine feuerfeste Form geben und bei 160°C ca. 1–1½ Stunden schmoren lassen. Den Knochen auslösen und das Fleisch in der passierten und abgeschmeckten Sauce warmstellen.

2 Lammrücken
Salz, Pfeffer
3 EL Pflanzenöl
1 Knoblauchzehe, püriert
1 Zweig Rosmarin, fein gehackt

Die Rücken würzen, scharf anbraten und mit der Knoblauch-Rosmarinmischung bestreichen. Bei 120°C ca. 8–10 Minuten rosa braten.

Dazu passen Kürbis-Polenta und Paprika-Chutney.

2 lamb shanks
Salt, pepper
3 tbsp vegetable oil
1 small carrot, diced
½ celery root, diced
1 onion, diced
1 clove of garlic, halved
2 twigs rosemary
250 ml red wine

Season lamb shanks and sear. Remove the meat from the pan and sear the vegetables in the same pan. Add garlic and rosemary and deglaze with red wine. Place the meat with the vegetables in an ovenproof dish and braise at 320°F for 1–1½ hours. Debone the shanks and keep the meat warm in the strained and seasoned sauce.

2 lamb filets
Salt, pepper
3 tbsp vegetable oil
1 clove of garlic, mashed
1 twig rosemary, finely chopped

Season the filets, sear and brush with the garlic-rosemary mixture. Bake at 250°F for approx. 8–10 minutes until medium-rare.

Serve with pumpkin polenta and bell pepper chutney.

2 jarrets d'agneau
Sel, poivre
3 c. à soupe d'huile végétale
1 petite carotte, coupée en dés
½ bulbe de céleri, coupé en dés
1 oignon, coupé en dés
1 gousse d'ail, coupée en deux
2 branches de romarin
250 ml de vin rouge

Assaisonner les jarrets d'agneau et les saisir à feu vif. Retirer la viande de la poêle et y faire revenir les légumes. Ajouter l'ail et le romarin, puis verser le vin rouge. Mettre la viande et les légumes dans un moule ininflammable et faire cuire à 160 °C pendant env. 1–1 ½ heure. Enlever les os et conserver la viande au chaud dans la sauce qui aura été filtrée et assaisonnée.

2 selles d'agneau
Sel, poivre
3 c. à soupe d'huile végétale
1 gousse d'ail, réduite en purée
1 branche de romarin, finement hachée

Assaisonner les selles d'agneau, les saisir à feu vif et les frotter avec la préparation à base d'ail et de romarin. Faire rôtir à 120 °C pendant env. 8–10 minutes pour obtenir une viande rose.

Proposer en accompagnement une polenta au potiron et de la chutney au poivron.

2 codillos de cordero
Sal, pimiento
3 cucharadas de aceite vegetal
1 zanahoria pequeña, en dados
½ bulbo de apio, en dados
1 cebolla, en dados
1 diente de ajo, cortado por la mitad
2 ramitos de romero
250 ml de vino tinto

Sazone los codillos de cordero y fríalos a fuego fuerte. Saque la carne de la sartén y sofría la verdura en ella. Incorpore el ajo y el romero y vierta dentro el vino tinto. Coloque el cordero y la verdura en un molde resistente al calor y ase los ingredientes durante aprox. 1–1 ½ horas a 160 °C. Quite el hueso y reserve la carne caliente en la salsa colada y sazonada.

2 lomos de cordero
Sal, pimienta
3 cucharadas de aceite vegetal
1 diente de ajo, hecho puré
1 ramito de romero, finamente picado

Sazone los lomos, fríalos a fuego fuerte y úntelos con la mezcla de ajo y romero. Áselos después aprox. 8–10 minutos a 120 °C hasta que estén medio hechos.

Un buen acompañamiento es polenta de calabaza y *chutney* de pimiento.

2 stinchi d'agnello
Sale, pepe
3 cucchiai di olio vegetale
1 piccola carota tagliata a dadini
½ bulbo di sedano tagliato a dadini
1 cipolla tagliata a dadini
1 spicchio d'aglio tagliato a metà
2 rami di rosmarino
250 ml di vino rosso

Condire gli stinchi d'agnello e rosolarli a fuoco vivo. Estrarre la carne dalla padella e rosolare nella stessa padella le verdure. Aggiungere l'aglio e il rosmarino e bagnare con il vino rosso. Mettere la carne e le verdure in una pirofila e lasciarle cuocere in forno a 160 °C per circa 1 ora–1 ½. Disossare la carne e tenerla al caldo nella salsa condita e passata al passaverdura.

2 schiene d'agnello
Sale, pepe
3 cucchiai di olio vegetale
1 spicchio d'aglio passato
1 rametto di rosmarino finemente tritato

Condire le schiene d'agnello, rosolarle a fuoco vivo e spennellarle con il trito d'aglio e di rosmarino. Cuocerle in forno a 120 °C per circa 8–10 minuti.

Servire con polenta di zucca e con chutney di peperoni.

IMA Multibar

Design: Jose Ortels | Chef: Emre Erkan
Owners: David & Karen Ardinast

Kleine Bockenheimer Straße 14 | 60313 Frankfurt | Innenstadt
Phone: +49 69 90 02 56 65
www.ima-multibar.com
Subway: Alte Oper, Hauptwache
Opening hours: Mon–Wed 11 am to 9 pm, Thu–Sat 11 am to 1:30 pm & cocktail bar
open from 9:30 pm, Sun closed
Average price: € 7
Cuisine: International

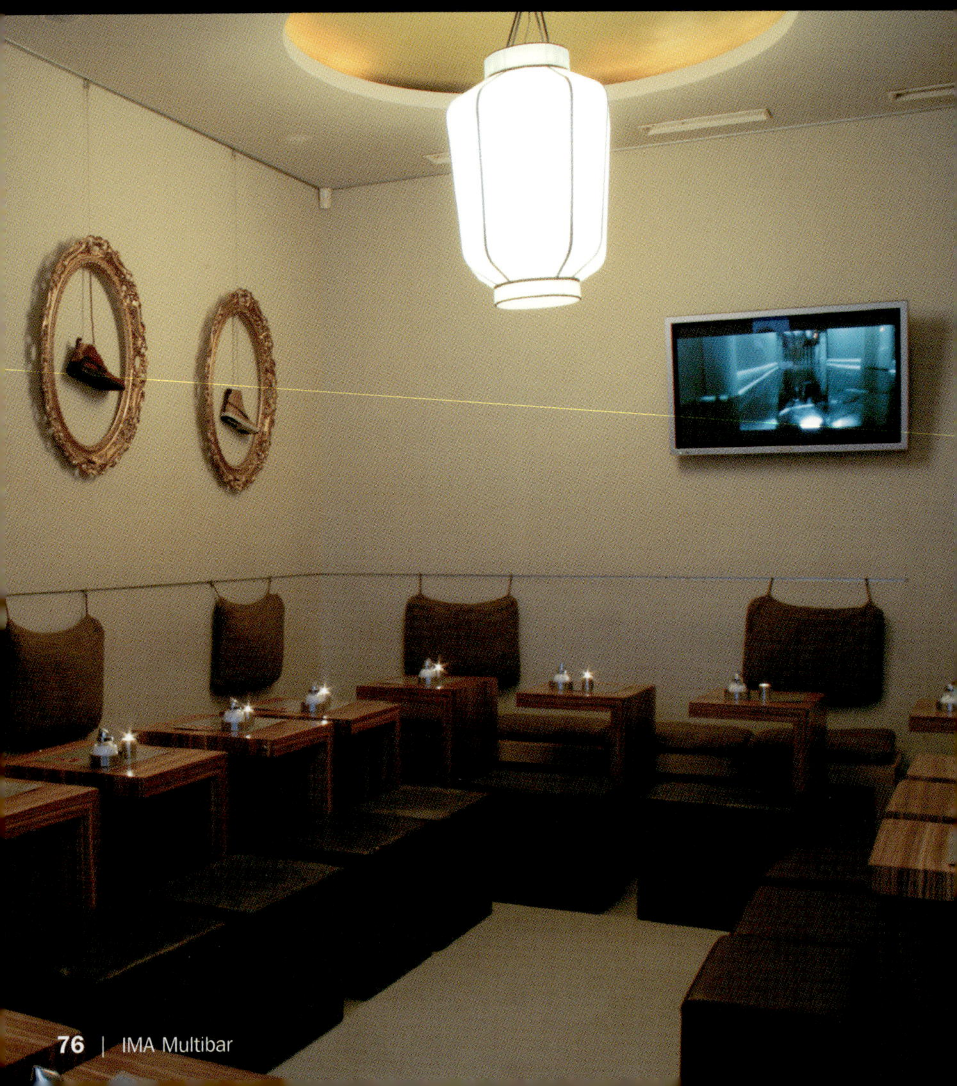

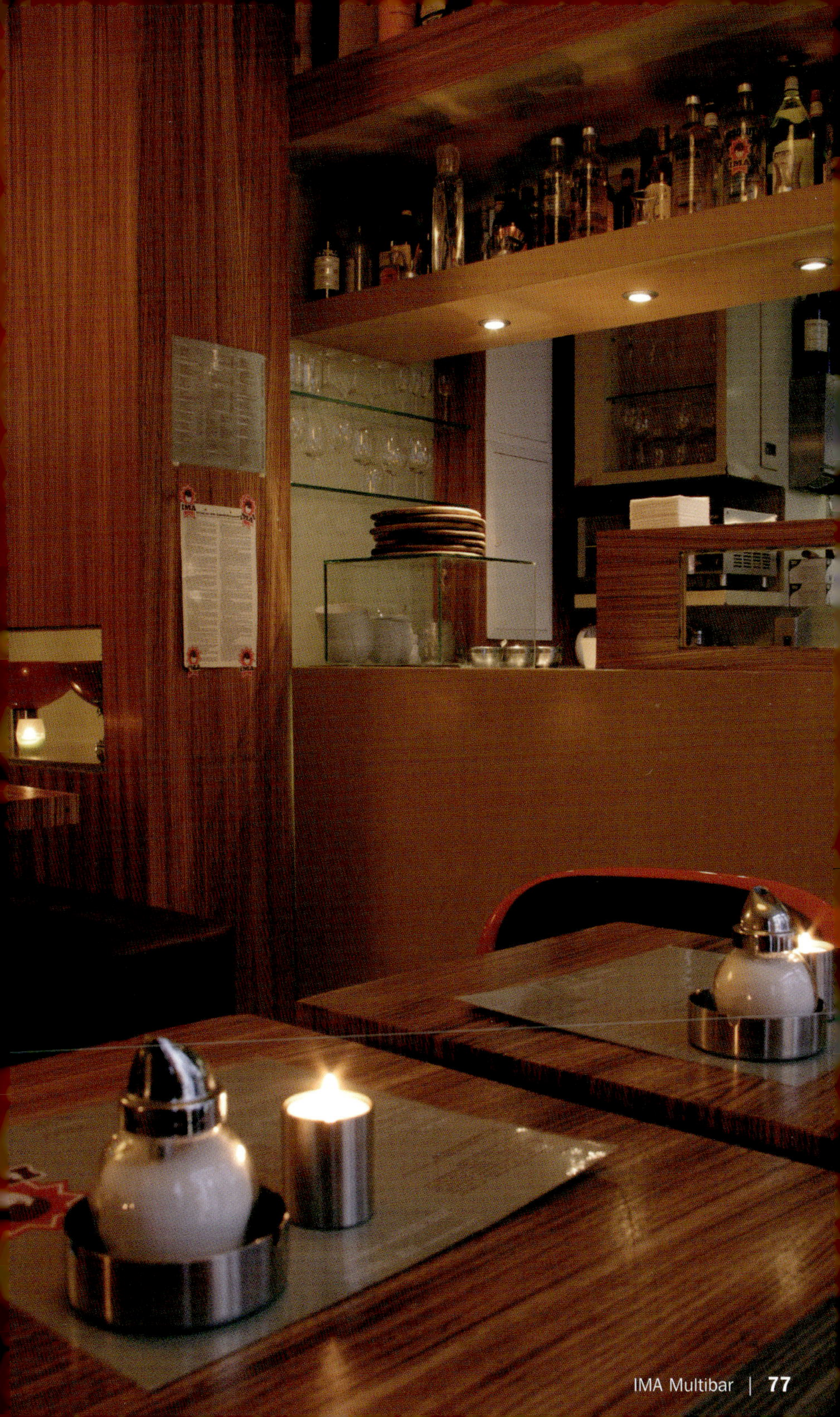

Rinderfilet
mit gelben Linsen und Granatapfel

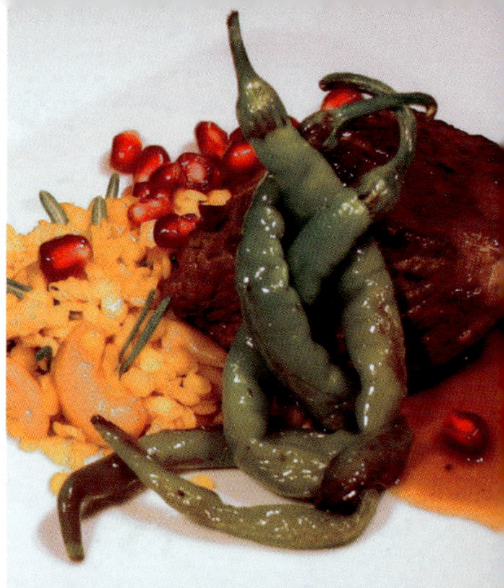

Beef Filet with Yellow Lentils and
Pomegranate

Filet de boeuf aux lentilles jaunes et à la
grenade

Filete de ternera con lentejas amarillas
y granada

Filetto di manzo con lenticchie gialle
e melagrana

4 Scheiben Rinderfilet, à 200 g
Salz, Pfeffer
3 EL Pflanzenöl

350 g gelbe Linsen
750 ml Geflügelbrühe
2 EL Butter
2 Zweige Rosmarin
50 g Cashewkerne
Salz, Pfeffer, Kreuzkümmel

150 ml Rotwein
120 ml Bratensauce
1 Granatapfel, die Kerne ausgelöst
20 grüne Chilischoten

Die Linsen mit dem Geflügelfond aufkochen und ca. 12 Minuten köcheln lassen. Die Rosmarinnadeln in der Butter anschwitzen, die Cashewkerne zugeben und mit den gekochten Linsen mischen. Abschmecken und warmstellen.
Den Rotwein um die Hälfte einreduzieren lassen, mit Bratensauce auffüllen und die Granatapfelkerne einrühren.
Die Rinderfiletscheiben würzen, von beiden Seiten 1 Minute scharf anbraten und warmstellen. In derselben Pfanne die Chilischoten scharf anbraten.
Die Linsen auf vier Tellern verteilen, das Rinderfilet anlegen und mit Sauce beträufeln. Jeweils 5 Chilischoten auf Fleisch und Linsen verteilen und servieren.

4 slices beef filet, 7 oz each
Salt, pepper
3 tbsp vegetable oil

12 oz yellow lentils
750 ml chicken stock
2 tbsp butter
2 twigs rosemary
1½ oz cashew nuts
Salt, pepper, cumin

150 ml red wine
120 ml gravy
1 pomegranate, the seeds set aside
20 green chilies

Bring the lentils with the chicken stock to a boil and simmer for approx. 12 minutes. Sauté the rosemary needles in butter, add the cashew nuts and combine with the cooked lentils. Season and keep warm.
Reduce the red wine to one half, fill up with gravy and stir in the pomegranate seeds.
Season the beef filet slices, sear from both sides for 1 minute and keep warm. Sear the chilies in the same pan.
Divide the lentils onto four plates, place the beef filet beside it and drizzle with sauce. On each plate spread 5 chilies across the meat and lentils.

4 tranches de filet de boeuf de 200 g chacune
Sel, poivre
3 c. à soupe d'huile végétale

350 g de lentilles jaunes
750 ml de bouillon de vollaille
2 c. à soupe de beurre
2 branches de romarin
50 g de noix de cajou
Sel, poivre, cumin

150 ml de vin rouge
120 ml de jus de rôti
1 grenade, épépinée, conserver les pépins
20 piments verts

Amener les lentilles à ébullition avec le fond de volaille et laisser mijoter pendant env. 12 minutes. Faire revenir les aiguilles de romarin dans le beurre, ajouter les noix de cajou et mélanger avec les lentilles cuites. Assaisonner et conserver au chaud.
Réduire le vin rouge de moitié, compléter avec la sauce de rôti et ajouter les pépins de la grenade.
Saler et poivrer les tranches de filet de boeuf, les saisir des deux côtés à feu vif pendant 1 minute et conserver au chaud. Faire revenir à feu vif les piments dans la même poêle.
Répartir les lentilles sur quatre assiettes, disposer le filet de boeuf et arroser de sauce. Placer dans chaque assiette 5 piments sur la viande et sur les lentilles et servir.

4 filetes de ternera, de 200 g cada uno
Sal, pimienta
3 cucharadas de aceite vegetal

350 g de lentejas amarillas
750 ml de caldo de volatería
2 cucharadas de mantequilla
2 ramitas de romero
50 g de anacardos
Sal, pimienta, comino

150 ml de vino tinto
120 ml de salsa de asado
1 granada, las pepitas sueltas
20 guindillas verdes

Cueza las lentejas con el caldo de volatería y deje que hierva a fuego lento durante aprox. 12 minutos. Rehogue las agujas del romero en la mantequilla, añada los anacardos e incorpore las lentejas cocidas. Sazone y reserve caliente.
Reduzca el vino tinto a la mitad, añada la salsa de asado e incorpore las pepitas de la granada.
Sazone los filetes, fríalos a fuego fuerte durante 1 minuto por cada lado y resérvelos calientes. Sofría en esa misma sartén las guindillas.
Reparta las lentejas en cuatro platos, coloque sobre ellas los filetes y vierta por encima la salsa. Disponga sobre la carne y las lentejas 5 guindillas por plato y sirva.

4 fette di filetto di manzo di 200 g ciascuna
Sale, pepe
3 cucchiai di olio vegetale

350 g di lenticchie gialle
750 ml di brodo di pollo o di tacchino
2 cucchiai di burro
2 rami di rosmarino
50 g di noci di acagiù
Sale, pepe, cumino

150 ml di vino rosso
120 ml di sugo d'arrosto
I semi di 1 melagrana
20 peperoncini verdi

Portare a cottura le lenticchie nel fondo di pollo e lasciar cuocere a fuoco lento per circa 12 minuti. Rosolare nel burro gli aghi di rosmarino, unire i noci di acagiù e mescolarli alle lenticchie cotte. Assaggiare, regolare il condimento e tenere in caldo.
Far restringere il vino rosso della metà, aggiungere il sugo d'arrosto ed incorporarvi i semi di melagrana.
Condire le fette di filetto, rosolarle a fuoco vivo da entrambi i lati per 1 minuto e tenerle in caldo. Rosolare a fuoco vivo nella stessa padella i peperoncini.
Ripartire le lenticchie in quattro piatti, disporvi il filetto di manzo e pillottarlo con la salsa. Ripartire 5 peperoncini su ogni filetto e sulle lenticchie e servire.

Kabuki

Design & Owner: Kiyoshi Tsutsumi | Chef: Shunichi Komiyama

Kaiserstraße 42 | 60329 Frankfurt | Bahnhofsviertel
Phone: +49 69 23 43 53
www.kabuki-restaurant.com
Subway: Willy-Brandt-Platz
Opening hours: Mon–Fri noon to 2 pm and 6 pm to 10:30 pm,
Sat–Sun 6 pm to 10:30 pm
Average price: € 32
Cuisine: Japanese, Tepan-Yaki

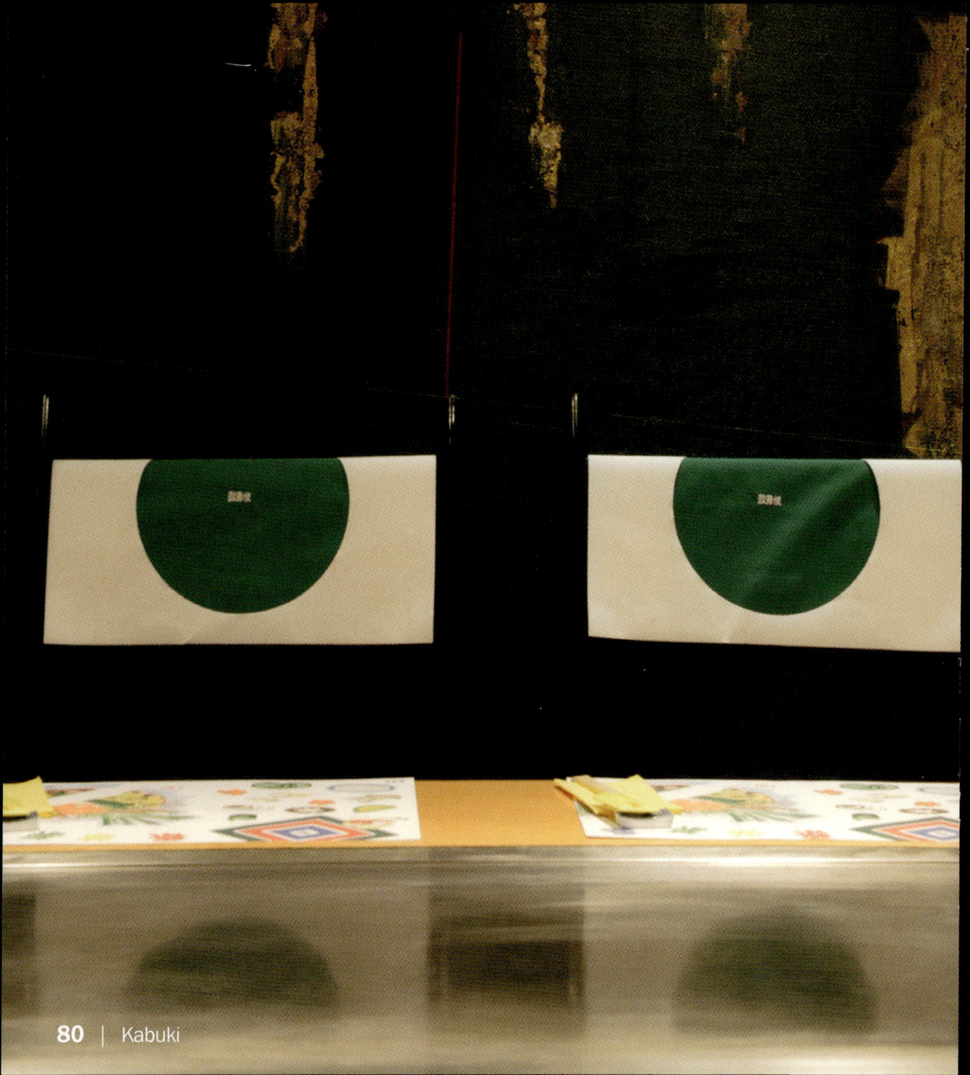

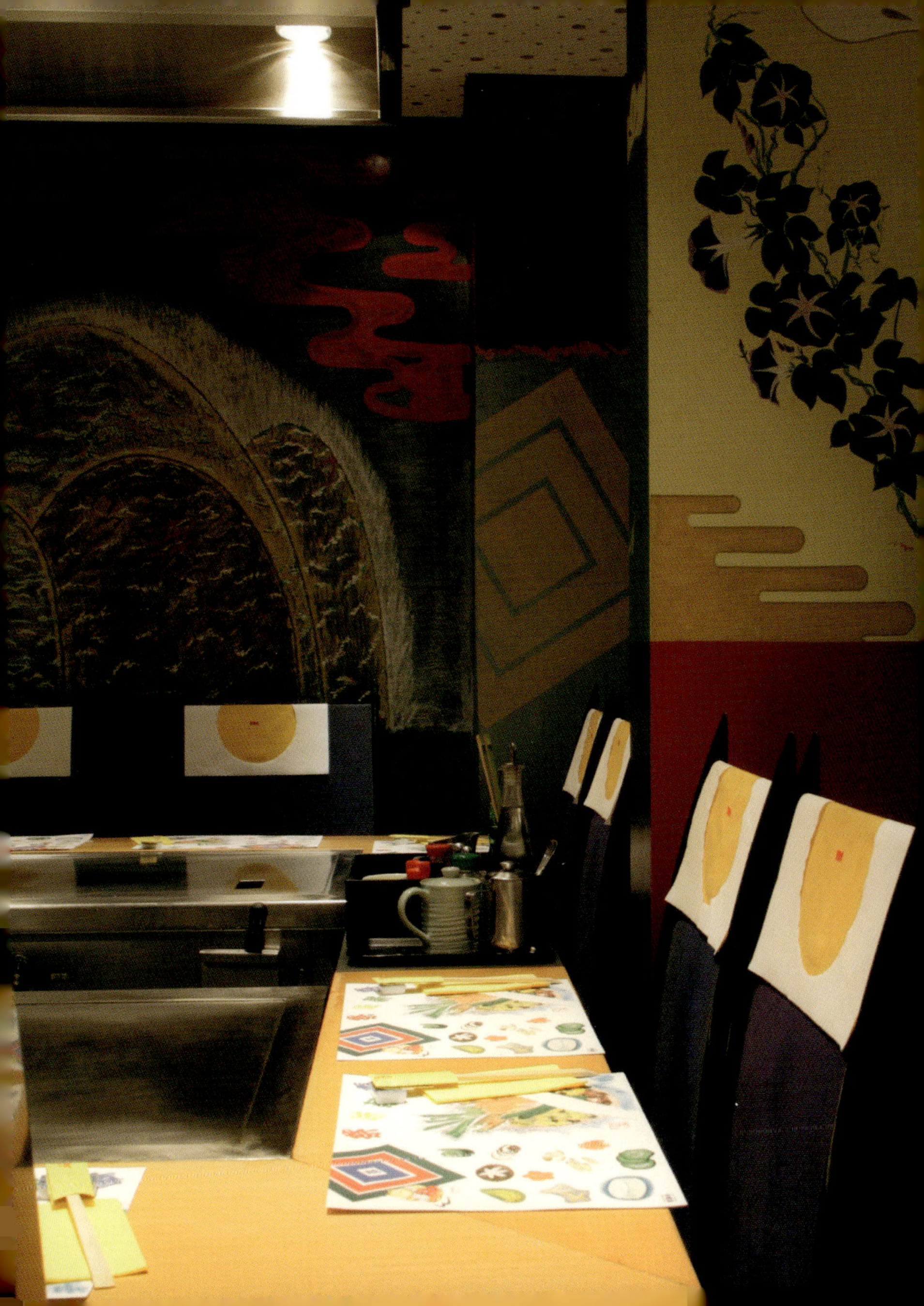

King Kamehameha Club

Design: Kay Mack | Owner: Madjid Djamegari

Hanauer Landstraße 192, Union Gelände | 60314 Frankfurt | Ostend
Phone: +49 69 4 80 03 70
www.king-kamehameha.de
Subway: Schwedler Straße
Opening hours: Thu 9 pm to 4 am, Fri–Sat 10 pm to 5 am, Sun–Wed closed
Average cocktail price: € 7

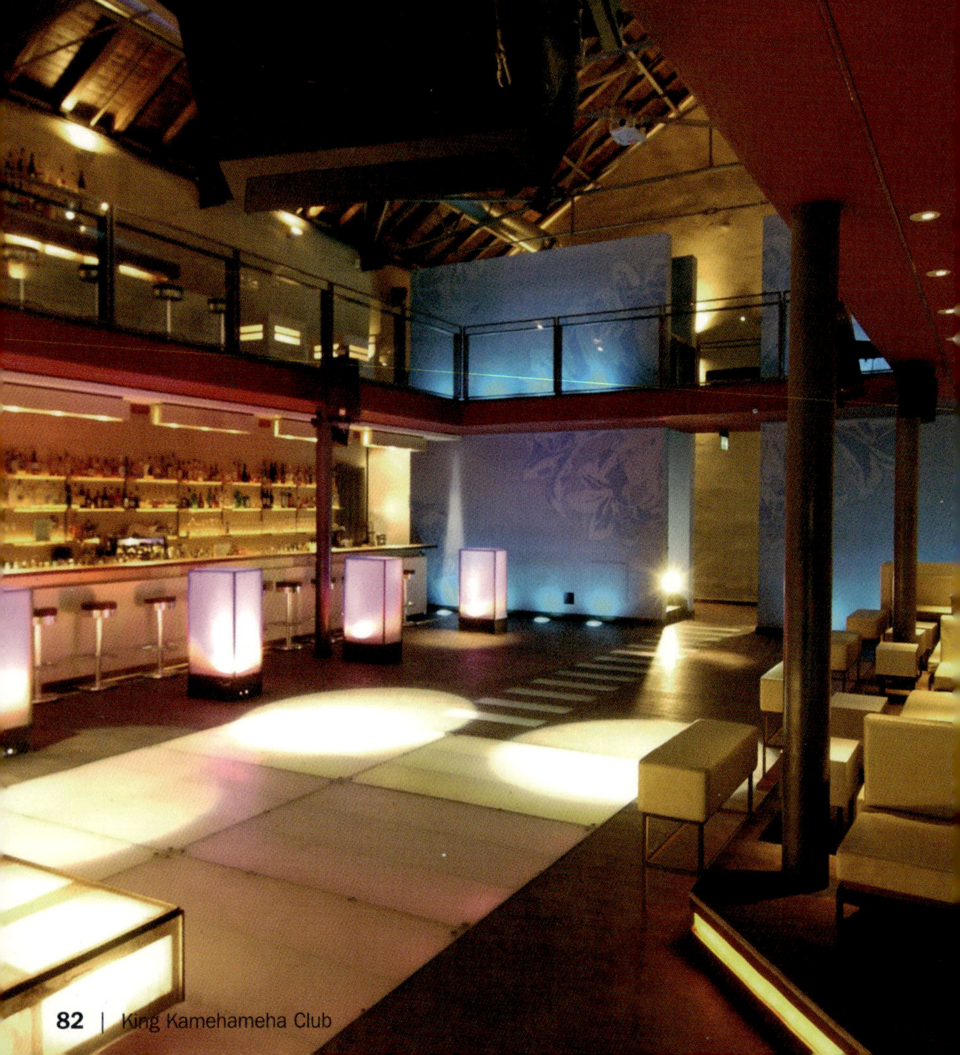

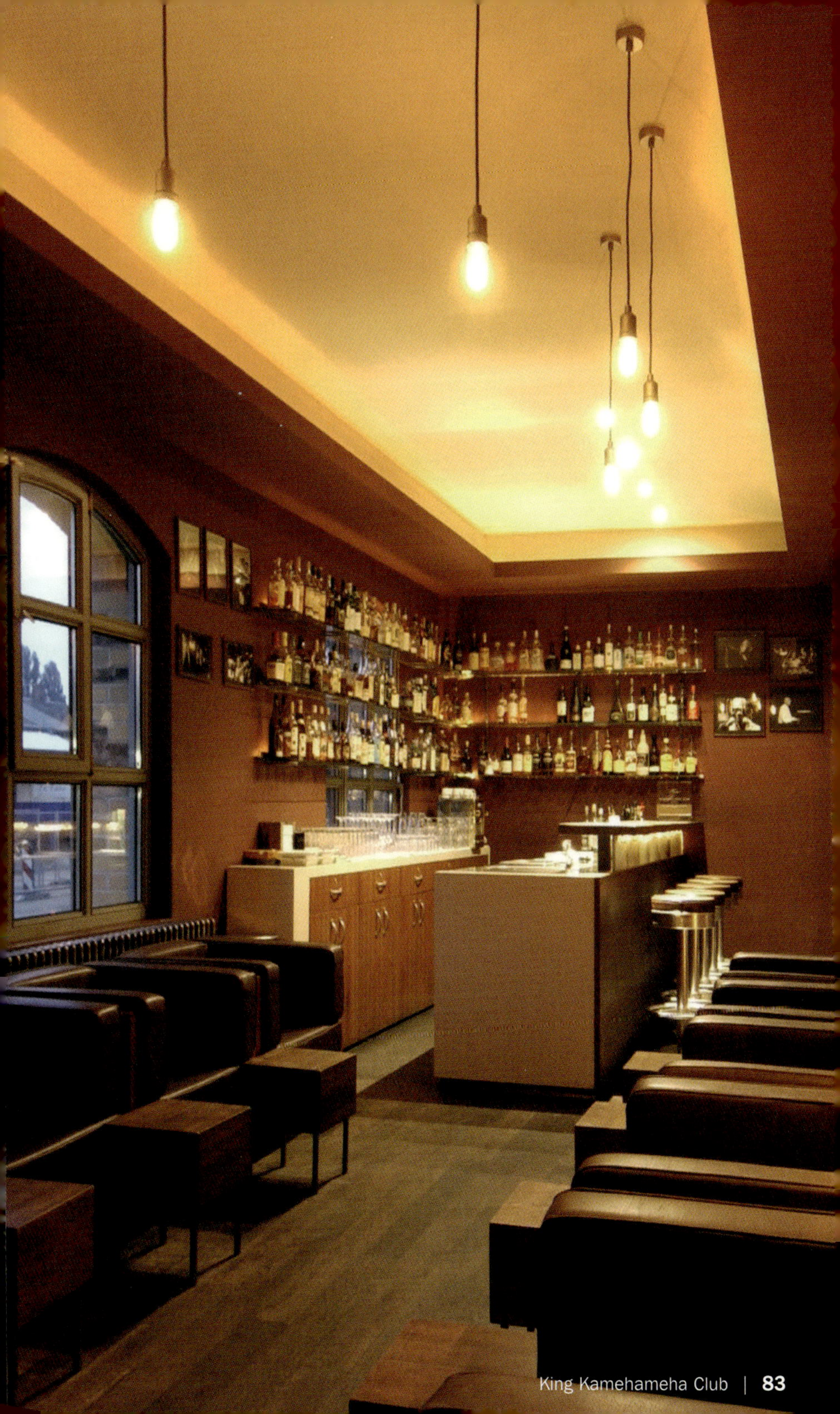

Medici

Design: Prof. Alfred Grazioli
Chef & Owners: Stamatios & Christos Simiakos

Weißadlergasse 2 | 60311 Frankfurt | Stadtmitte
Phone: +49 69 21 99 07 94
www.restaurantmedici.de
Subway: Hauptwache
Opening hours: Mon–Sat 11 am to 1 am, Sun closed
Average price: € 15
Cuisine: Modern European

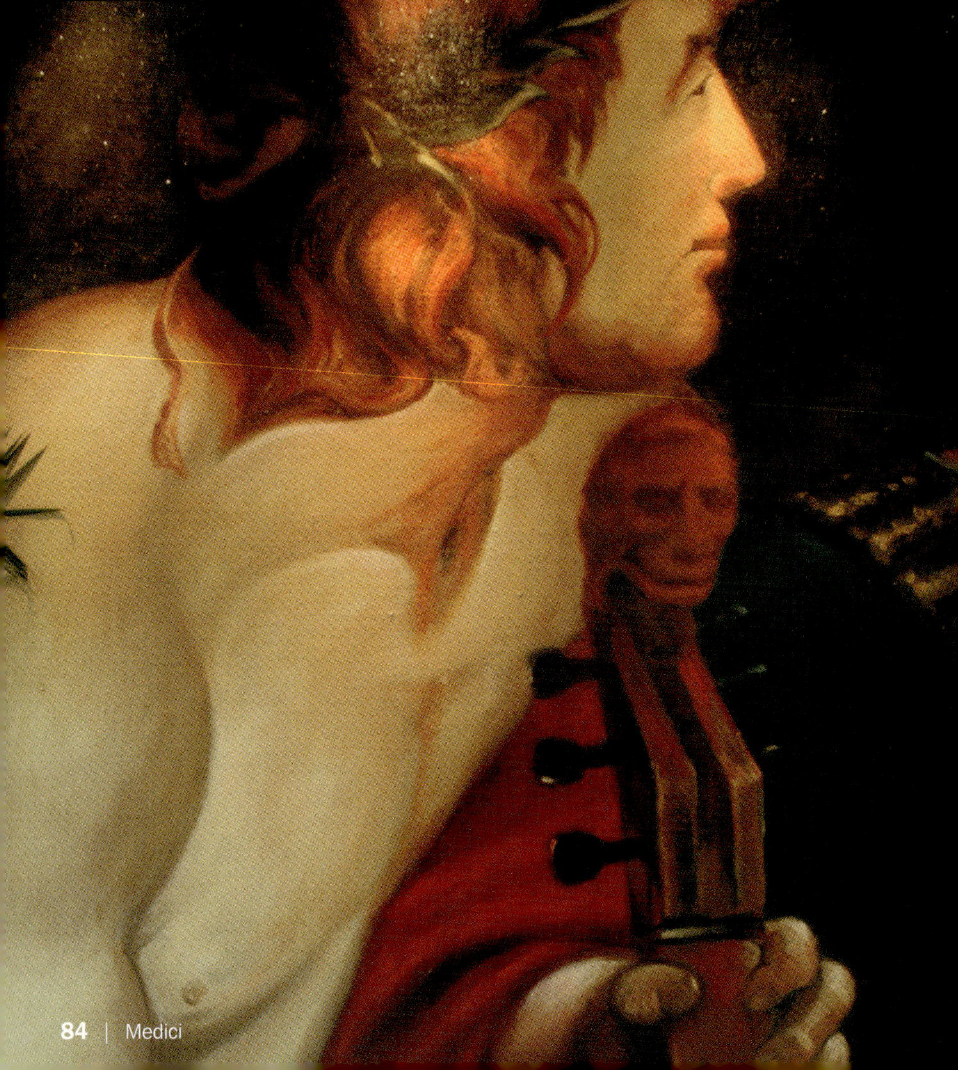

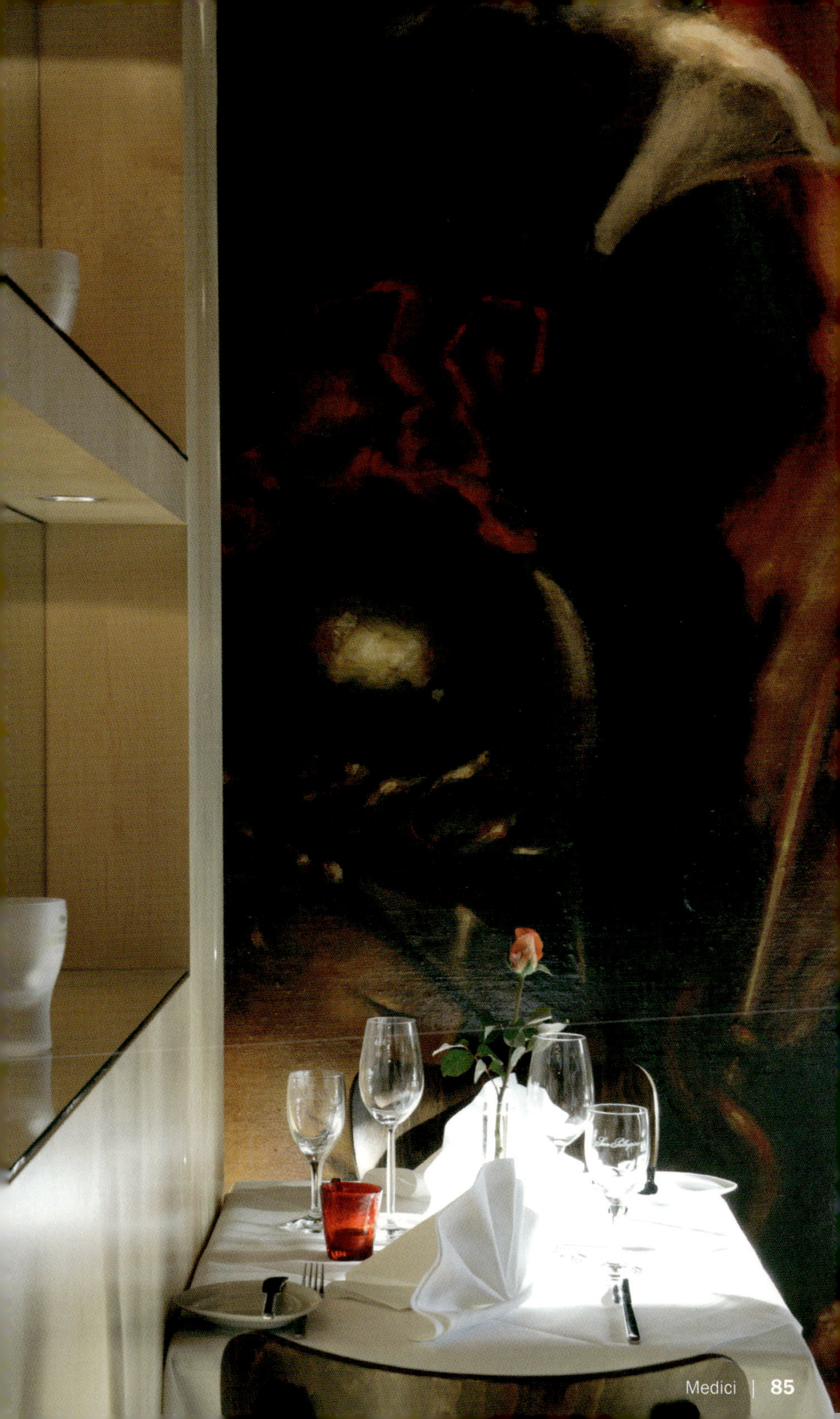

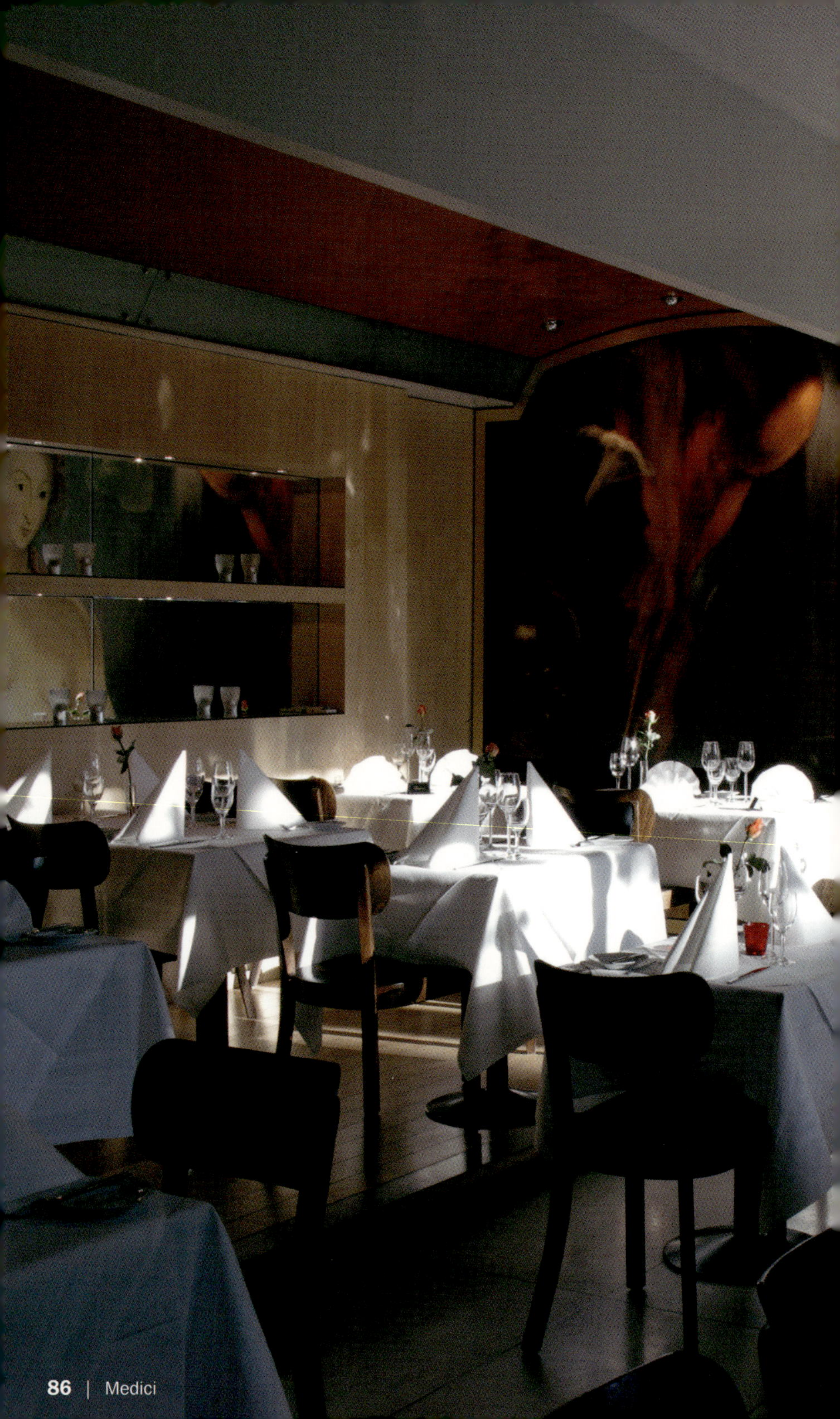

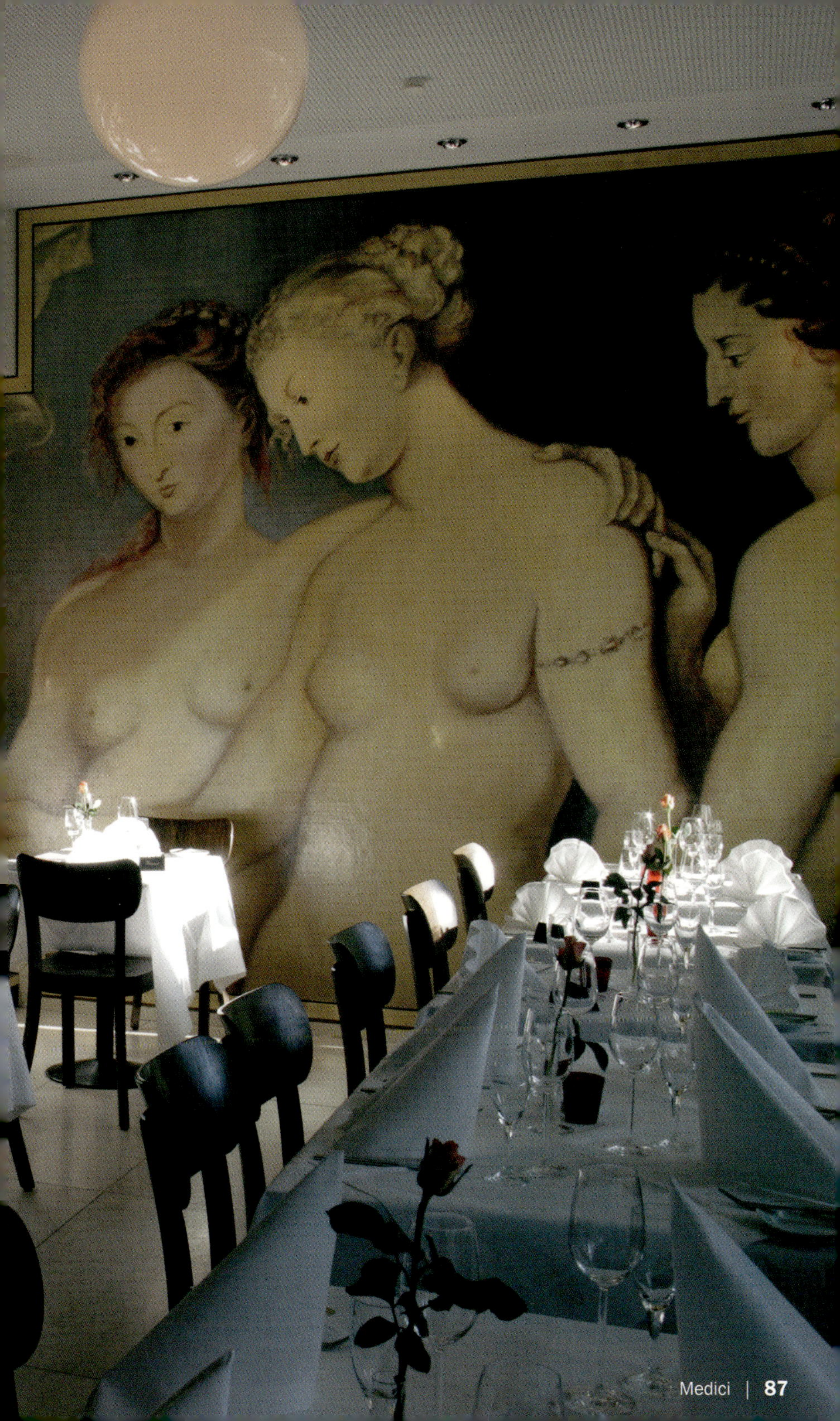

Nougatmousse

Chocolate Nougat Mousse

Mousse au praliné

Mousse de praliné

Mousse di nocciolato

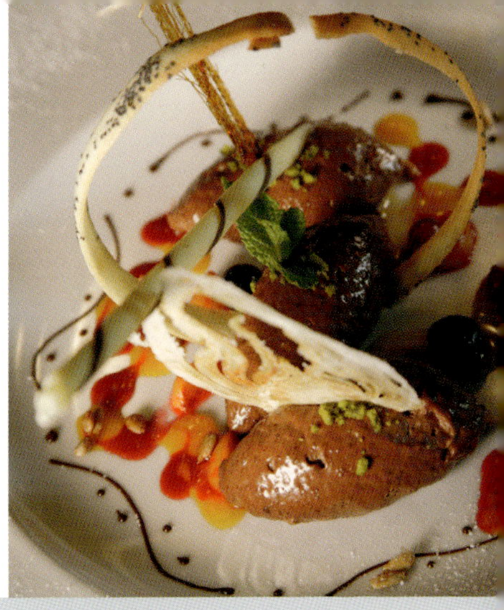

450 g Nougat
6 Eigelbe
50 g Zucker
100 ml Crème de Cacao
650 g geschlagene Sahne

Verschiedene Früchte, Frucht- und Schokoladensauce und Minze zur Dekoration

Den Nougat klein schneiden und im Wasserbad auflösen. In der Zwischenzeit die Eigelbe mit Zucker und Likör in einem Wasserbad warm aufschlagen (ca. 80 °C), dann in Eiswasser kaltschlagen (ca. 30 °C).
Den geschmolzenen Nougat einrühren und die Sahne rasch unterheben. In eine Form füllen und kaltstellen.
Für jeden Teller drei Nocken abstechen und mit Früchten, Frucht- und Schokoladensauce und Minze dekorieren.
Evtl. mit Hippen, Karamellgittern und Schokoladenspiralen garnieren.

1 lb chocolate nougat (gianduja)
6 egg yolks
1½ oz sugar
100 ml Crème de Cacao
1 lb 7 oz whipped cream

Different fruits, fruit and chocolate sauce and mint leaves for decoration

Cut the nougat in small pieces and heat up in a double boiler. In the meantime whisk egg yolks with sugar and liquor in a double boiler (approx. 180 °F), then whisk on ice water (approx. 90 °F) to cool.
Stir in the melted nougat cream and quickly fold under the whipped cream. Pour into a container and chill.
Place three scoops on each plate and decorate with fruits, fruit- and chocolate sauce and mint leaves.
Garnish with wafers and sugar spirals if desired.

450 g de praliné
6 jaunes d'œufs
50 g sucre
100 ml de Crème de Cacao
650 g de crème liquide battue

Différents fruits, sauce au fruit et au chocolat et
de la menthe pour la décoration

Couper le praliné en petits morceaux et le faire
fondre au bain-marie. Pendant ce temps, battre
à chaud les jaunes d'œufs avec le sucre et la
liqueur dans le bain-marie (env. 80 °C), puis battre à froid dans de l'eau glacée (env. 30 °C).
Ajouter le praliné fondu et incorporer rapidement
la crème liquide. Verser dans un moule et mettre
au frais.
Former trois boules par assiette et décorer avec
les fruits, la sauce au fruit et au chocolat et la
menthe.
Garnir éventuellement de cigarettes russes, de
motifs en caramel et de spirales en chocolat.

450 g de turrón de chocolate y almendras
6 yemas
50 g de azúcar
100 ml de licor Crème de Cacao
650 g de nata batida

Diferentes frutos, salsas de fruta y de chocolate
y menta para decorar

Corte el turrón de chocolate y almendras en
trozos pequeños y deshágalos al baño maría.
Entre tanto bata al baño maría (aprox. 80 °C) las
yemas con el azúcar y el licor y después en agua
fría (aprox. 30 °C).
Añada el terrón deshecho, añada la nata y bata
rápidamente. Rellene un molde con la mezcla e
introdúzcalo en el frigorífico.
Ponga en cada plato tres montoncitos de mousse
y decore con los frutos, las salsas de fruta y de
chocolate y la menta.
Si lo desea puede decorar con barquillos, trocitos
de caramelo y espirales de chocolate.

450 g di nocciolato
6 tuorli d'uovo
50 g di zucchero
100 ml di Crème di Cacao
650 g di panna montata

Per la guarnizione: frutta varia, succo di frutta,
salsa di cioccolato e menta

Triturare il nocciolato e scioglierlo a bagnomaria.
Nel frattempo, sempre a bagnomaria, sbattere a
caldo (ca. 80 °C) i tuorli d'uovo con lo zucchero
ed il liquore, quindi sbatterli a freddo (ca. 30 °C)
in acqua ghiacciata.
Incorporare il nocciolato sciolto ed unire velo-
cemente la panna. Versare il composto in uno
stampo e mettere in frigorifero.
Disporre in ogni piatto tre noci di mousse e guarnirle con la frutta, il succo di frutta, la salsa di
cioccolato e la menta.
Eventualmente, guarnire anche con wafer, ghiri-
gori di caramello e spirali di cioccolato.

Meyer's

Design: Seidel Architekten | Chef: Jens Dudek
Owner: Gregor Meyer

Große Bockenheimer Straße 54 | 60313 Frankfurt | Innenstadt
Phone: +49 69 91 39 70 70
www.meyer-frankfurt.de
Subway: Alte Oper
Opening hours: Mon–Sat noon to midnight, Sun closed
Average price: € 18
Cuisine: International
Special features: Fine food shop

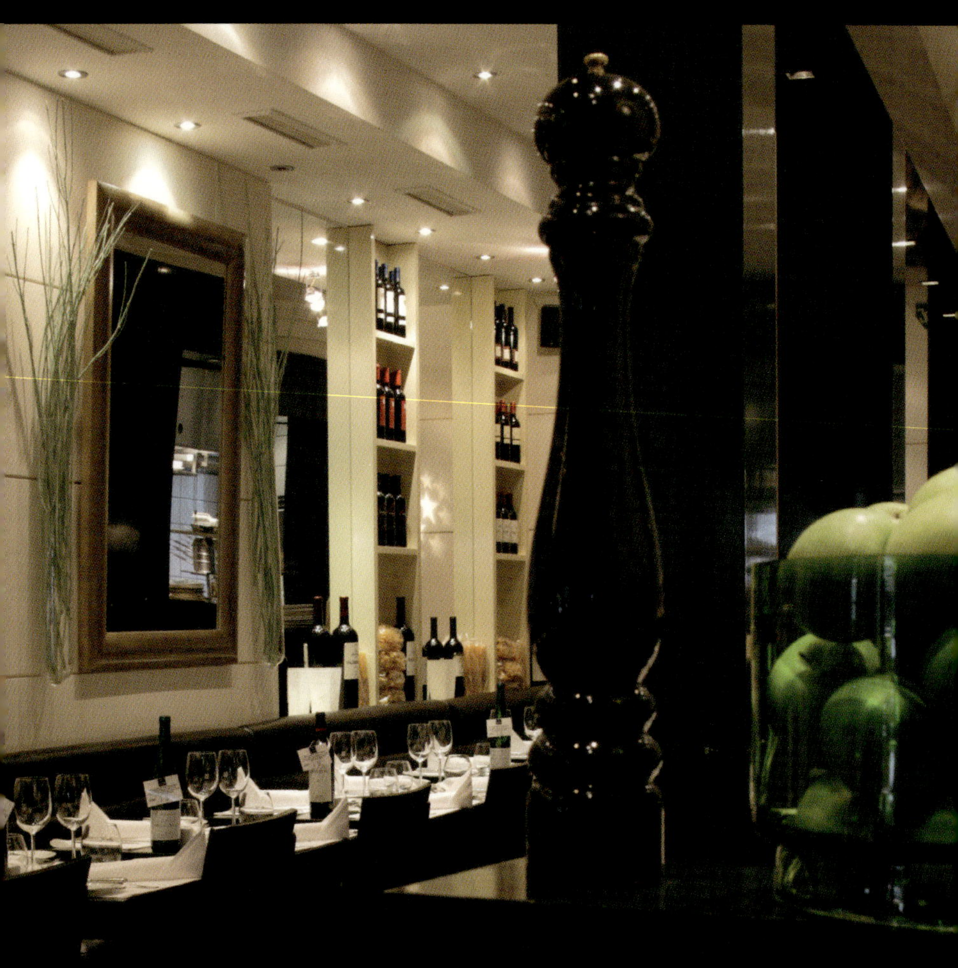

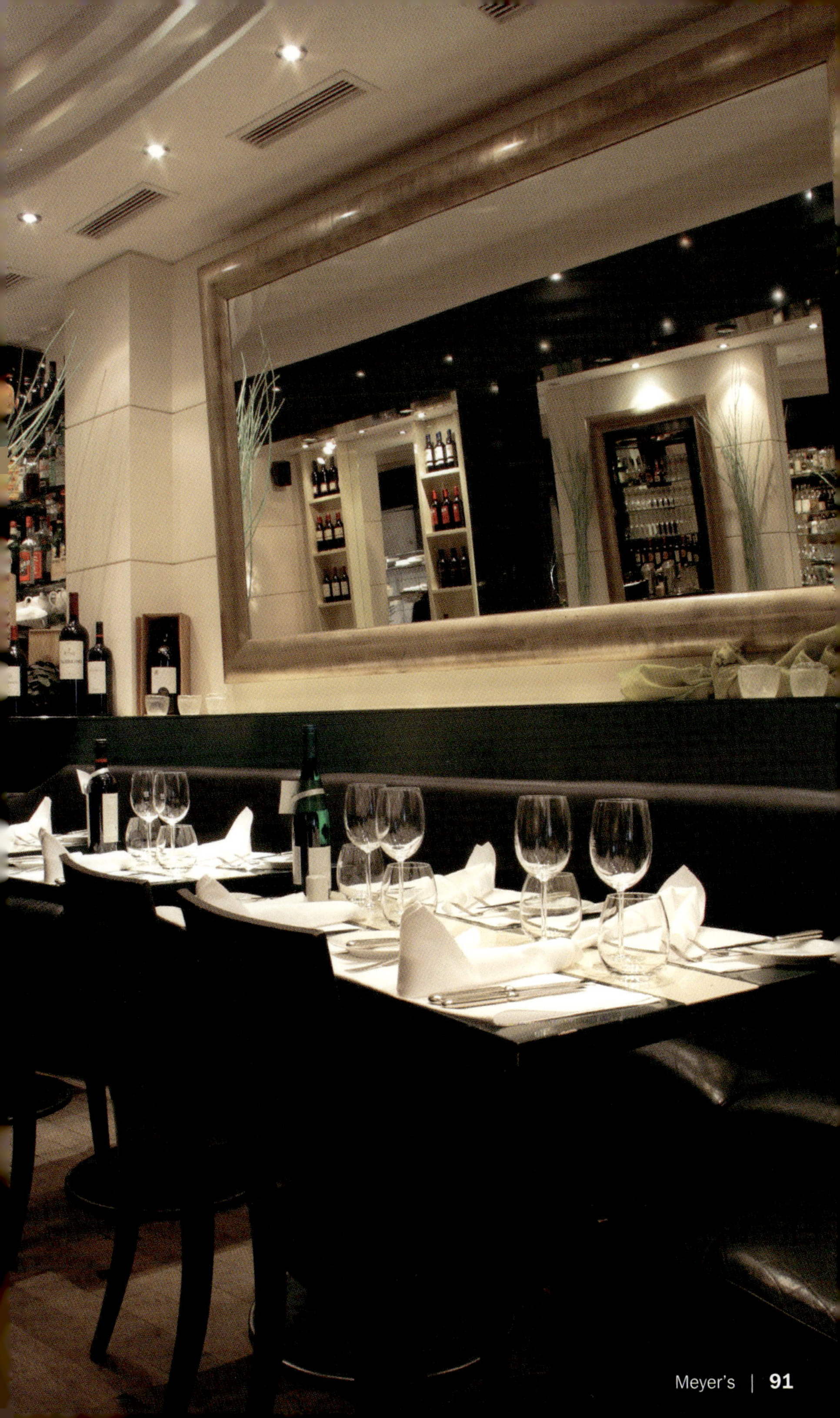

Micro

Design: 3deluxe, Nik Schweiger | Chef: Mario Lohninger
Owners: Sven Väth, Matthias Martinsohn, Mario Lohninger

Carl-Benz-Straße 21 | 60386 Frankfurt | Ostend
Phone: +49 69 90 02 00
www.cocoonclub.net
Subway: Dieselstraße
Opening hours: Tue–Thu 7 pm to 3 am, Fri–Sat 7 pm to 6 am
Average price: € 7
Cuisine: International

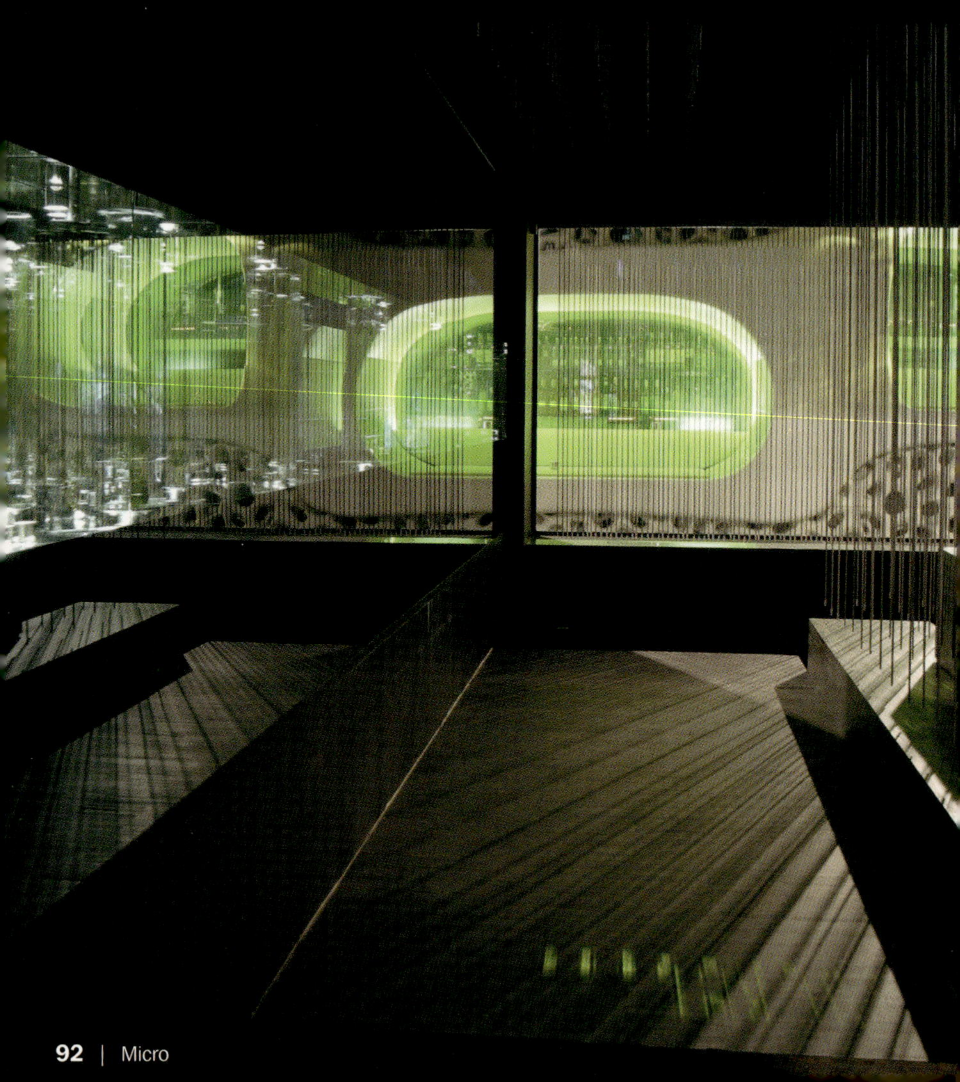

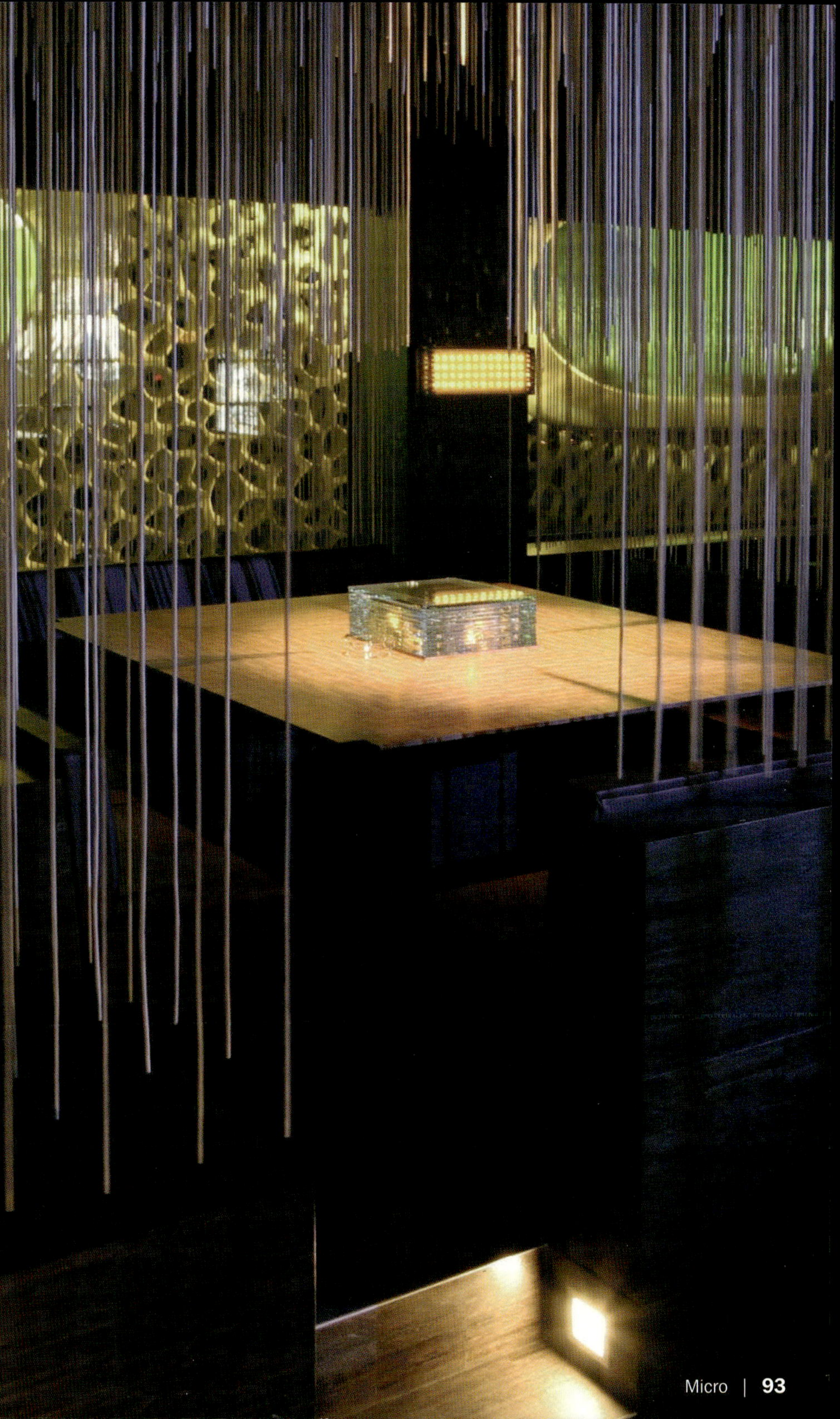

MoschMosch

Design: Superreal | Chef: Sam Tran
Owner: MoschMosch GmbH

Wilhelm-Leuschner-Straße 78 | 60329 Frankfurt | Hauptbahnhof
Phone: +49 69 24 00 37 37
www.moschmosch.com
Subway: Hauptbahnhof
Opening hours: Mon–Fri 11 am to 11 pm, Sat from 5:30 pm to 11 pm, Sun closed
Average price: € 7
Cuisine: Japanese, Ramen

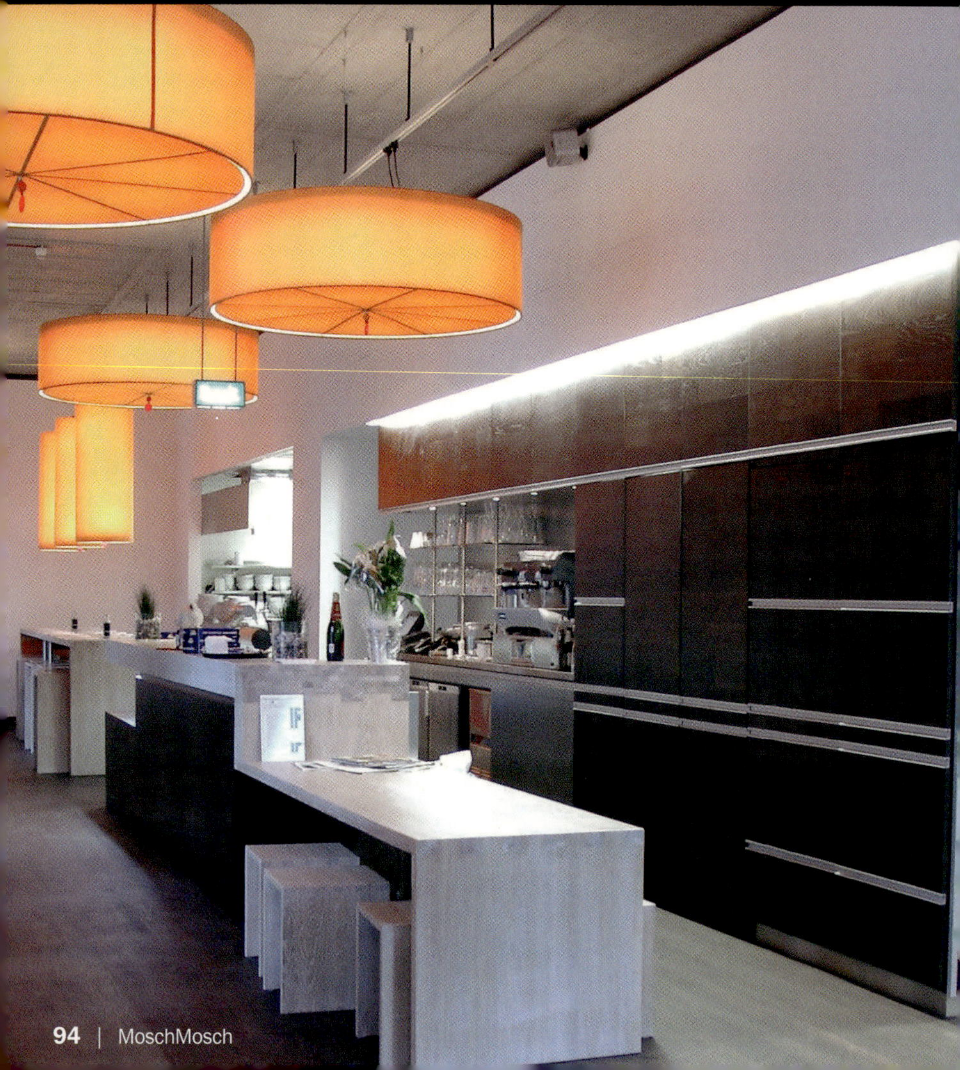

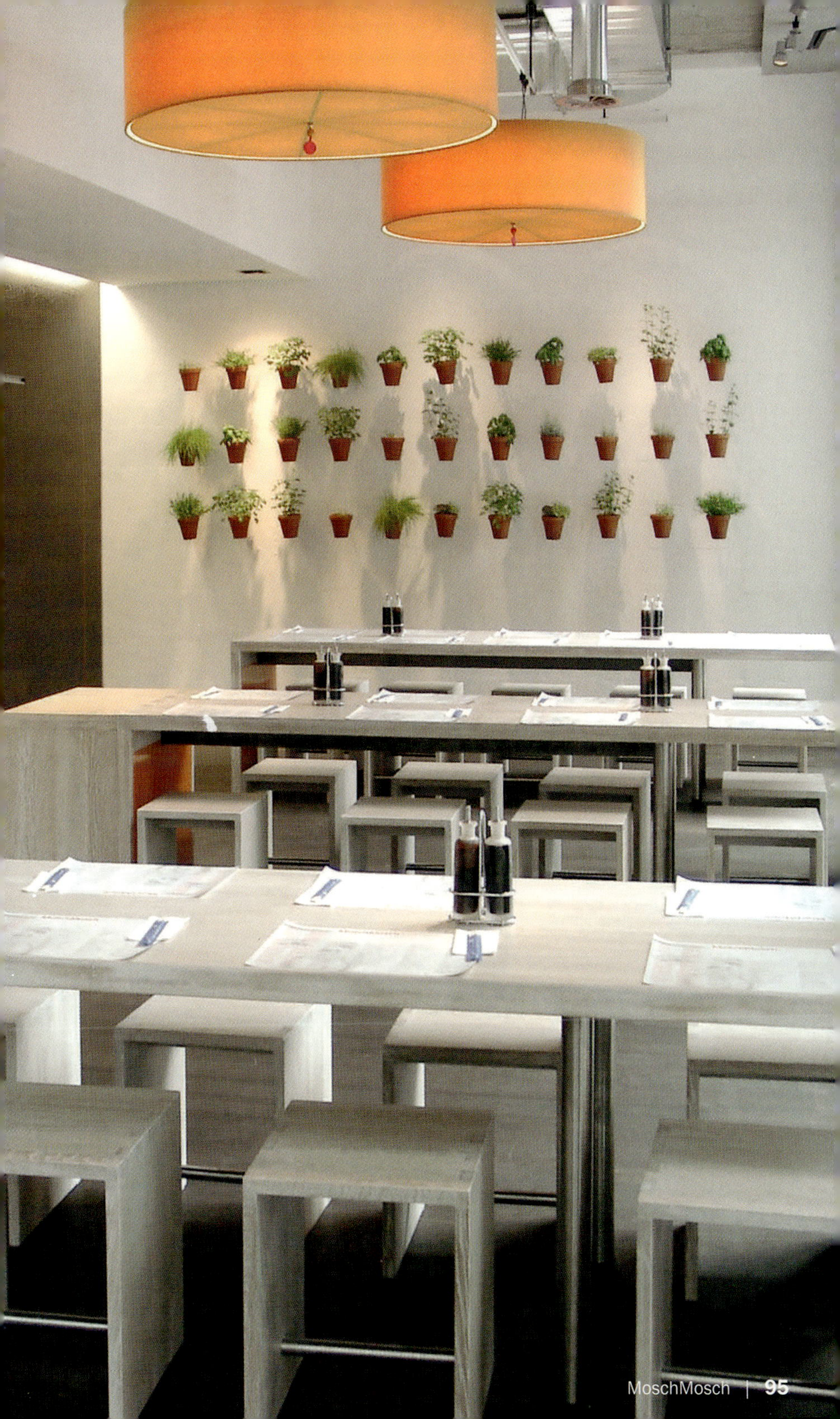

Ramen-Nudeln
mit Rindfleisch

Ramen Noodles with Beef

Nouilles râmen au boeuf

Fideos ramen con ternera

Ramen con carne di manzo

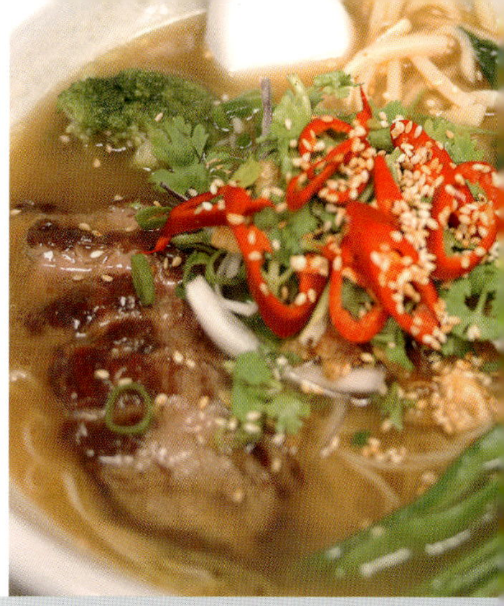

500 g Ramen-Nudeln, al dente
1 l Geflügelbrühe
4 Rinderfiletsteaks, à 120 g, gebraten und in Streifen geschnitten
400 g gemischtes gedämpftes Gemüse (z. B. Brokkoli, Zuckerschoten, Karotten, Spinat, etc.)
100 g frische Sojasprossen
30 g Korianderblätter
2 rote Chilischoten, in Ringen
1 Frühlingszwiebel, in Ringen
2 EL Sesam

8 EL helle Misopaste
4 EL Sojasauce
4 TL Mirin
4 TL Sesamöl

Alle Zutaten mischen und auf vier Suppenschüsseln verteilen.

Die Hälfte der heißen Brühe auf die vier Schüsseln verteilen und die Nudeln auf die Suppe geben. Die Rinderfiletsteakstreifen in die Schüsseln geben, das Gemüse und die Sojasprossen darauf setzen und mit der restlichen Brühe übergießen. Mit Koriander, Chili, Frühlingszwiebeln und Sesam garnieren und sofort servieren.

1 lb 1½ oz ramen noodles, cooked al dente
1 l chicken stock
4 beef filet steaks, 4 oz each, seared and cut into strips
1 lb mixed steamed vegetables (e.g. broccoli, sugar snap peas, carrots, spinach, etc.)
3 oz fresh soy sprouts
1 oz cilantro leaves
2 red chilies, sliced
1 spring onion, sliced
2 tbsp sesame seeds

8 tbsp light miso paste
4 tbsp soy sauce
4 tsp mirin wine
4 tsp sesame oil

Combine all ingredients and spoon into four soup bowls.

Add one half of the hot stock into the four bowls and put the noodles on top. Divide the beef filet strips amongst the bowls, place the vegetables and soy sprouts on top and pour the leftover chicken stock into the bowls. Garnish with cilantro, chilies, spring onion and sesame seeds and serve immediately.

500 g de nouilles râmen, cuites al dente
1 l de bouillon de volaille
4 steaks de filet de boeuf, de 120 g chacun, cuits
et coupés en lamelles
400 g de mélange de légumes cuits à la vapeur
(par ex. brocolis, pois gourmands, carottes, épi-
nard, etc.)
100 g de germes de soja fraîches
30 g de feuilles de coriandre
2 piments rouges, coupés en rondelles
1 oignon grelot, coupé en tranches
2 c. à soupe de sésame

8 c. à soupe de pâte miso claire
4 c. à soupe de sauce soja
4 c. à café de Mirin
4 c. à café d'huile de sésame

Mélanger tous les ingrédients et répartir dans quatre assiettes creuses.

Repartir la moitié du bouillon chaud dans les quatre assiettes creuses et ajouter les nouilles dans la soupe. Repartir les lamelles des steaks de filet de boeuf dans les assiettes creuses, ajouter les légumes et les pousses de soja et verser par-dessus le bouillon restant. Garnir avec la coriandre, le piment, l'oignon grelot et le sésame et servir immédiatement.

500 g de fideos ramen, *al dente*
1 l de caldo de volatería
4 filetes de ternera, de 120 g cada uno, fritos y
cortados en tiras
400 g de mezcla de verduras cocidas (p.ej. brécol,
tirabeques, zanahorias, espinacas, etc.)
100 g de brotes de soja frescos
30 g de hojas de cilantro
2 guindillas rojos, en aros
1 cebolleta, en aros
2 cucharadas de sésamo

8 cucharadas de pasta miso clara
4 cucharadas de salsa de soja
4 cucharaditas de Mirin
4 cucharaditas de aceite de sésamo

Mezcle todos los ingredientes y reparta la mezcla en cuatro cuencos soperos.

Reparta la mitad del caldo caliente entre los cuatro cuencos e incorpore los fideos. Reparta las tiras de carne entre los cuencos, coloque encima la verdura y los brotes de soja y vierta por encima el resto del caldo. Decore con cilantro, las guindillas, la cebolleta y el sésamo y sirva inmediatamente.

500 g di ramen (tipica pasta asiatica, n.d.t.) cotti
al dente
1 l di brodo di pollo o tacchino
4 bistecche di filetto di manzo di 120 g ciascuna,
arrostite e tagliate a strisce
400 g di verdure miste cotte al vapore (ad es. broccoli, piselli dolci, carote, spinaci ecc.)
100 g di germogli freschi di soia
30 g di foglie di coriandolo
2 peperoncini rossi tagliati ad anelli
1 cipollotto tagliato ad anelli
2 cucchiai di sesamo

8 cucchiai di pasta di miso chiara
4 cucchiai di salsa di soia
4 cucchiaini di mirin
4 cucchiaini di olio di sesamo

Mescolare tutti gli ingredienti e ripartirli in quattro ciotole.

Versare la metà del brodo caldo nelle quattro scodelle e ripartivi la pasta. Distribuire nelle scodelle le strisce di carne, disporvi sopra le verdure ed i germogli di soia e ricoprire il tutto con il brodo restante. Guarnire con il coriandolo, il peperoncino, i cipollotti e il sesamo. Servire subito.

New Brick

Design: Peter Silling | Chef: Sven Krause
Owner: Lindner Hotels AG

Walther-von-Cronberg-Platz 1 | 60594 Frankfurt | Sachsenhausen
Phone: +49 69 6 64 01 43 03
www.lindner.de
Subway: Lokalbahnhof, Wasserweg
Opening hours: Mon–Sun 7 am to 11:30 pm
Average price: € 25
Cuisine: Californian
Special features: Open show kitchen

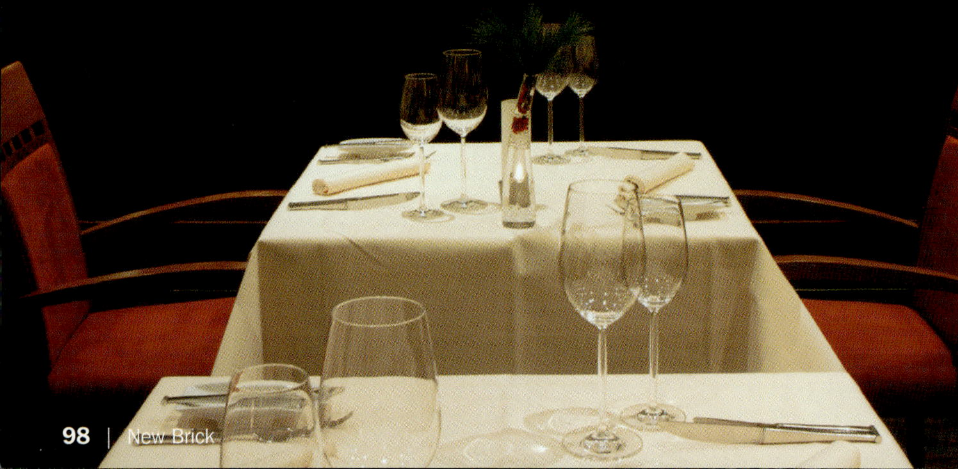

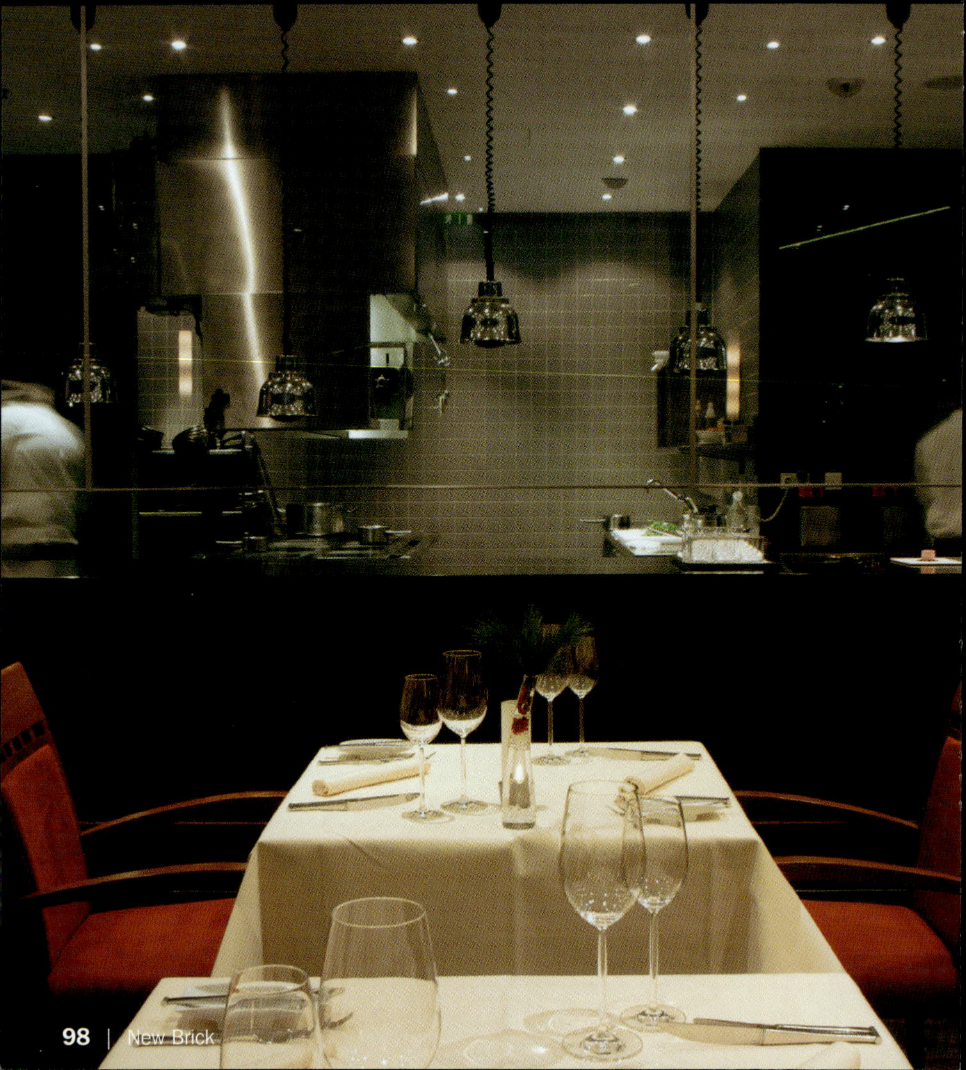

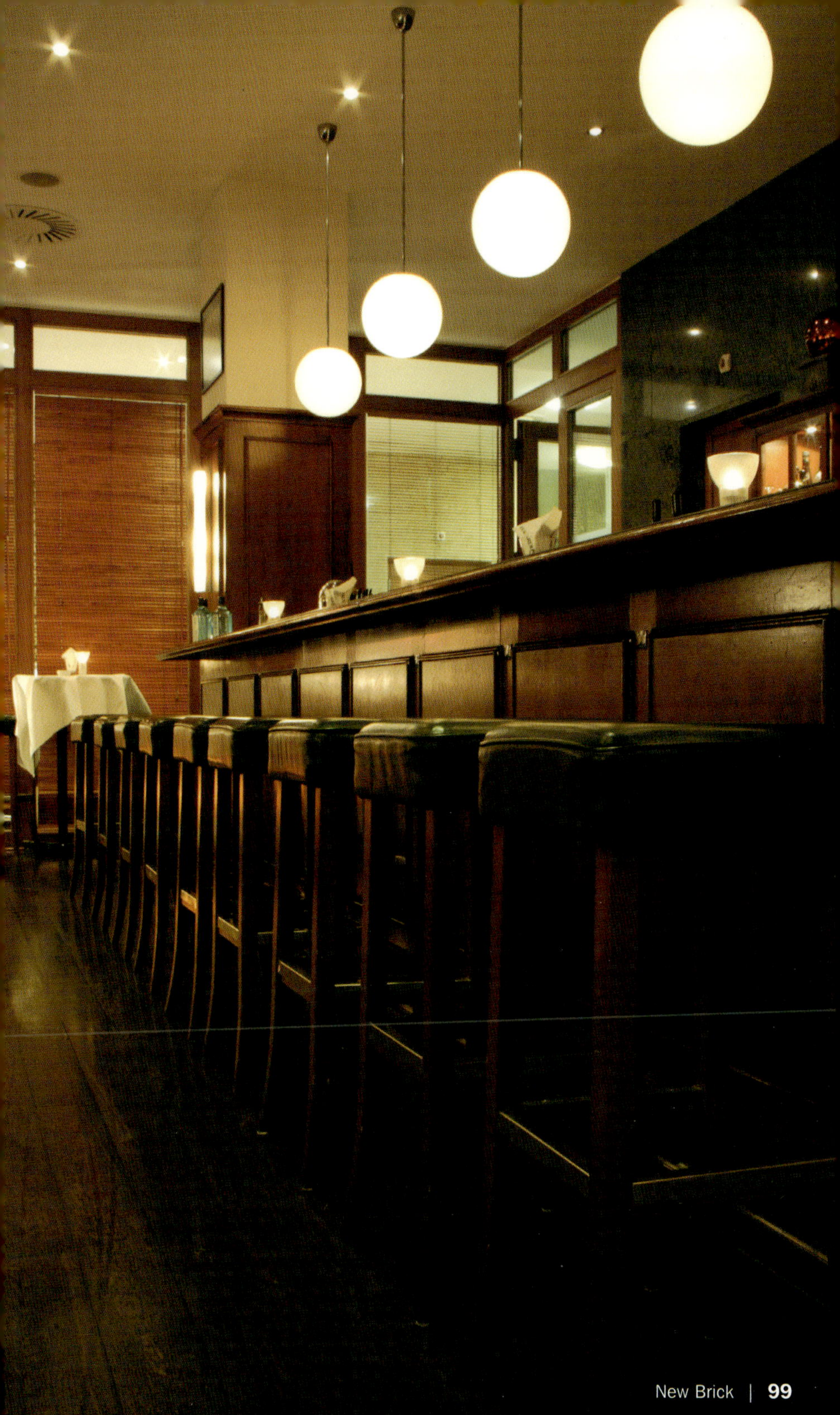

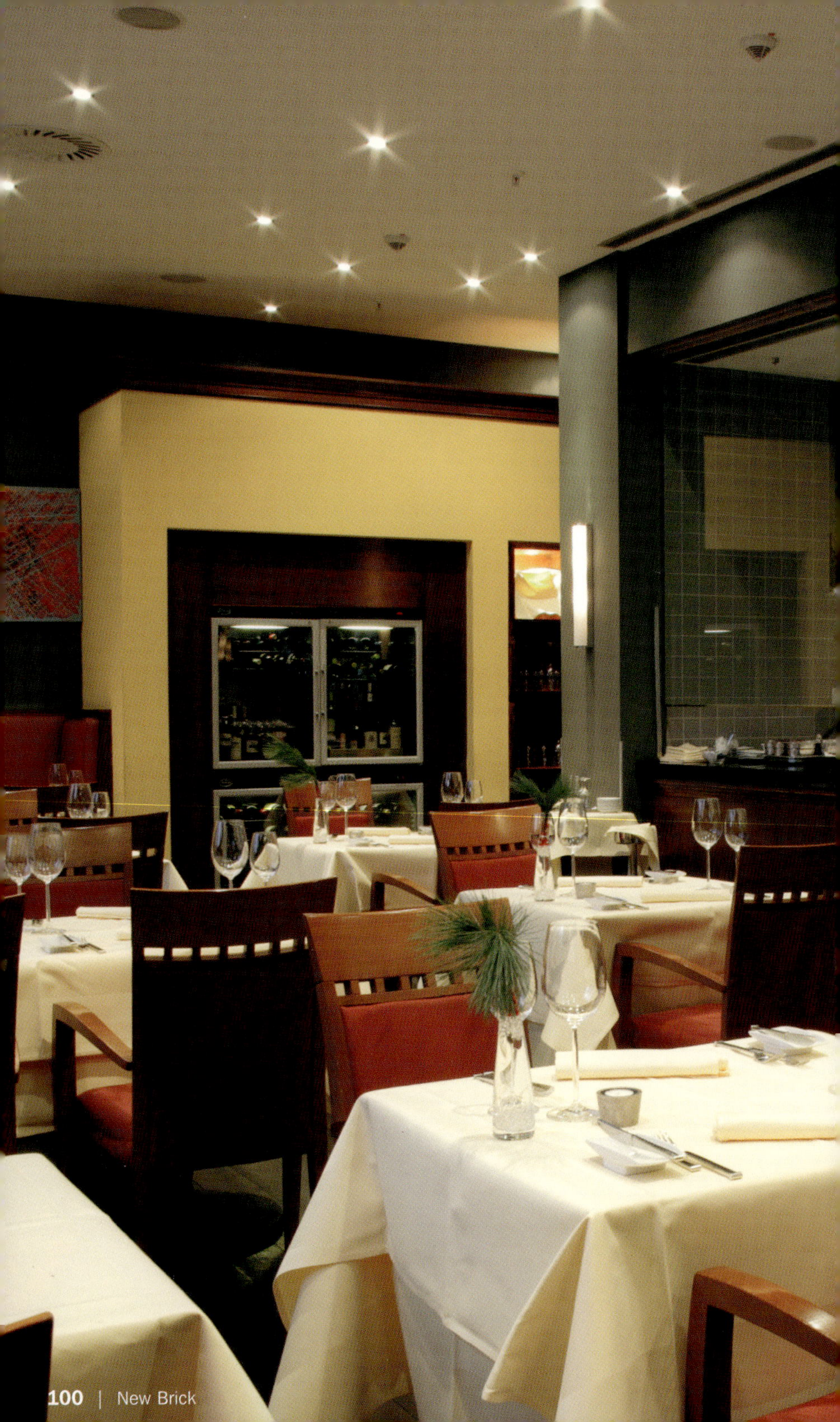

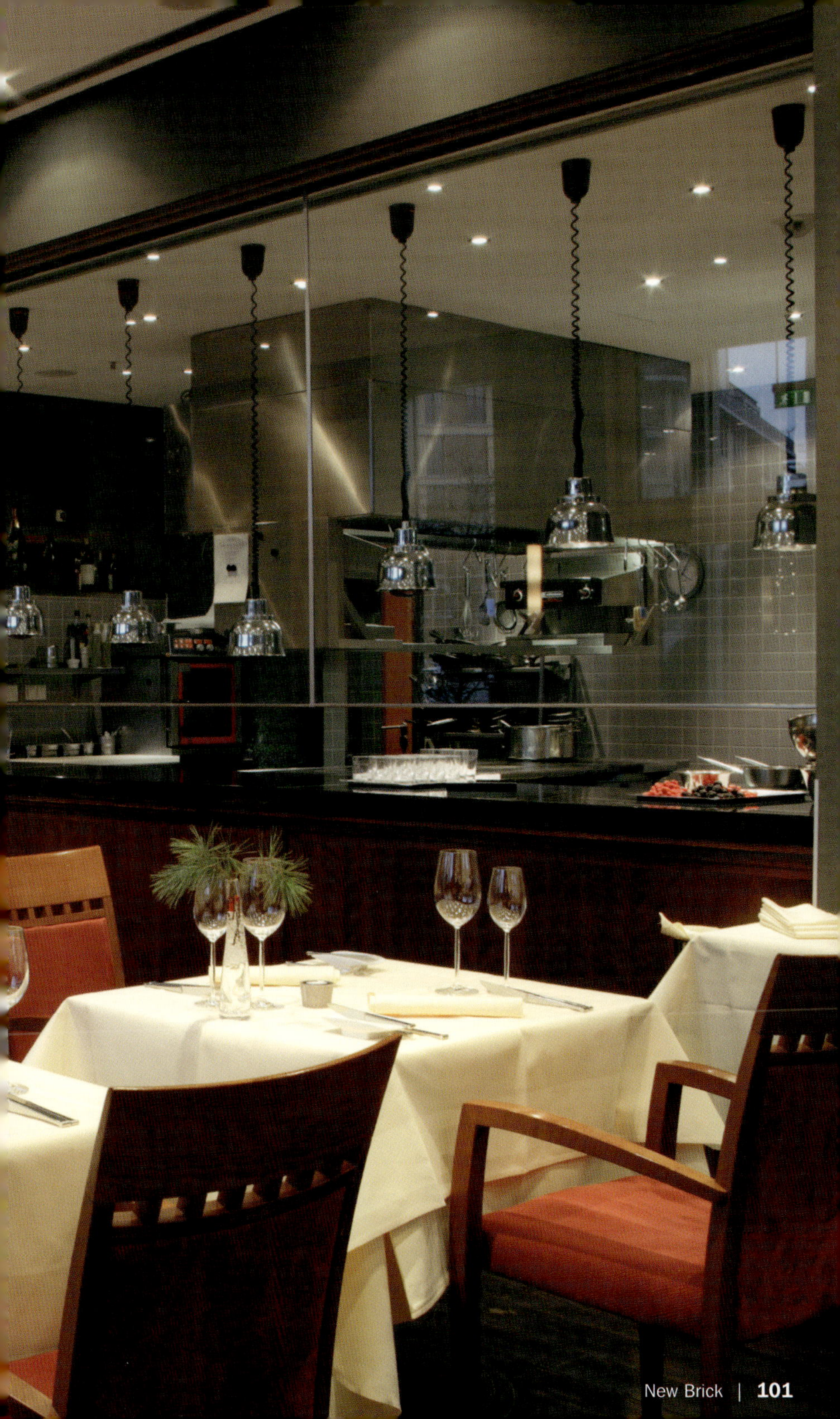

New Brick Blueberry Cheesecake

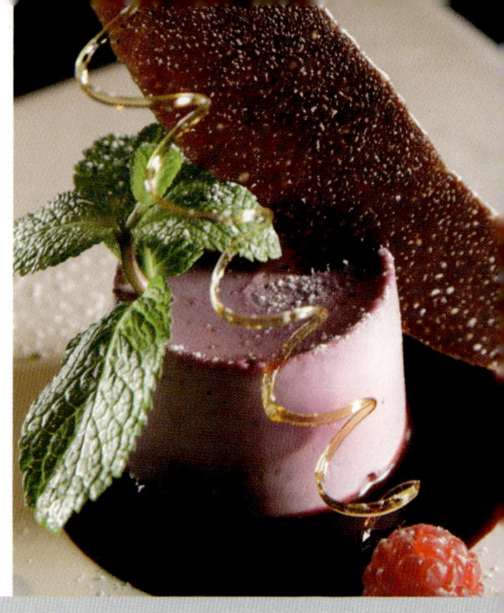

150 g Löffelbiskuit, zerbröselt
100 g flüssige Butter
250 g Sahne
250 g Frischkäse
150 g Zucker
6 Blatt Gelatine, eingeweicht
200 g Blaubeeren, püriert

Verschiedene Beeren, Fruchtsauce und Minze
zur Dekoration
Eventuell Hippen und Zuckerspiralen zur
Dekoration

Die Biskuitbrösel mit der Butter mischen und in vier kleine runde Formen füllen. Fest andrücken und kaltstellen.
Sahne, Frischkäse und Zucker mischen und glatt rühren.
4 EL des Blaubeerpürees erhitzen und die Gelatine darin auflösen. 3 EL Sahne-Frischkäsemischung in die Gelatine rühren und die Gelatinemischung zurück in die Sahne-Frischkäsemischung geben. Das Blaubeerpüree unterrühren und in die Formen füllen. Mind. 3 Stunden kaltstellen.
Die Cheesecakes mit einem heißen Messer aus den Formen lösen und mit verschiedenen Beeren, Fruchtsauce und Minze dekorieren.

5 oz sponge fingers, crushed
3 oz liquid butter
9 oz cream
9 oz cream cheese
5 oz sugar
6 leaves gelatin, soaked
7 oz blueberries, mashed

Different berries, fruit sauce and mint leaves for decoration
Wafers and sugar spirals for decoration, if desired

Combine the sponge finger crumbs with butter and fill into four small circular molds. Press in tightly and chill.
Combine cream, cream cheese and sugar and mix until smooth.
Heat up 4 tbsp mashed blueberries and dissolve the gelatin in it. Stir 3 tbsp cream cheese mixture into the gelatin and pour that mixture back into the cream cheese mixture. Stir in the mashed blueberries and pour into the molds. Chill for at least 3 hours.
Remove the cheesecakes with a hot knife from the molds and decorate with berries, fruit sauce and mint leaves.

150 g de biscuits cuillères, réduits en miettes
100 g de beurre liquide
250 g de crème liquide
250 g de fromage frais
150 g sucre
6 feuilles de gélatine, ramollies
200 g de myrtilles, réduites en purée

Différentes baies, de la sauce aux fruits et de la menthe pour la décoration
Eventuellement cigarettes russes et spirales en sucre pour la décoration

Mélanger les miettes de biscuit au beurre et répartir dans quatre petits moules ronds. Les tasser fermement et mettre au frais.
Mélanger la crème liquide, le fromage frais et le sucre pour obtenir un mélange lisse.
Faire chauffer 4 c. à soupe de la purée de myrtilles et y faire fondre la gélatine. Verser 3 c. à soupe de cette préparation à base de crème liquide et de fromage frais dans la gélatine, puis ajouter ce mélange dans la préparation à base de crème liquide et de fromage frais. Incorporer la purée de myrtilles et verser dans les moules. Mettre au frais pendant au moins 3 heures.
Démouler les cheese-cakes à l'aide d'un couteau brûlant et décorer avec différentes baies, la sauce aux fruits et de la menthe.

150 g de bizcochos, desmenuzados
100 g de mantequilla líquida
250 g de nata
250 g de queso fresco
150 g de azúcar
6 láminas de gelatina, reblandecida
200 g de arandanos, hechos puré

Diferentes bayas, salsa de fruta y menta para decorar
Si lo desea, barquillos y espirales de azúcar para decorar

Mezcle las migas de bizcocho con la mantequilla y rellene cuatro moldes pequeños y redondos con la mezcla. Presione bien y resérvelos en el frigorífico.
Mezcle la nata con el queso fresco y el azúcar y remueva bien hasta conseguir una mezcla uniforme.
Caliente 4 cucharadas del puré de arándanos y deshaga dentro las láminas de gelatina. Añada 3 cucharadas de la mezcla de nata y queso, remueva y devuelva la mezcla a la nata con el queso. Añada el puré de arándanos, remueva y repártalo entre los moldes. Resérvelos en el frigoríficodurante 3 horas como mínimo.
Separe los pastales de queso de los moldes con un cuchillo caliente y decore con las bayas, la salsa de fruta y la menta.

150 g di biscotti savoiardi sbriciolati
100 g di burro fuso
250 g di panna
250 g di formaggio fresco
150 g di zucchero
6 fogli di gelatina ammorbiditi
200 g di mirtilli passati

Per la guarnizione: frutti di bosco, succo di frutta e menta
Eventualmente wafer e spirali di zucchero per la guarnizione

Mescolare i savoiardi sbriciolati e il burro e ripartirli in quattro formine rotonde. Comprimere bene e mettere in frigorifero.
Mescolare la panna, il formaggio fresco e lo zucchero fino ad ottenere un composto omogeneo.
Riscaldare 4 cucchiai di purea di mirtilli e sciogliervi la gelatina. Incorporare nella gelatina 3 cucchiai del composto di panna e formaggio e versare quindi nuovamente il tutto nel composto di panna e formaggio. Incorporarvi la purea di mirtilli e versare il composto nelle formine. Tenere in frigorifero per almeno 3 ore.
Estrarre con un coltello caldo le cheesecake dalle formine e guarnirle con i frutti di bosco, il succo di frutta e la menta.

Nizza

Design: Hubert J. Pumpe, Elke Pumpe-Krüger | Chef: Martin A. Stachel | Owners: Stefanos Kirgiannakis, Asterios Kokkinoplitis

Untermainkai 17 | 60329 Frankfurt | Bahnhofsviertel
Phone: +49 69 2 99 20 75 11
www.nizzamain.de
Subway: Willy-Brandt-Platz
Opening hours: Mon–Sat 3 pm to midnight, Sun noon to midnight
Average price: € 35 menu
Cuisine: Mediterranean
Special features: Banquet and casino

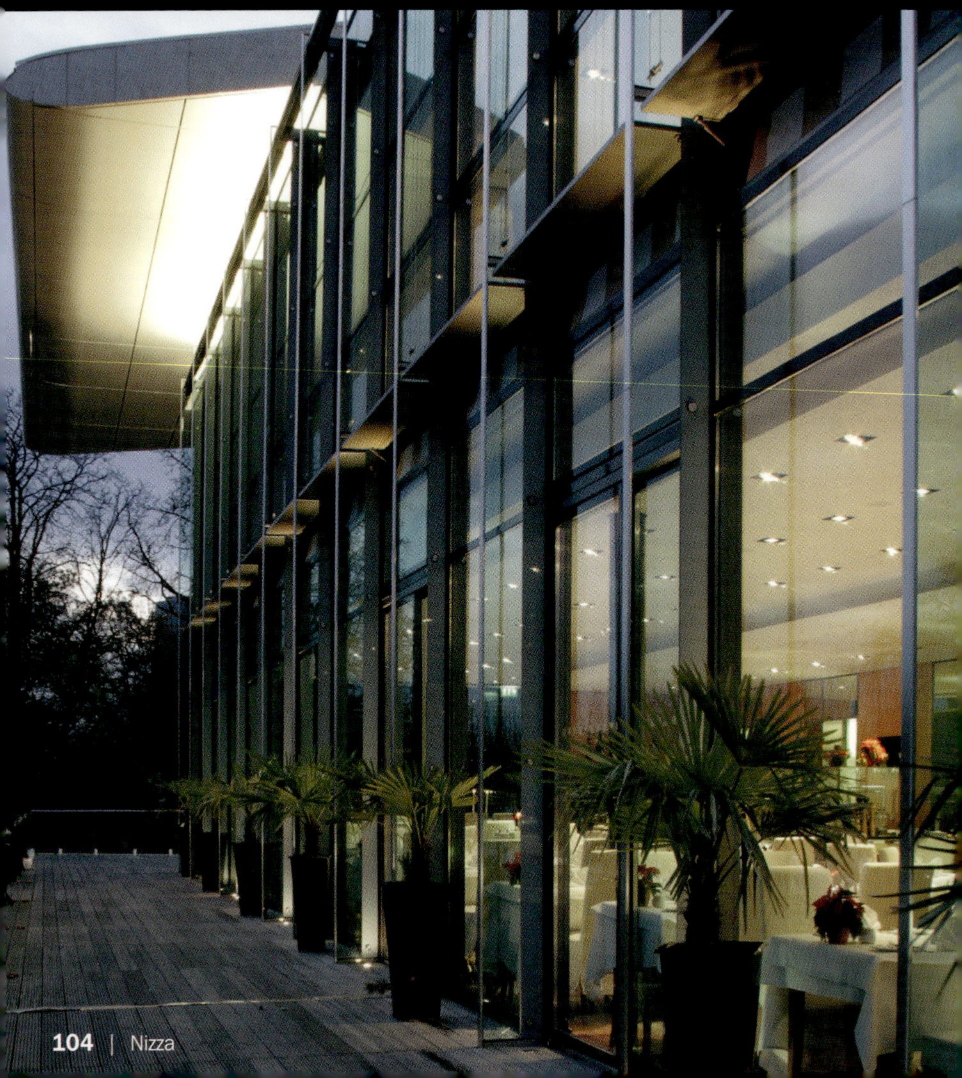

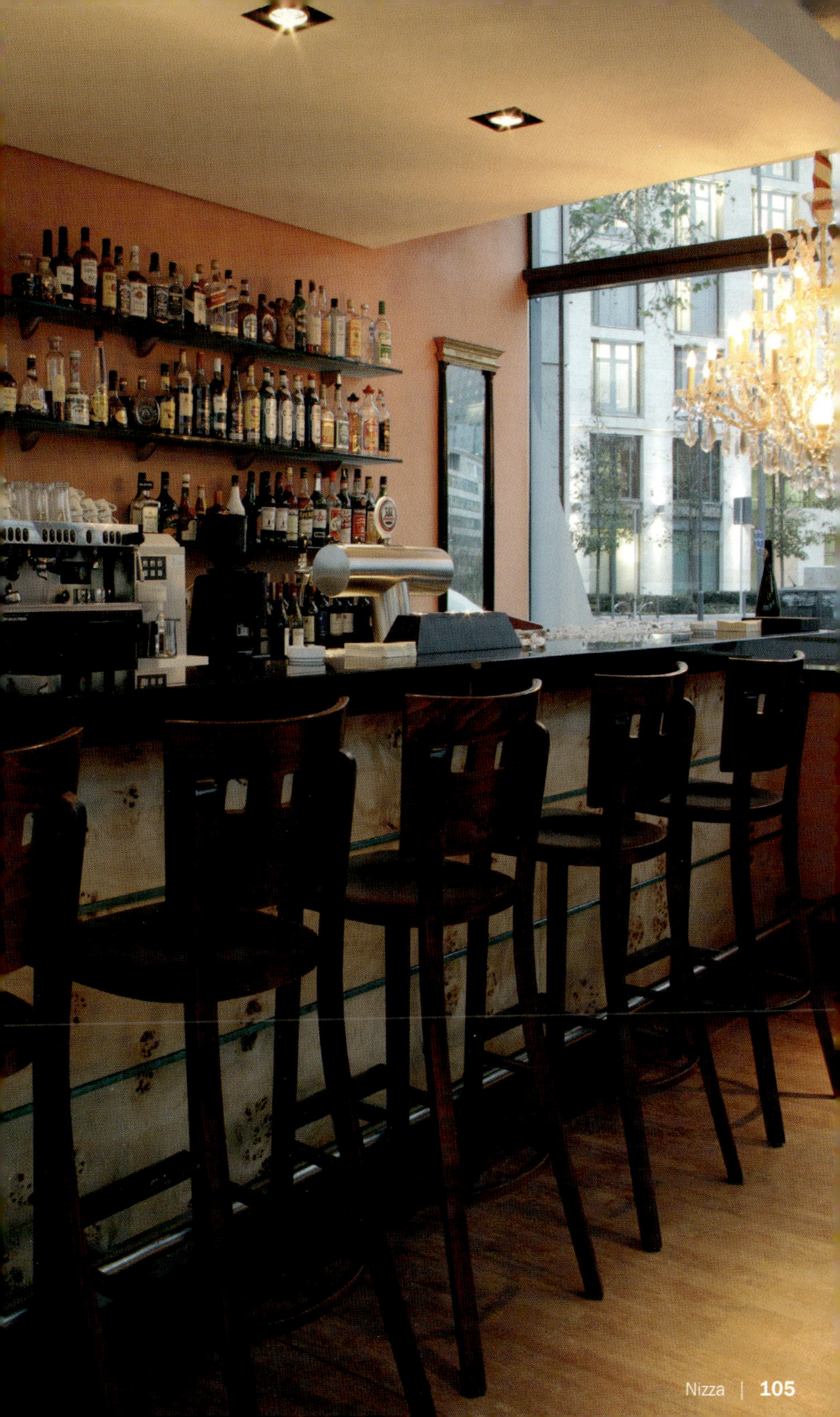

Opéra

Chef: Christoph Gessner | Owners: Gerd Käfer, Roland Kuffler

Opernplatz 1 | 60313 Frankfurt | Innenstadt
Phone: +49 69 1 34 02 15
www.opera-restauration.de
Subway: Opernplatz
Opening hours: Daily noon to 1 am
Average price: € 24
Cuisine: International with French influences
Special features: Placed in the historical old entrance hall of the opera

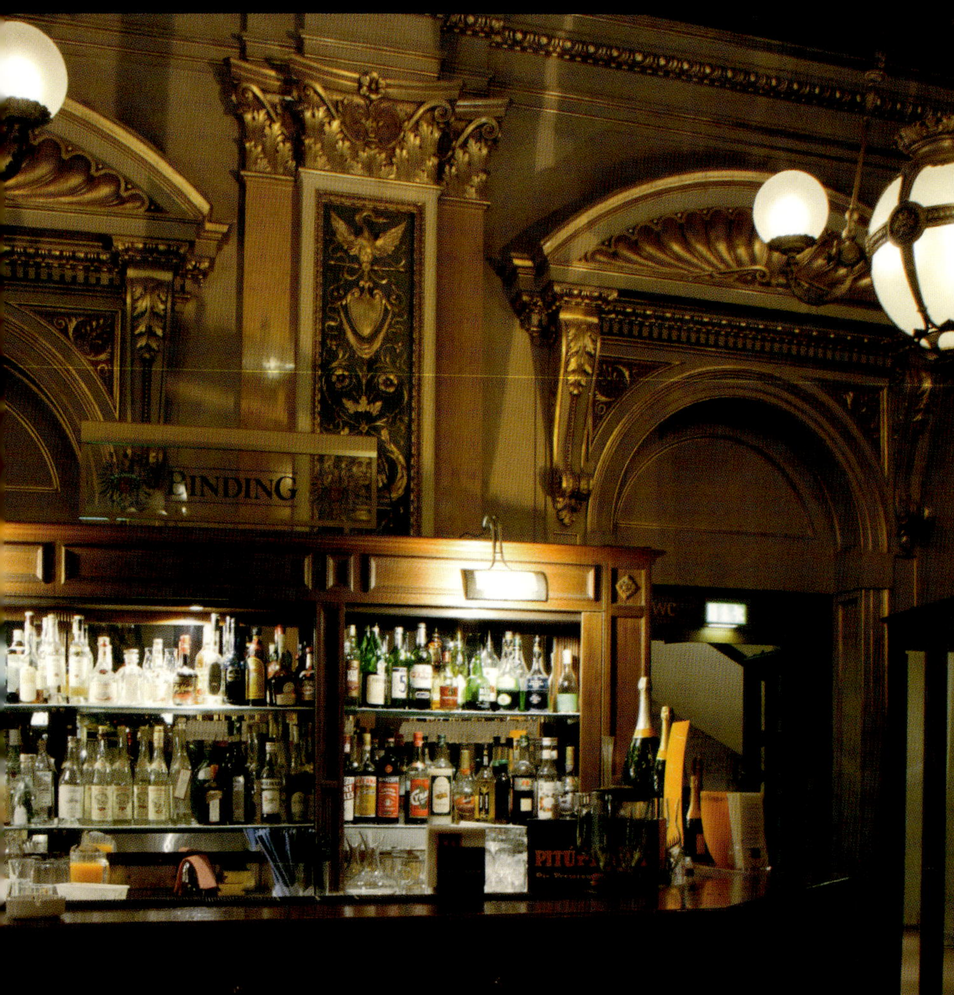

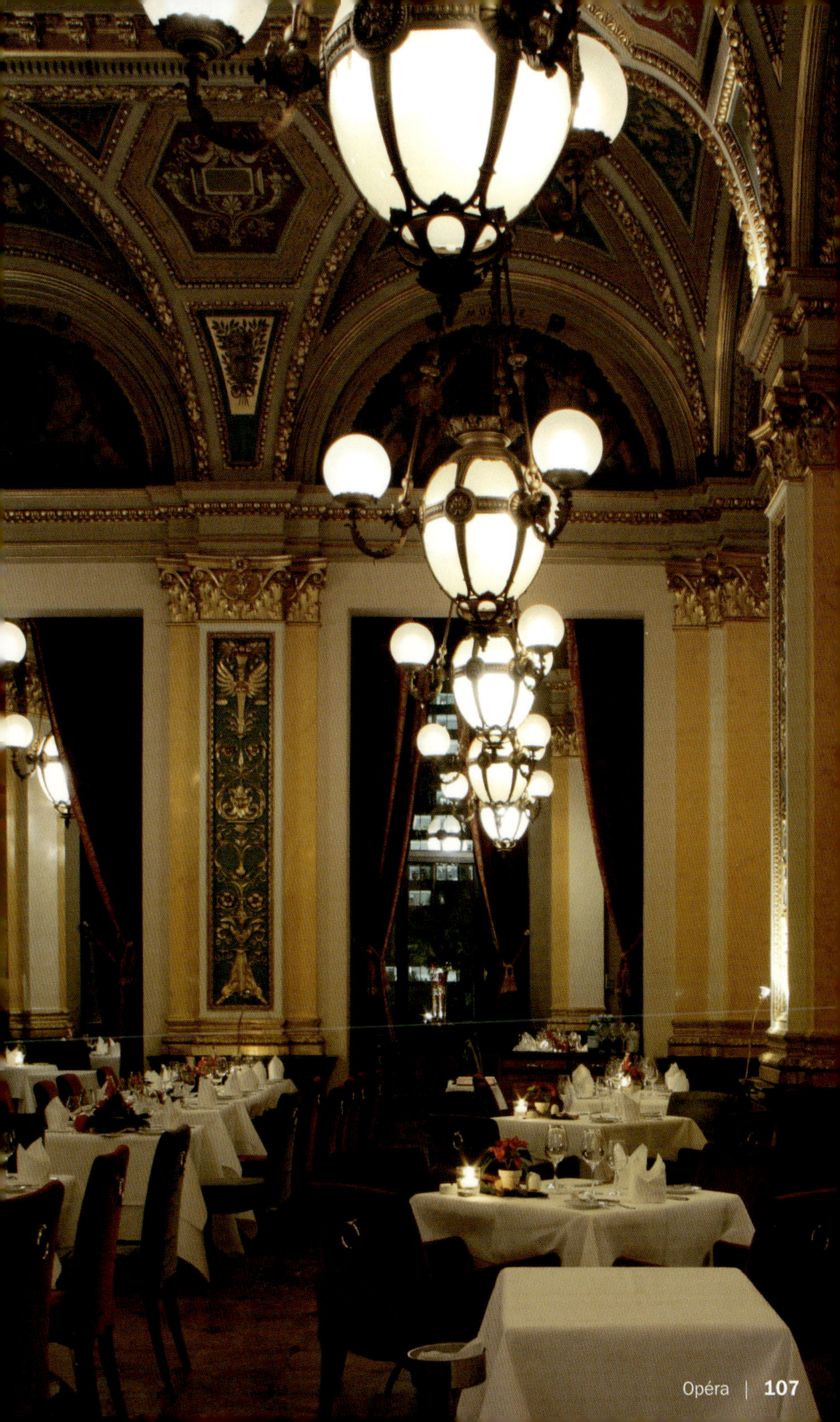

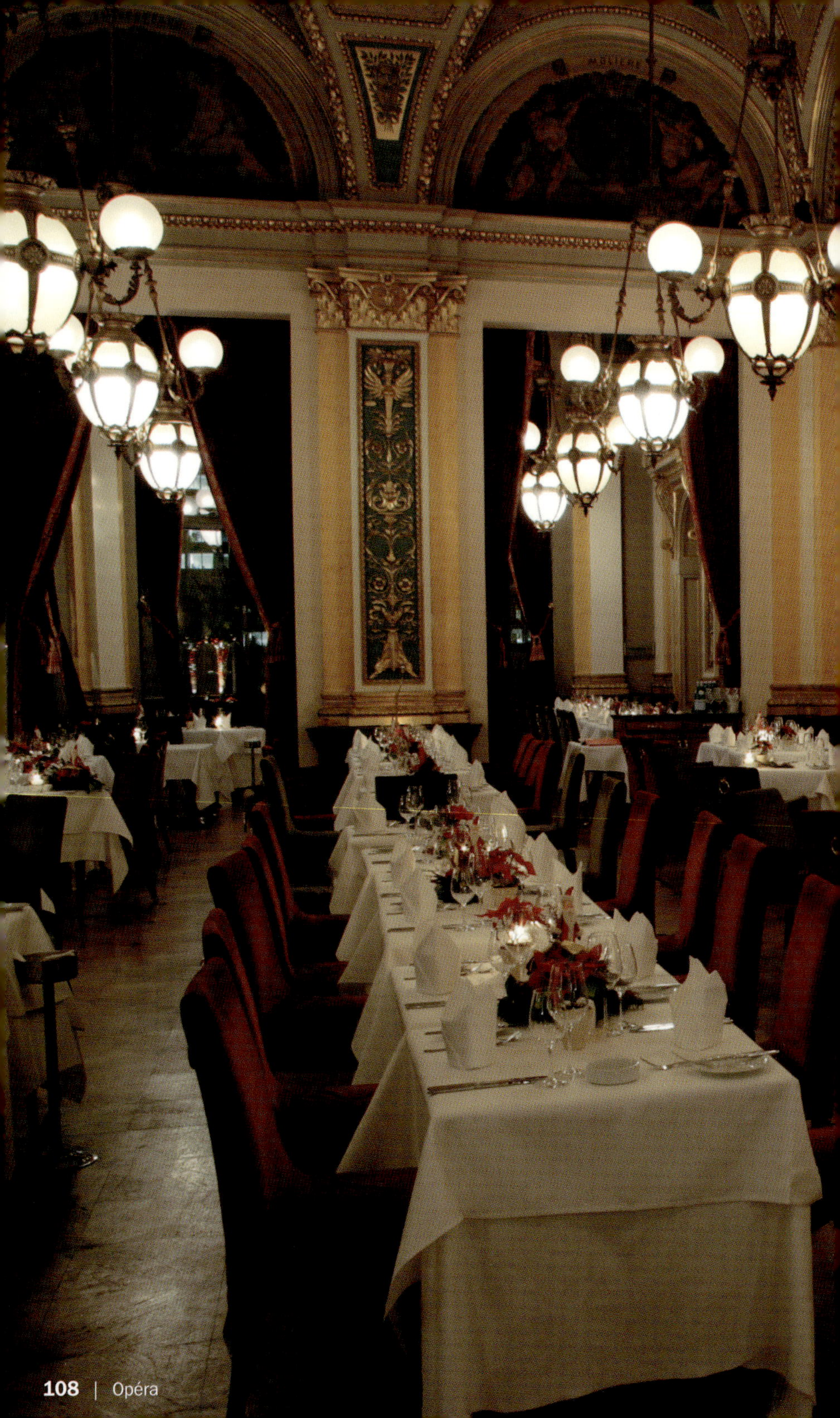

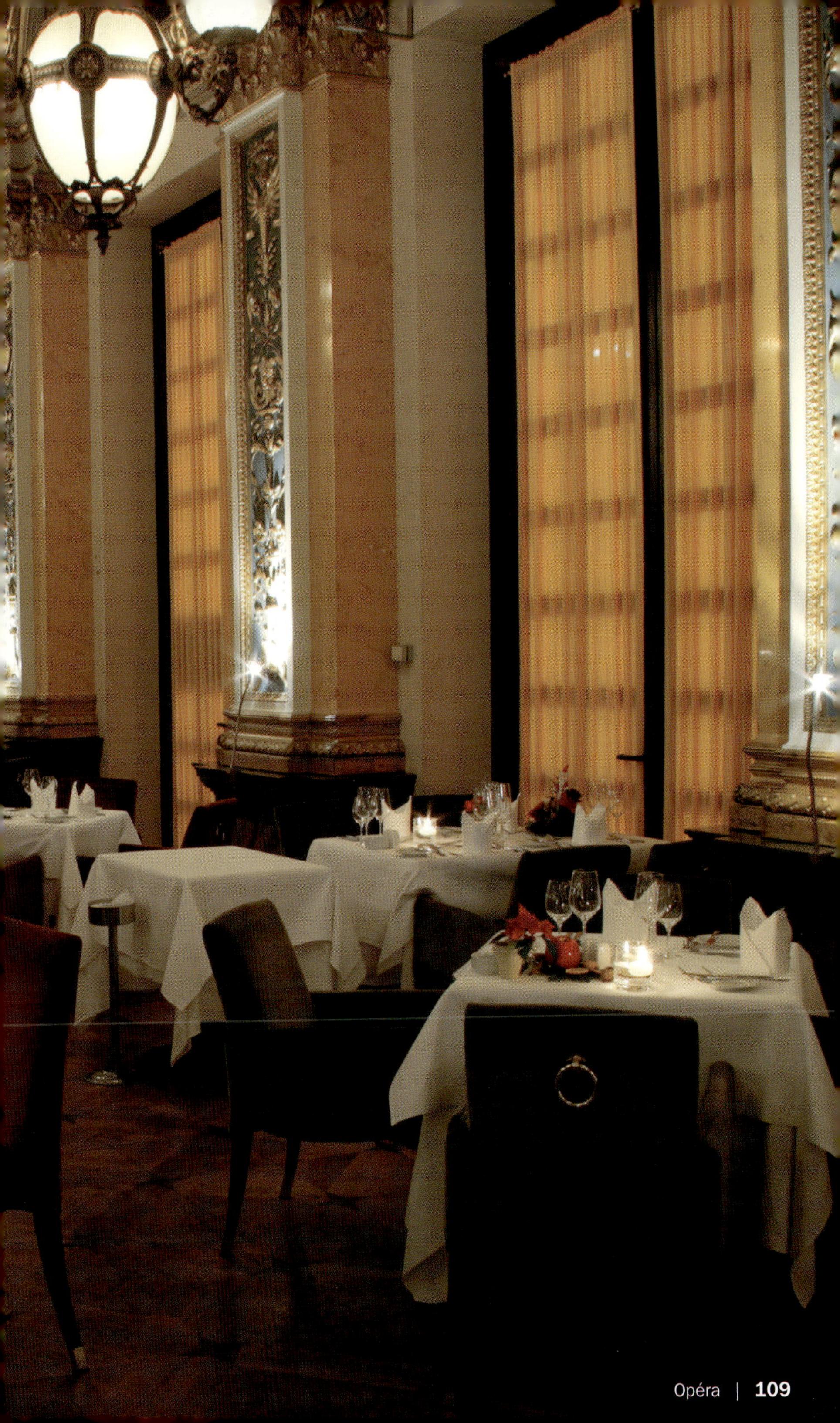

Rama V

Design: artforyou GmbH | Chef & Owner: Aree Rackwitz

Vilbeler Straße 32 | 60313 Frankfurt | Innenstadt
Phone: +49 69 21 99 64 88
Subway: Konstabler Wache
Opening hours: Daily noon to 3 pm and 6 pm to 1 am, Sun 6 pm to 1 am
Average price: € 8
Cuisine: Thai

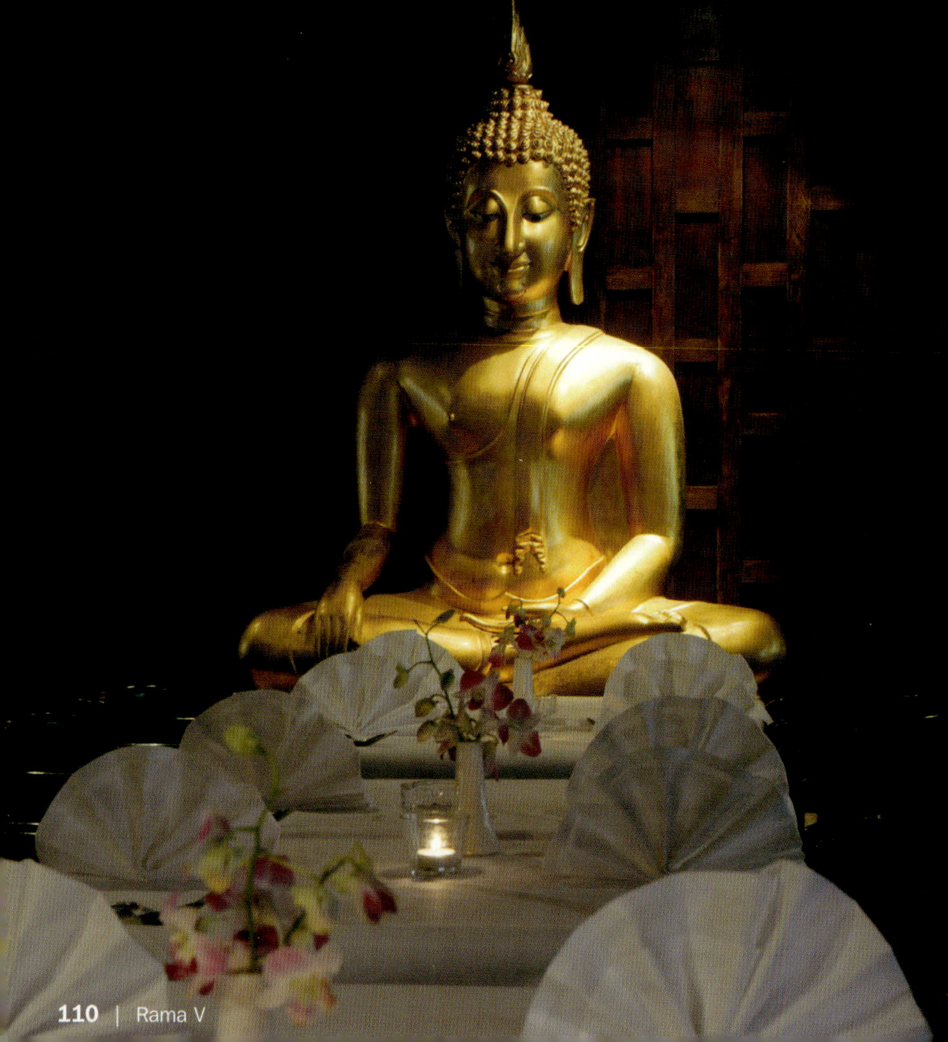

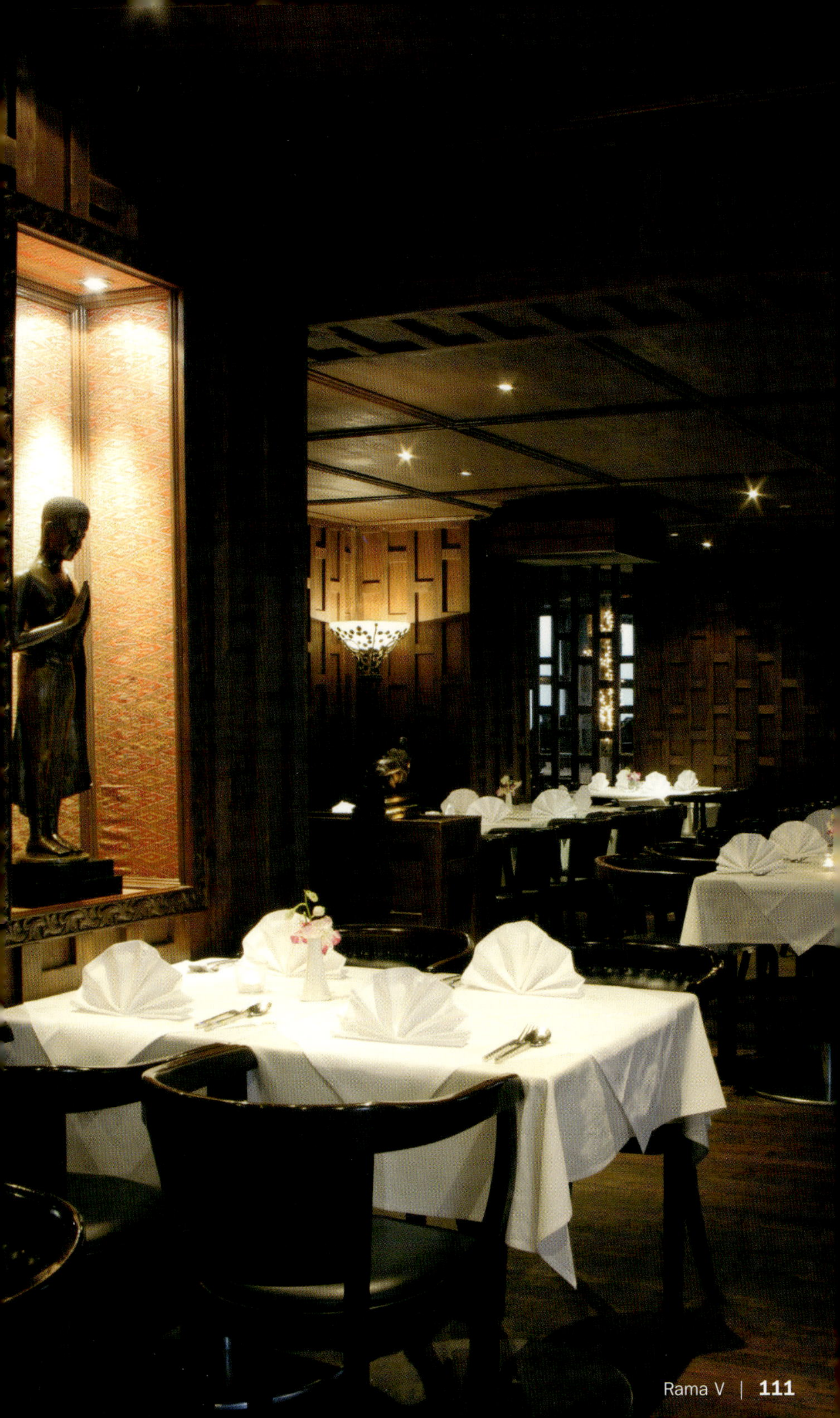

Rindfleisch

in rotem Curry und Kokosnussmilch

Beef with Red Curry and Coconut Milk

Viande de bœuf au curry rouge et au lait
de coco

Filete de ternera en curry rojo y leche
de coco

Carne di manzo al curry rosso con latte
di noce di cocco

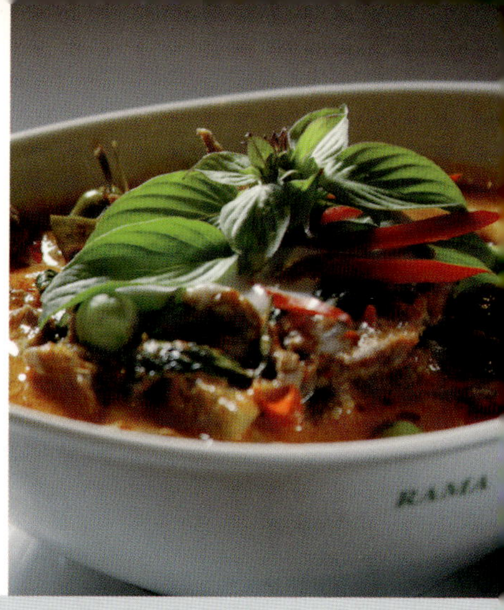

450 g Rinderfilet
5 EL Pflanzenöl
3 EL rote Currypaste
2 rote Chilischoten, entkernt und in Streifen
500 ml Kokosnussmilch
100 g Makua Puang (thailändische Baby-
Auberginen), gewürfelt
200 g Aubergine, gewürfelt
4 Zweige süßes Basilikum, gezupft
6 Limettenblätter, gezupft
3 EL Fischsauce
Salz, Pfeffer, Zucker

Das Rinderfilet in daumenlange Streifen schneiden. Die Currypaste in Pflanzenöl anschwitzen,
die Rindfleischstreifen zugeben und ca. 2 Minuten braten. Die Chilischoten zugeben und mit
Kokosnussmilch ablöschen. Das Gemüse zufü-
gen, die Kräuter unterrühren und mit Fischsauce,
Salz, Pfeffer und Zucker würzen. Kurz aufkochen
lassen und sofort mit Reis servieren.

1 lb beef filet, cut into strips
5 tbsp vegetable oil
3 tbsp red curry paste
2 red chilies, seeded and cut into strips
500 ml coconut milk
3½ oz makua puang (Thai baby eggplants),
diced
7 oz eggplant, diced
4 twigs sweet basil, picked
6 lime leaves, picked
3 tbsp fish sauce
Salt, pepper, sugar

Cut the beef filet in thumb-long strips. Sauté curry
paste in vegetable oil, add the beef strips and
sear for approx. 2 minutes. Add the chilies and
deglaze with coconut milk. Add the vegetables,
stir in the herbs and season with fish sauce, salt,
pepper and sugar. Bring to a quick boil and serve
immediately with rice.

450 g de filet de bœuf
5 c. à soupe d'huile végétale
3 c. à soupe de pâte de curry rouge
2 piments rouges, épépinés et coupés en lamelles
500 ml de lait de coco
100 g de makua puang (petites aubergines thaïlandaises), coupées en dés
200 g d'aubergines, coupées en dés
4 branches de basilic, effeuillées
6 feuilles de citron vert, coupées en petits morceaux
3 c. à soupe de sauce de poisson
Sel, poivre, sucre

Couper le filet de bœuf en lamelles de la taille d'un pouce. Faire revenir la pâte de curry dans l'huile végétale, ajouter les lamelles de filet de bœuf et faire frire pendant env. 2 minutes. Ajouter les piments et verser le lait de coco. Ajouter les légumes, puis les herbes et assaisonner avec la sauce de poisson, le sel, le poivre et le sucre. Amener à ébullition pendant un bref instant et servir immédiatement avec le riz.

450 g de filete de ternera
5 cucharadas de aceite vegetal
3 cucharadas de pasta de curry roja
2 guindillas rojas, despepitadas y en juliana
500 ml de leche de coco
100 g de *makua puang* (berenjenas baby tailandesas), en dados
200 g de berenjena, en dados
4 ramitas de albahaca dulce, arrancadas
6 hojas de lima, arrancadas
3 cucharadas de salsa de pescado
Sal, pimienta, azúcar

Corte el filete de ternera en tiras del tamaño de un pulgar. Sofría la pasta de curry en aceite vegetal, incorpore las tiras de ternera y fríalas durante aprox. 2 minutos. Incorpore las guindillas y la leche de coco. Añada la verdura, las hierbas y sazone con la salsa de pescado, la sal, la pimienta y el azúcar. Deje que hierva brevemente y sirva inmediatamente con arroz.

450 g di filetto di manzo
5 cucchiai di olio vegetale
3 cucchiai di pasta di curry rosso
2 peperoncini rossi tagliati a strisce e privati dei semi
500 ml di latte di noce di cocco
100 g di makua puang (piccole melanzane tailandesi) tagliate a dadini
200 g di melanzane tagliate a dadini
4 rametti di basilico dolce, le foglioline sminuzzate
6 foglioline sminuzzate di limetta
3 cucchiai di sugo di pesce
Sale, pepe, zucchero

Tagliare il filetto di manzo in strisce della lunghezza di un pollice. Rosolare la pasta di curry nell'olio vegetale, aggiungere le strisce di carne e lasciar cuocere per circa 2 minuti. Unire i peperoncini e bagnare con il latte di cocco. Aggiungere le verdure, incorporare le erbe e condire con la salsa di pesce, sale, pepe e zucchero. Dare un bollore e servire subito con del riso.

Silk

Design: 3deluxe, Nik Schweiger | Chef: Mario Lohninger
Owners: Sven Väth, Matthias Martinsohn, Mario Lohninger

Carl-Benz-Straße 21 | 60386 Frankfurt | Ostend
Phone: +49 69 90 02 00
www.cocoonclub.net
Subway: Dieselstraße
Opening hours: Tue–Thu 7 pm to 3 am, Fri–Sat 7 pm to 6 am, Sun–Mon closed
Average menu price: € 76
Cuisine: Modern eclectic blend
Special features: 10 course menu, menu start 8 pm

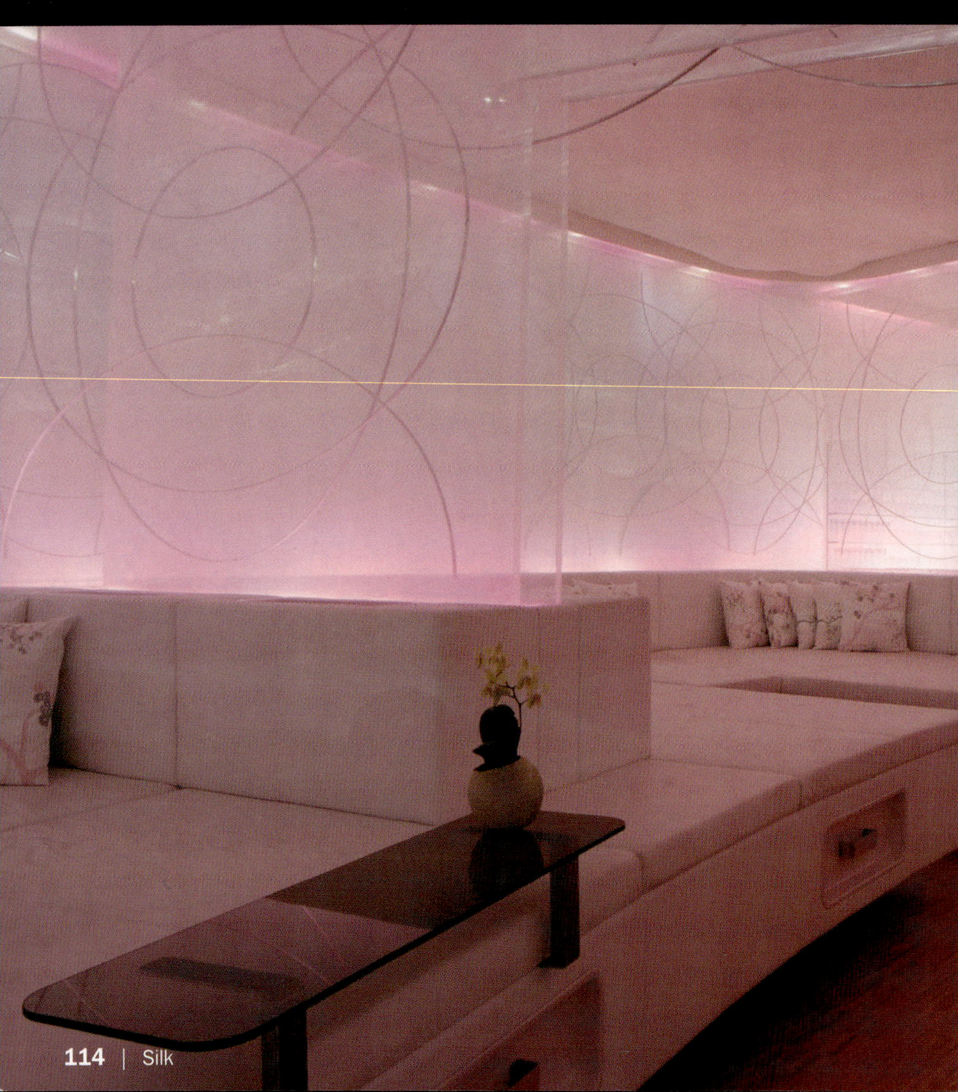

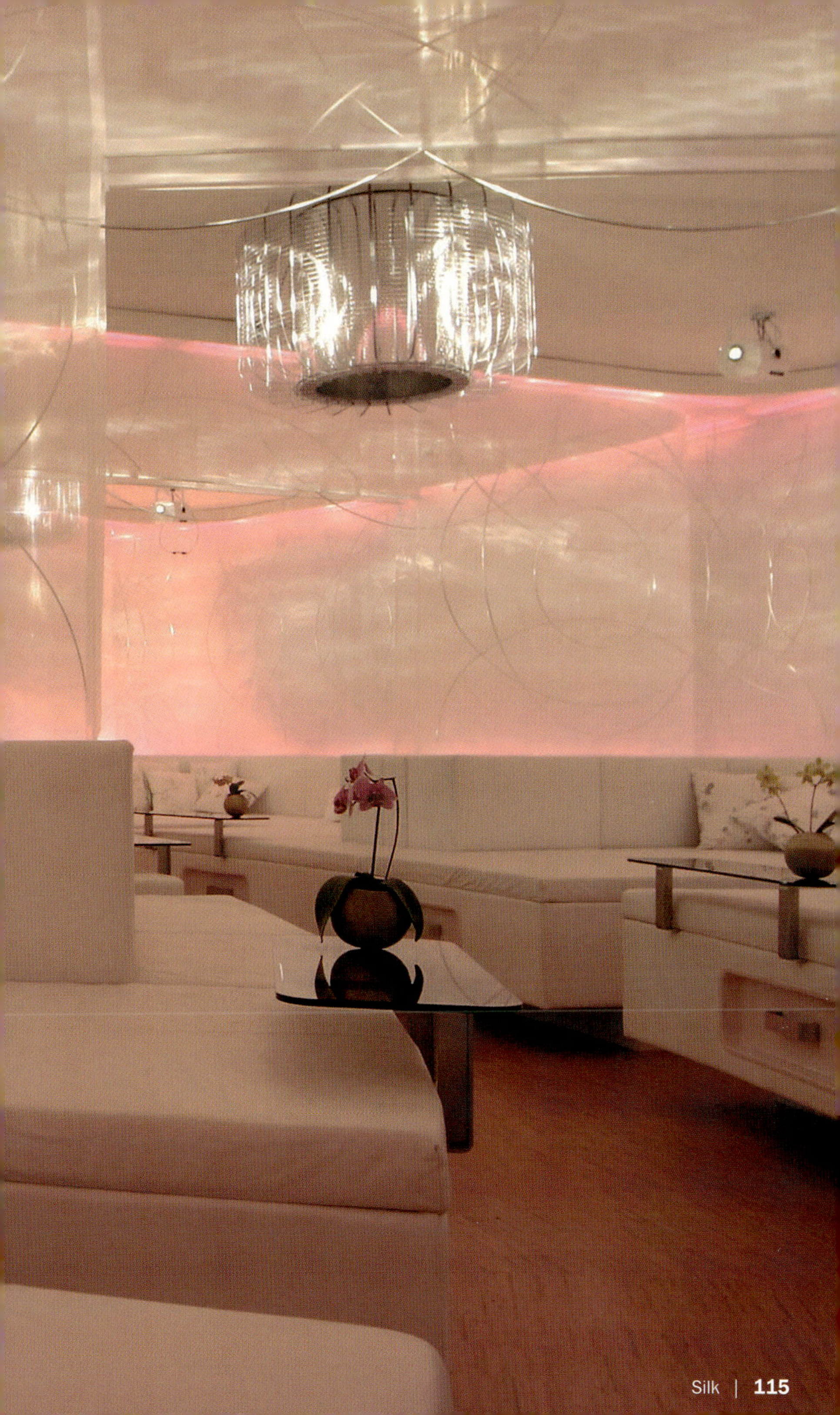

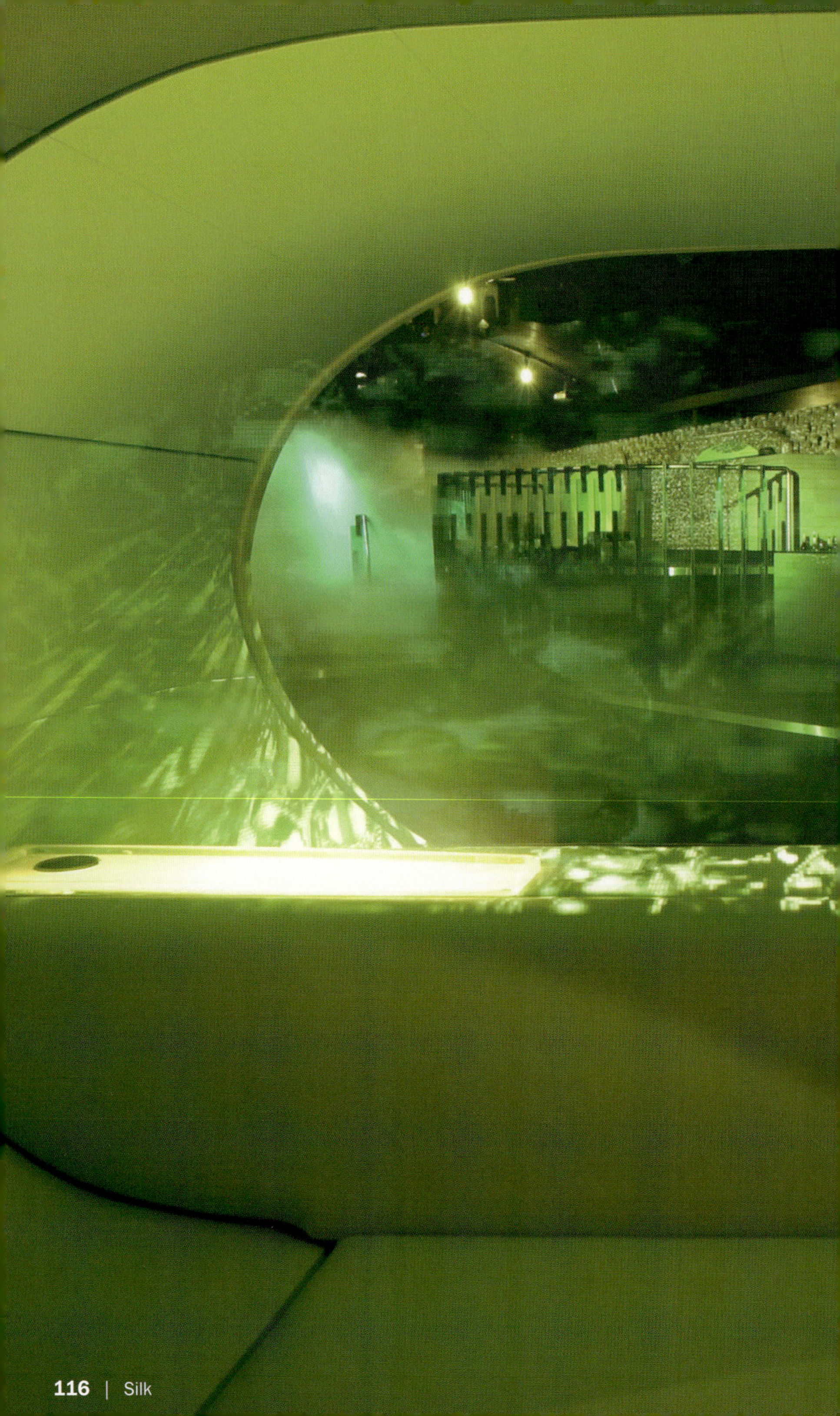

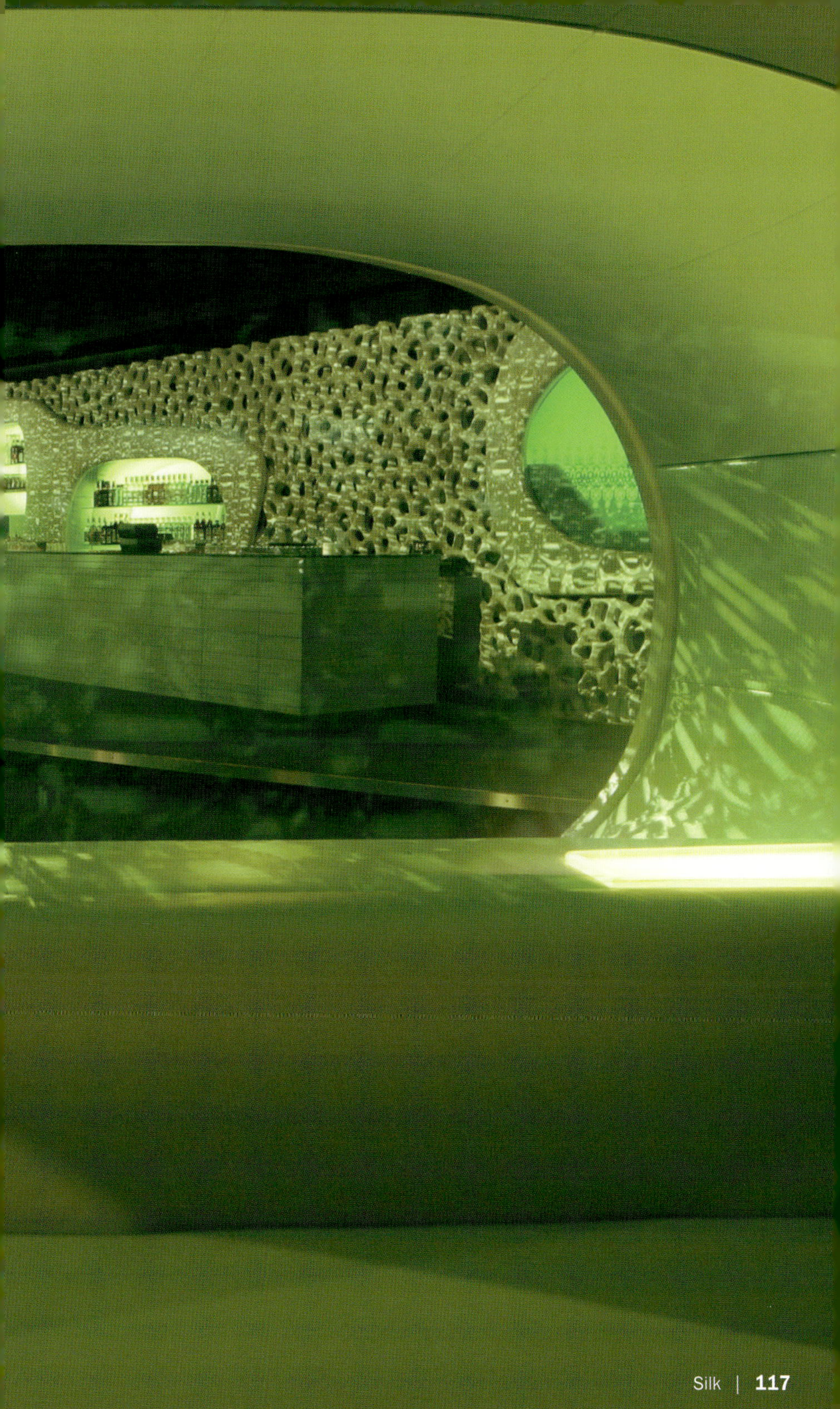

Tigerpalast

Chef: Martin Göschel
Owners: Margareta Dillinger, Johnny Klinke

Heiligkreuzgasse 16–20 | 60313 Frankfurt | Innenstadt
Phone: +49 69 92 00 22 25
www.tigerpalast.de
Subway: Konstabler Wache
Opening hours: Tue–Sat 6 pm to 1 am, Sun–Mon closed
Average price: € 38
Cuisine: Mediterranean
Special features: Varieté theatre

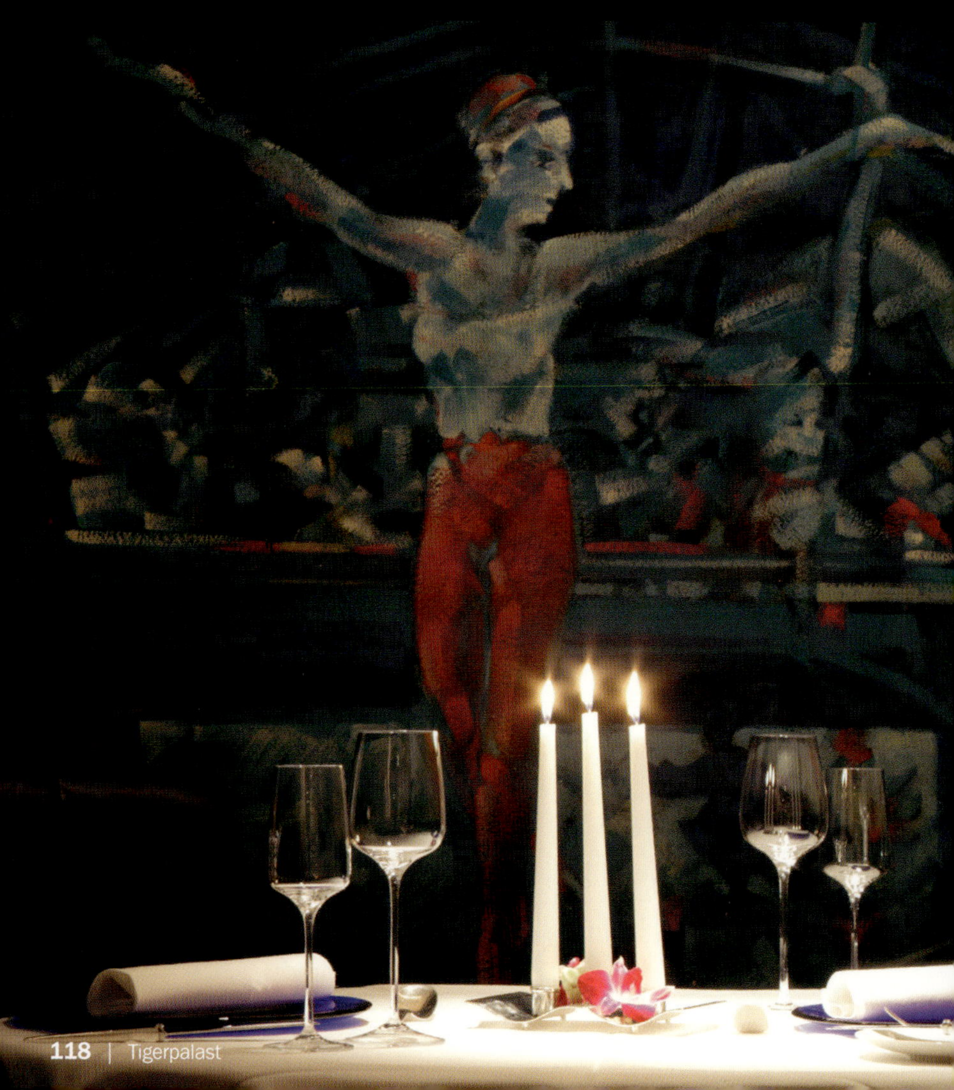

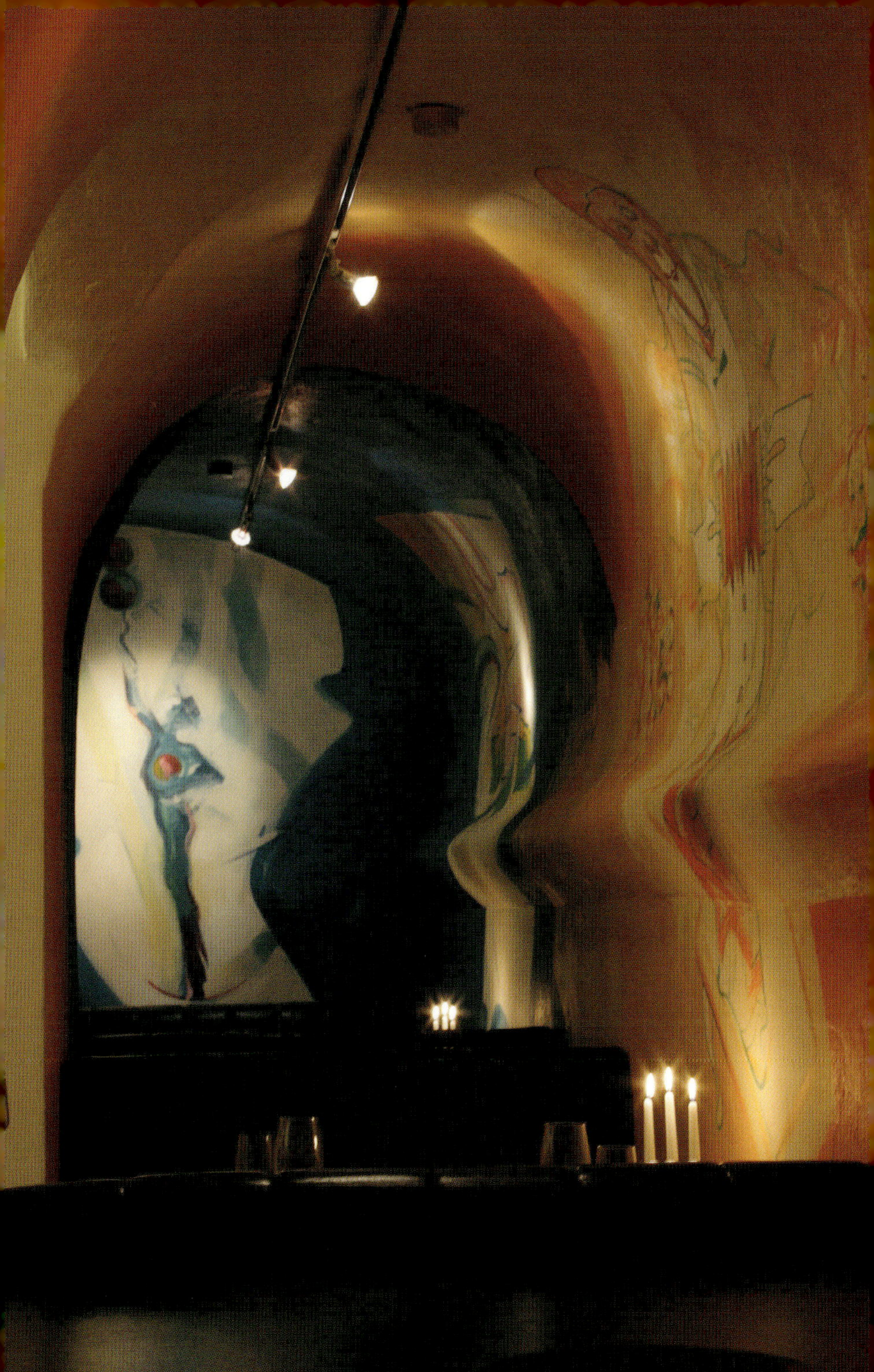

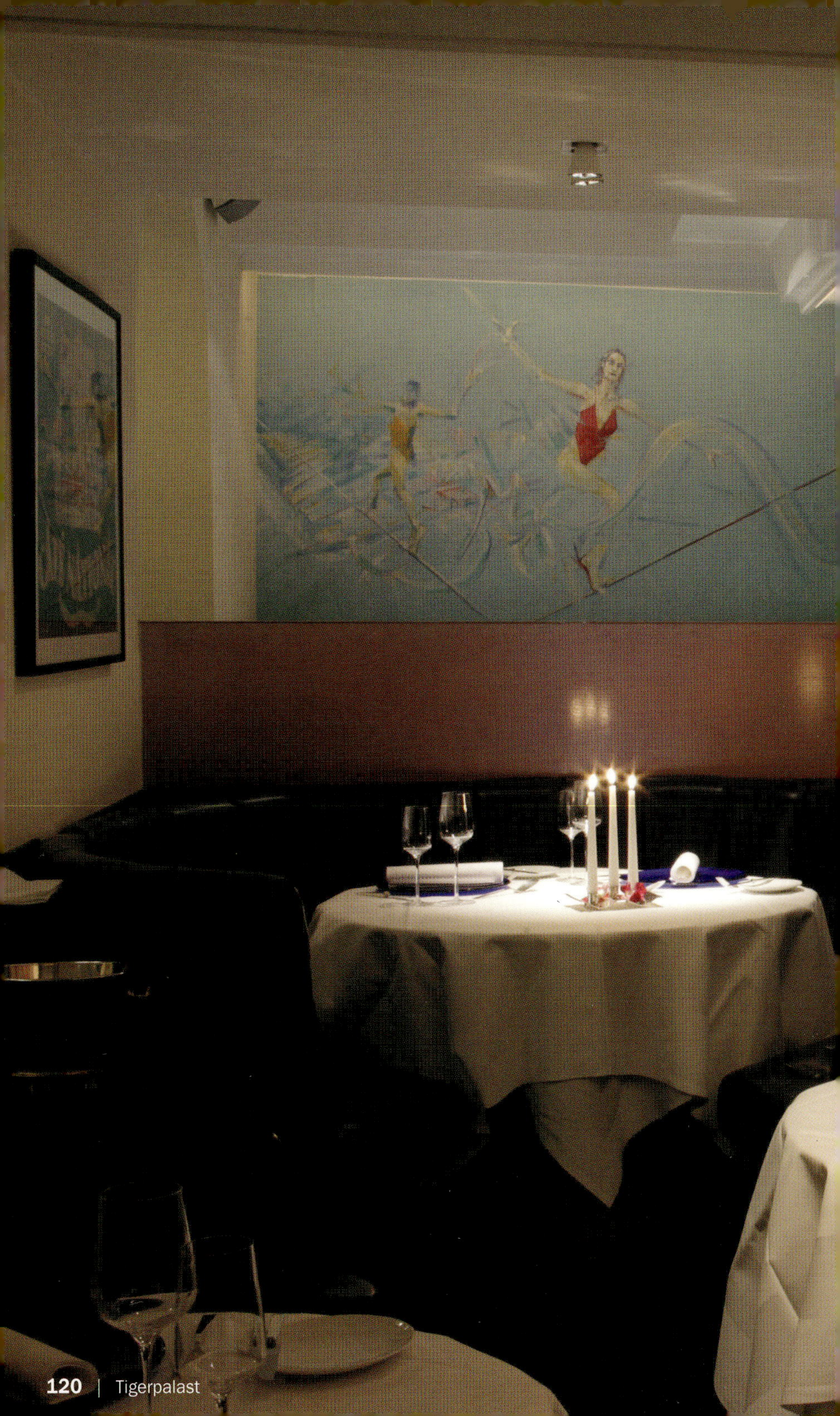

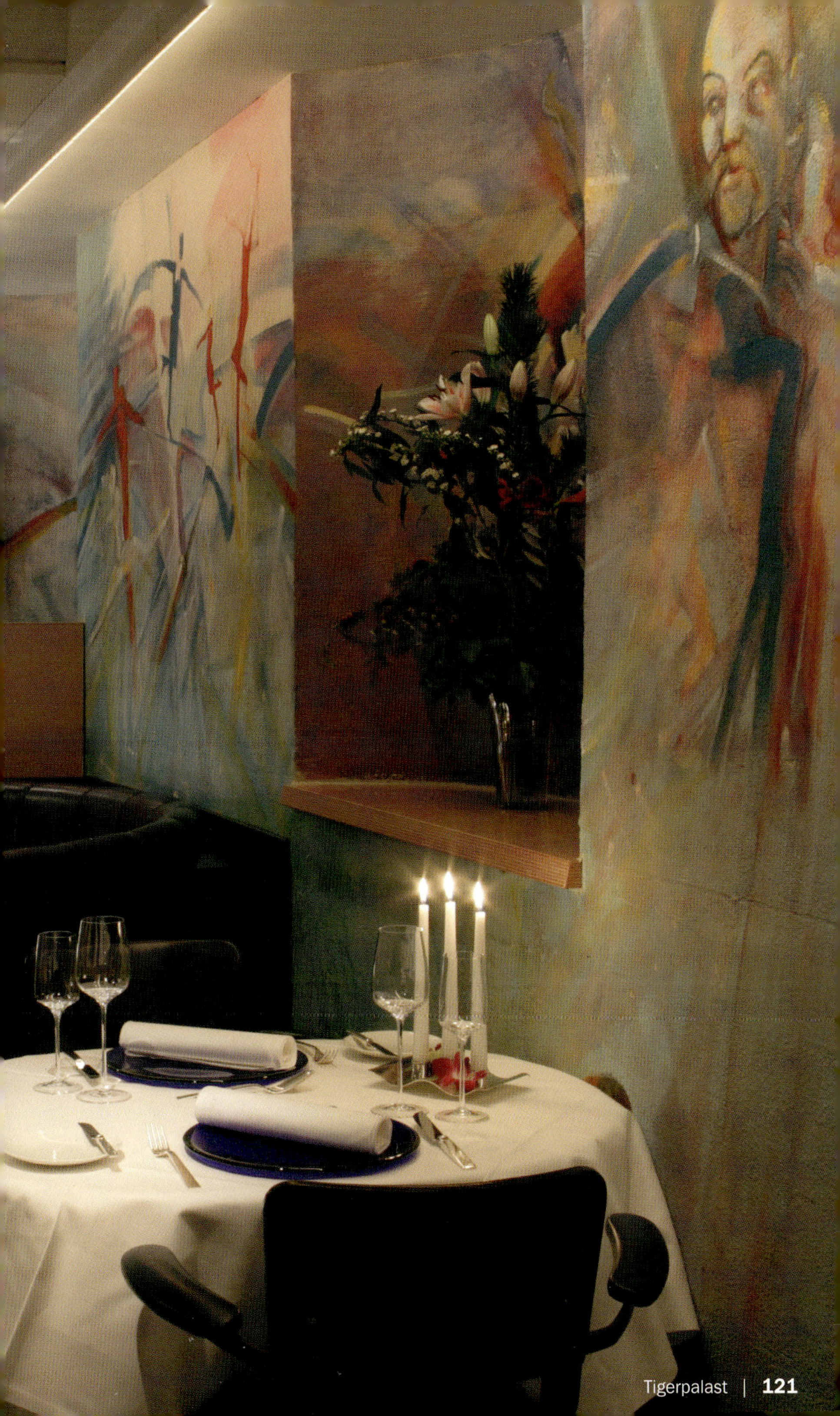

Kalbszungenterrine

mit Felchenkaviar

Cured Veal Tongue Terrine with Whitefish Caviar

Terrine de langue de veau saumurée au caviar de corégone

Aspic de lengua de ternera en salmuera con caviar de corégono

Terrina di lingua di vitello salmistrata con uova di lavarello

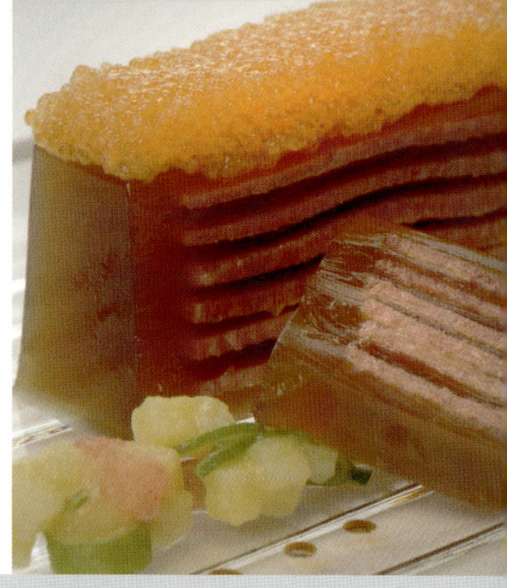

1 gepökelte Kalbszunge
2 Schalotten, halbiert
1 Knoblauchzehe, halbiert
Je 1 Stück Karotte, Sellerieknolle und Lauch, ca. 5 cm
1 Lorbeerblatt
1 Nelke
2 Wacholderbeeren

Alle Zutaten in einen Topf geben und mit Wasser bedecken. Zum Kochen bringen und ca. 2 Stunden leise köcheln lassen. Die Kalbszunge aus dem Sud nehmen und abkühlen lassen. Den Sud abseihen und auf 240 ml einreduzieren lassen. Die abgekühlte Kalbszunge in 2 mm starke Scheiben schneiden.

240 ml reduzierter Zungenfond
1 TL Senf
4 Blatt Gelatine, eingeweicht

Den Fond erhitzen, den Senf einrühren und die Gelatine darin auflösen. Kaltstellen.
Die Kalbszungenscheiben abwechselnd mit dem erkalteten, aber noch flüssigen Gelee in eine Kastenform schichten und kaltstellen.

150 g Crème fraîche
2 EL Wasabi

Mischen und evtl. abschmecken.

4 EL Felchenkaviar
Kartoffelsalat als Beilage

Zum Servieren die Terrine in Scheiben schneiden, den Kaviar auf die Terrine geben und mit Kartoffelsalat und Wasabicreme garnieren.

1 cured veal tongue
2 shallots, halved
1 clove of garlic, halved
1 piece of carrot, celery root and leek each, approx. 2 inches
1 bay leave
1 clove
2 juniper berries

Combine all ingredients in a pot and cover with water. Bring to a boil and let simmer gently for approx. 2 hours. Remove the veal tongue from the fond and cool down. Strain the fond and reduce to 240 ml. Cut the cool veal tongue in ½ inch thin slices.

240 ml reduced tongue fond
1 tsp mustard
4 leaves gelatin, soaked

Heat up the tongue fond, stir in the mustard and dissolve the gelatin in it. Chill.
Layer the tongue slices alternately with the cold but still liquid tongue jelly in a square dish and chill.

5 oz crème fraîche
2 tbsp wasabi

Mix and season, if necessary.

4 tbsp whitefish caviar
Potato salad as side dish

To serve cut the terrine in slices, place the caviar on the terrine and garnish with potato salad and wasabi cream.

1 langue de veau saumurée
2 échalotes, coupées en deux
1 gousse d'ail, coupée en deux
1 morceau de carotte, de bulbe de céleri et de poireau d'env. 5 cm
1 feuille de laurier
1 clou de girofle
2 graines de genièvre

Mettre tous les ingrédients dans une casserole et recouvrir d'eau. Amener à ébullition et laisser mijoter pendant env. 2 heures. Retirer la langue de veau du bouillon et laisser refroidir. Filtrer le bouillon et faire réduire à 240 ml. Couper la langue refroidie en tranches de 2 mm d'épaisseur.

240 ml de fond de langue réduit
1 c. à café de moutarde
4 feuilles de gélatine, ramollies

Réchauffer le fond, mélanger la moutarde et y faire fondre la gélatine. Mettre au frais.
Disposer les tranches de langue de veau dans un moule à cake en alternant avec la gelée refroidie, mais encore liquide, et mettre au frais.

150 g de crème fraîche
2 c. à soupe de wasabi

Mélanger et rectifier éventuellement l'assaisonnement.

4 c. à soupe de caviar de corégone
Salade de pommes de terre en accompagnement

Pour servir, couper la terrine en tranches, disposer le caviar sur la terrine et garnir de salade de pommes de terre et de crème de wasabi.

1 lengua de ternera en salmuera.
2 chalotes, en mitades
1 diente de ajo, cortado por la mitad
1 zanahoria, bulbo de apio y puerro, aprox. 5 cm
1 hoja de laurel
1 clavo
2 enebrinas

Ponga todos los ingredientes en una cazuela y cúbralos con agua. Lleve a ebullición y deje que hierva a fuego lento durante aprox. 2 horas. Saque la lengua del caldo y deje que se enfríe. Cuele el caldo y redúzcalo hasta 240 ml. Corte la lengua en rodajas de 2 mm.

240 ml del caldo de lengua reducido
1 cucharadita de mostaza
4 láminas de gelatina, reblandecidas

Caliente el caldo, incorpore la mostaza y diluya dentro la gelatina. Reserve en el frigorífico.
En un molde rectangular, haga capas alternas con las rodajas de lengua y la gelatina fría pero todavía líquida en un molde rectangular. Introdúzcalo después en el frigorífico.

150 g de nata fresca espesa
2 cucharadas de *wasabi*

Mezcle los ingredientes y sazone si es necesario.

4 cucharadas de caviar de corégono
Ensalada de patata como acompañamiento

Para servir corte áspic en rodajas, ponga encima el caviar y decore con la ensalada de patata y crema de *wasabi*.

1 lingua di vitello salmistrata
2 scalogni tagliati a metà
1 spicchio d'aglio tagliato a metà
1 pezzo di carota, di bulbo di sedano ed di porro, di circa 5 cm ciascuno
1 foglia di alloro
1 chiodo di garofano
2 bacche di ginepro

Mettere in una pentola tutti gli ingredienti e ricoprirli d'acqua. Portarli ad ebollizione e lasciarli cuocere a fuoco lento per ca. 2 ore. Estrarre la lingua di vitello dal sugo e lasciarla raffreddare. Passare il sugo al setaccio e farlo restringere a 240 ml. Quando sarà fredda, tagliare la lingua a fette dello spessore di 2 mm.

240 ml di fondo di lingua ristretto
1 cucchiaino di senape
4 fogli di gelatina ammorbiditi

Riscaldare il fondo di lingua, incorporarvi la senape e sciogliervi la gelatina. Mettere in frigorifero.
Disporre a strati alternati le fette di lingua e la gelatina raffreddata ma ancora liquida in uno stampo rettangolare. Mettere in frigorifero.

150 g di crème fraîche
2 cucchiai di wasabi

Mescolare, assaggiare ed eventualmente regolare il condimento.

4 cucchiai di uova di lavarello
Come contorno: insalata di patate

Al momento di servire, affettare la terrina, disporvi sopra le uova di lavarello e guarnire con insalata di patate e crema di wasabi.

Villa Merton

Design: Union International Club | Chef: Hans Horberth
Owner: Kofler Company

Am Leonhardsbrunn 12 | 60487 Frankfurt | Bockenheim
Phone: +49 69 70 30 33
www.kofler-company.de
Subway: Bockenheimer Warte
Opening hours: Mon–Fri noon to 2 pm and 6 pm to 10 pm
Average price: € 25
Cuisine: International
Special features: Wine menu with 700 positions, meeting room for 60 persons

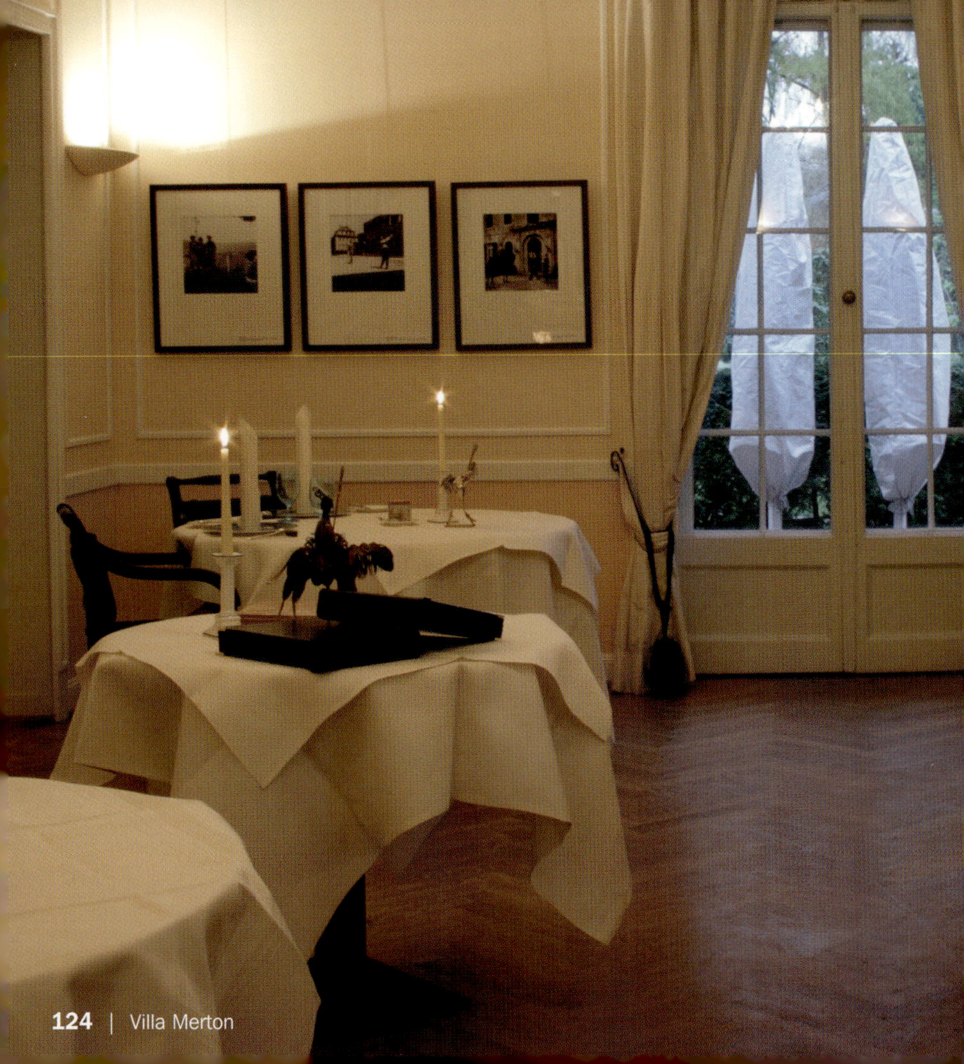

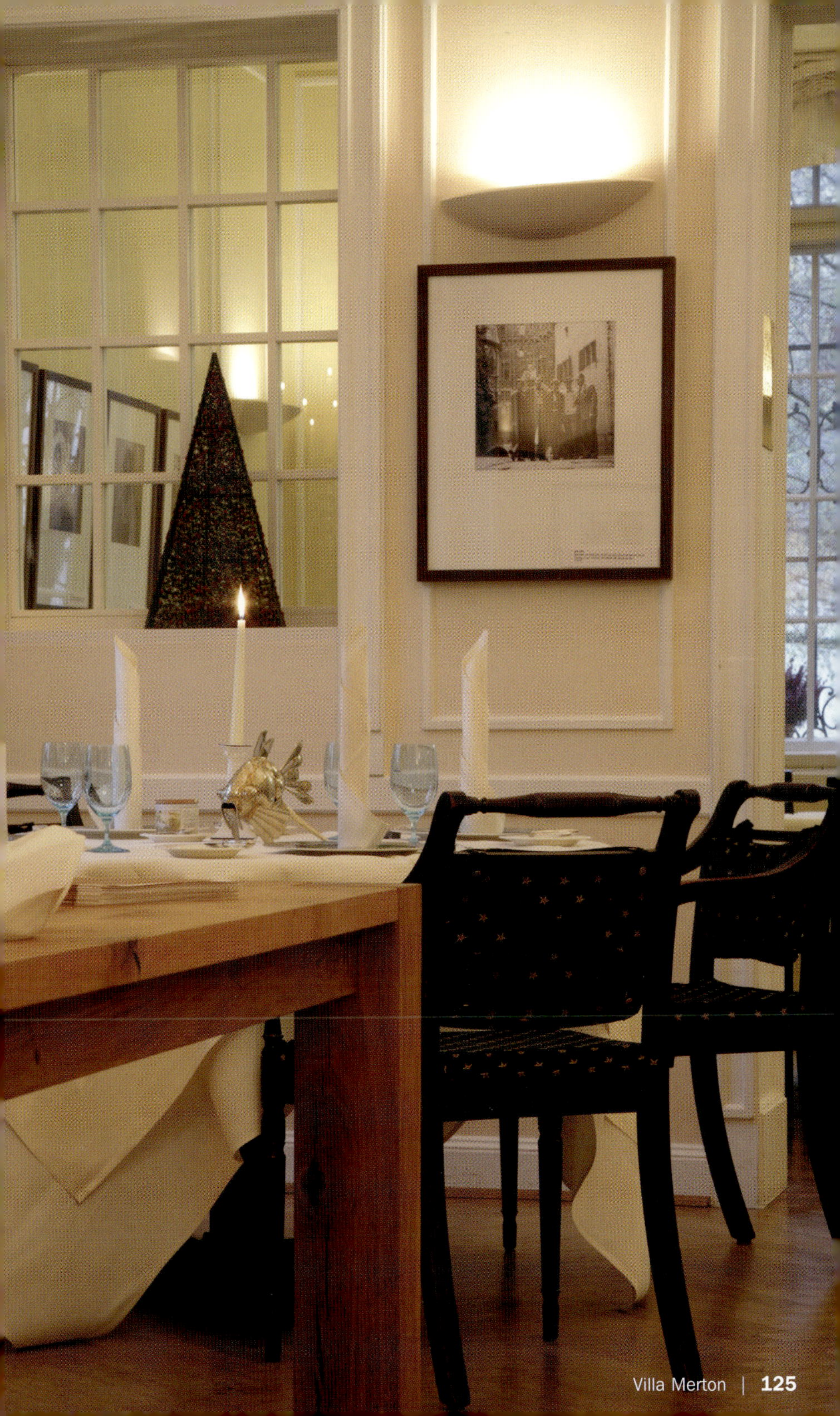

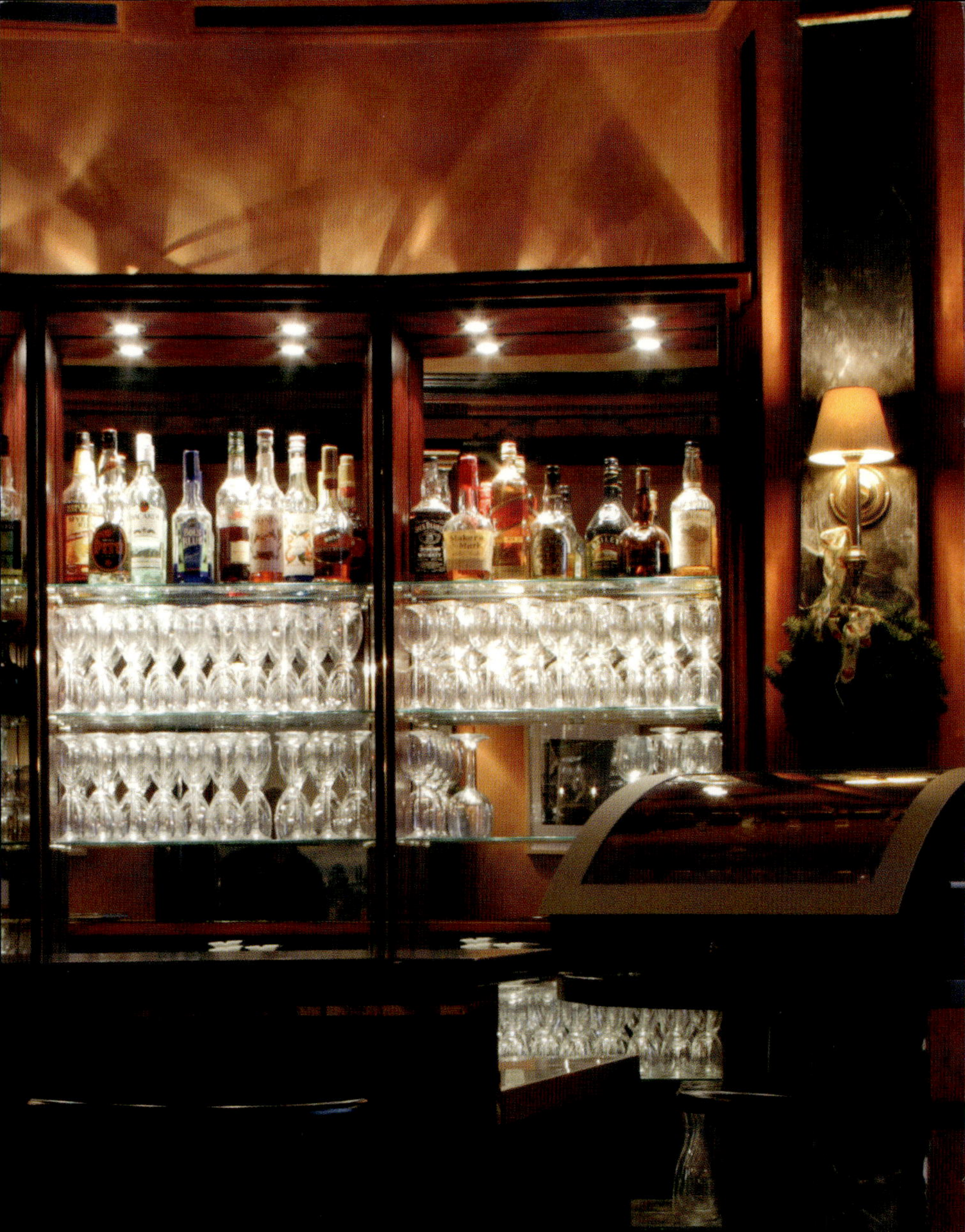

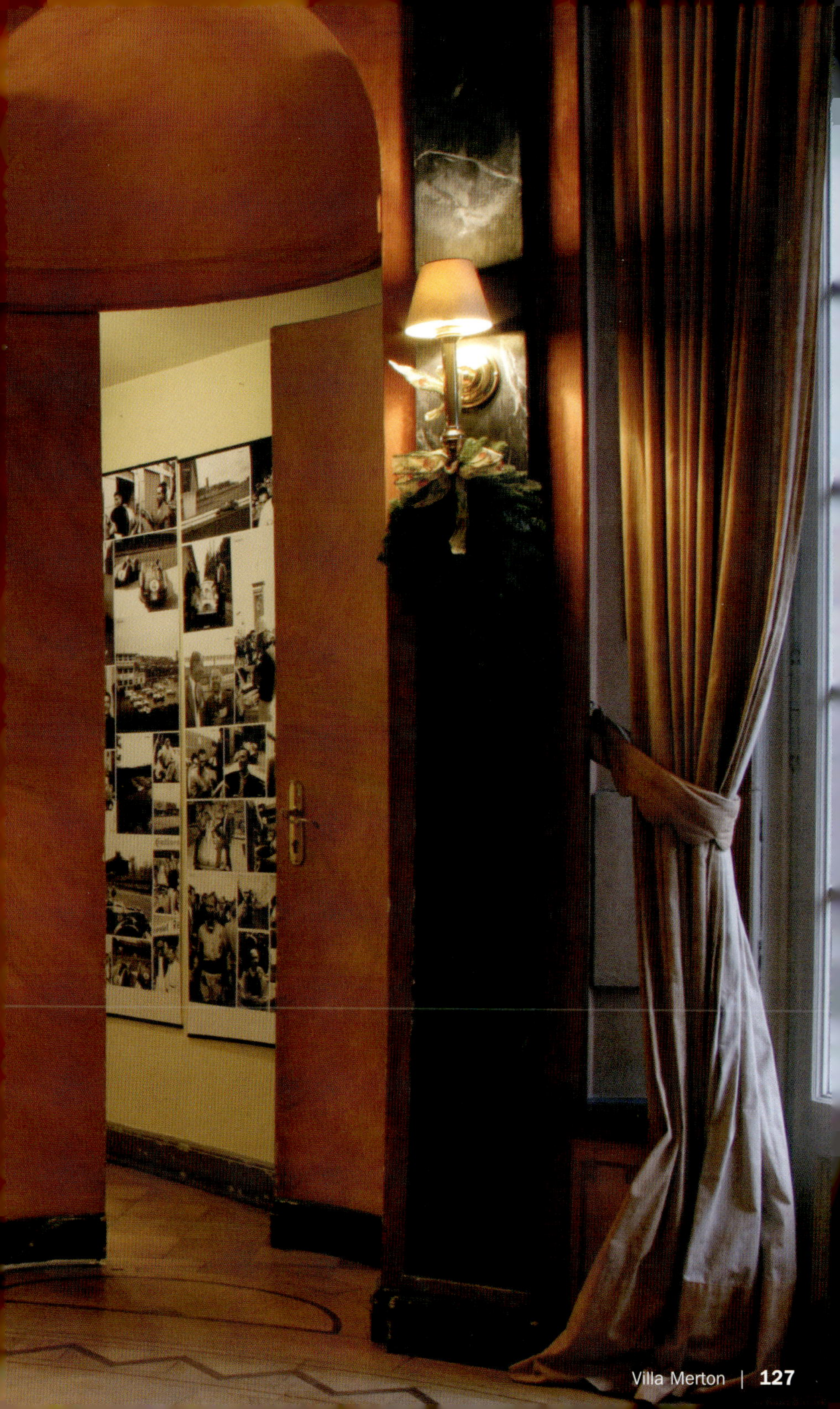

Jakobsmuschel

mit Kürbis, Zitronenwassergelee und Tomaten-Vinaigrette

Scallop with Pumpkin, Lemon Water Jelly and Tomato-Vinaigrette

Coquille Saint-Jacques au potiron, à la gelée d'eau citronnée et à la vinaigrette de tomates

Vieira con calabaza, jalea de agua de limón y tomates a la vinagreta

Capesanta con zucca, gelatina d'acqua e limone e vinaigrette al pomodoro

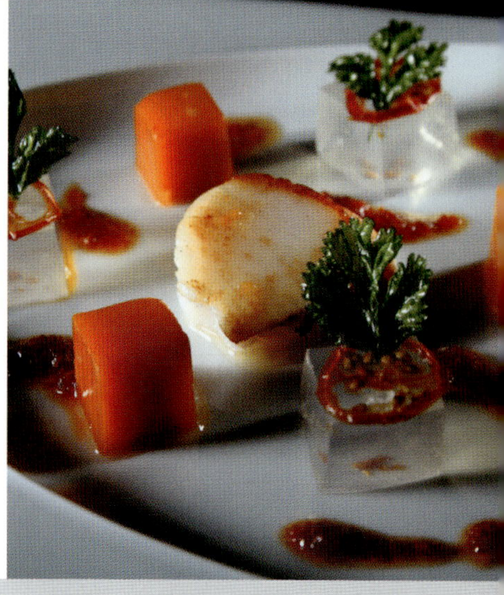

1 kg Muskatkürbis, geschält und entkernt,
in 3 x 3 cm breiten Würfeln
1 Schalotte, gewürfelt
1 TL weiße Pfefferkörner
500 ml Weißwein
500 ml Apfelsaft
2 Stangen Zitronengras
2 EL Honig
100 ml Essig
Korianderstängel, Salz
Alle Zutaten, außer dem Kürbis, mischen und aufkochen. Abseihen und in dem Sud die Kürbiswürfel bissfest blanchieren.

700 ml Wasser
Geriebene Schale und Saft von 2 Zitronen
5 Blatt Gelatine, eingeweicht
Wasser, Zitronenschale und Zitronensaft mischen, aufkochen, mit Salz würzen und die Gelatine in der heißen Flüssigkeit auflösen. In ein tiefes Blech gießen und mind. 5 Stunden kaltstellen. In 3 x 3 cm breite Würfel schneiden.

6 EL Olivenöl
2 EL weißer Essig
½ Knoblauchzehe
3 EL Tomatenmark
Salz, Pfeffer
Alle Zutaten in einem Mixer glatt mixen und abschmecken.

4 Jakobsmuscheln, ausgelöst
Salz, Pfeffer, 2 EL Olivenöl
Die Jakobsmuscheln würzen, von beiden Seiten 1 Minute anbraten und mit den Kürbiswürfeln, den Geleewürfeln sowie der Tomaten-Vinaigrette anrichten.

2 lb 3 oz pumpkin, peeled and seeded, cut in
1 x 1 inch cubes
1 shallot, diced
1 tsp white pepper corns
500 ml white wine
500 ml apple juice
2 sticks lemongrass
2 tbsp honey
100 ml vinegar
Twigs cilantro, salt
Combine all ingredients, except the pumpkin, and bring to a boil. Cook the pumpkin cubes in the stock until al dente.

700 ml water
Grated zest and juice of 2 lemons
5 leaves gelatin, soaked
Combine water, lemon zest and juice, bring to a boil, season with salt and dissolve the gelatin in the hot liquid. Pour into a deep dish and chill for at least 5 hours. Cut into 1 x 1 inch wide cubes.

6 tbsp olive oil
2 tbsp white vinegar
½ clove of garlic
3 tbsp tomato paste
Salt, pepper
Mix all ingredients in a blender until smooth and season.

4 scallops, shelled
Salt, pepper, 2 tbsp olive oil
Season the scallops, sear on both sides for 1 minute and arrange with pumpkin cubes, jelly cubes and tomato-vinaigrette.

1 kg de potiron, épluché et épépiné, coupé en dés de 3 x 3 cm
1 échalote, coupée en dés
1 c. à café de grains poivre blanc
500 ml vin blanc
500 ml de jus de pomme
2 branches de citronnelle
2 c. à soupe de miel
100 ml de vinaigre
Branches de coriandre, sel
Mélanger tous les ingrédients, sauf le potiron, et amener à ébullition. Filtrer et faire blanchir les dés de potiron dans le bouillon tout en veillant à ce qu'ils restent fermes sous la dente.

700 ml d'eau
L'écorce râpée et le jus de 2 citrons
5 feuilles de gélatine, ramollies

Mélanger l'eau, l'écorce de citron et le jus de citron, amener à ébullition, saler et dissoudre la gélatine dans le liquide brûlant. Verser sur une plaque creuse et mettre au frais pendant au moins 5 heures. Couper en dés de 3 x 3 cm.
6 c. à soupe d'huile d'olive
2 c. à soupe de vinaigre blanc
½ gousse d'ail
3 c. à soupe de concentré de tomate
Sel, poivre
Passer tous les ingrédients au mixer pour obtenir un mélange lisse et rectifier l'assaisonnement.

4 coquilles Saint-Jacques, décortiquées
Sel, poivre, 2 c. à soupe d'huile d'olive
Assaisonner les coquilles, les saisir des deux côtés pendant 1 minute et les disposer avec les dés de potiron, les dés de gelée et la vinaigrette de tomates.

1 kg de calabaza moscada, pelada y despepitada, en dados de 3 x 3 cm
1 chalote, en dados
1 cucharadita de granos de pimienta blanca
500 ml de vino blanco
500 ml de zumo de manzana
2 ramas de limoncillo
2 cucharadas de miel
100 ml de vinagre
Tallos de cilantro, sal
Mezcle todos los ingredientes excepto la calabaza y cuézalos. Áselos después por el colador y escalfe los dados de calabaza en el líquido.

700 ml de agua
La piel rallada y el zumo de 2 limones
5 láminas de gelatina, reblandecidas
Mezcle el agua, la piel de limón y el zumo y lleve a ebullición. Sazone con sal disuelva la gelatina en el líquido caliente. Viértalo en una bandeja de horno profunda y póngalo en el frigorífico durante un mínimo de 5 horas. Córtelo después de dados de 3 x 3 cm.

6 cucharadas de aceite de oliva
2 cucharadas de vinagre blanco
½ diente de ajo
3 cucharadas de concentrado de tomate
Sal, pimienta
Pase los ingredientes por la batidora y sazone.

4 vieiras, sin valvas
Sal, pimienta, 2 cucharadas de aceite de oliva
Sazone las vieiras, fríalas por ambos lados durante 1 minuto y dispóngalas en los platos con los dados de calabaza y de gelatina y con la vinagreta de tomate.

1 kg di zucca moscata, priva della buccia e dei semi, tagliata a dadini di 3 x 3 cm
1 scalogno tagliato a dadini
1 cucchiaino di pepe bianco in grani
500 ml di vino bianco
500 ml di succo di mela
2 bastoncini di cedronella
2 cucchiai di miele
100 ml di aceto
Mazzetti di coriandolo, sale
Mescolare tutti gli ingredienti tranne la zucca e portarli a cottura. Scolarli. Sbollentare al dente i dadini di zucca nel sugo ottenuto.

700 ml d'acqua
La buccia grattugiata ed il succo di 2 limoni
5 fogli di gelatina ammorbiditi
Mescolare l'acqua, la buccia ed il succo di limone, portarli a cottura, salare e sciogliere la gelatina nel liquido caldo. Versare il tutto in uno stampo alto. Tenere in frigorifero per almeno 5 ore. Ricavarne quindi dei dadini delle dimensioni di 3 x 3 cm.

6 cucchiai di olio d'oliva
2 cucchiai di aceto bianco
½ spicchio d'aglio
3 cucchiai di concentrato di pomodoro
Sale, pepe
Frullare tutti gli ingredienti fino ad ottenere una crema vellutata, assaggiare e regolare il condimento.

4 capesante private del guscio
Sale, pepe, 2 cucchiai di olio d'oliva
Condire le capesante, dorarle per 1 minuto da entrambi i lati e disporle nei piatti con i dadini di zucca, e di gelatina.

Walden

Design: nordisk büro design | Chef: Ajiou Fouzi
Owner: Thomas Klüber

Kleiner Hirschgraben 7 | 60311 Frankfurt | Altstadt
Phone: +49 69 92 88 27 00
www.walden-frankfurt.com
Subway: Hauptwache
Opening hours: Mon–Sat 9 am to 1 am, first floor Wed–Sat 8 pm to 2 am
Average price: € 12
Cuisine: Casual
Special features: Sunny terrace, first floor club, events

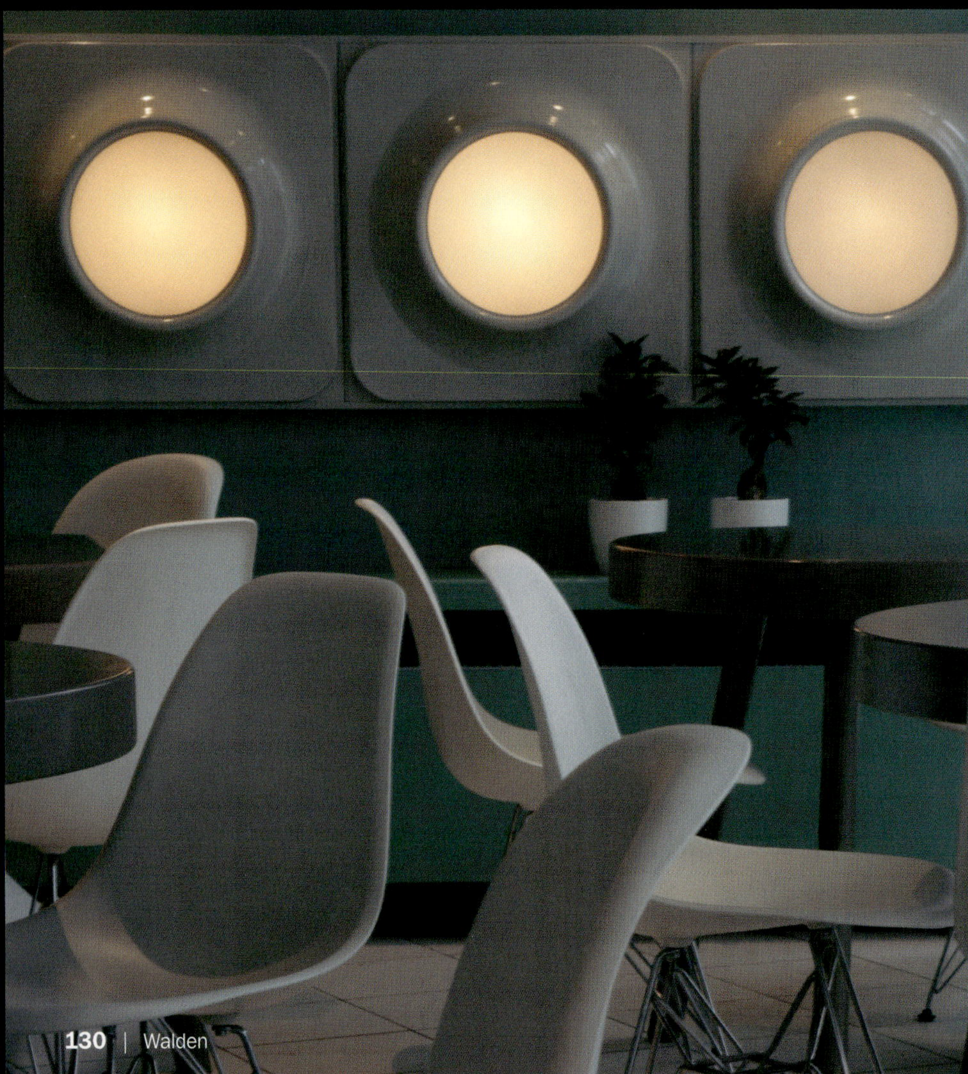

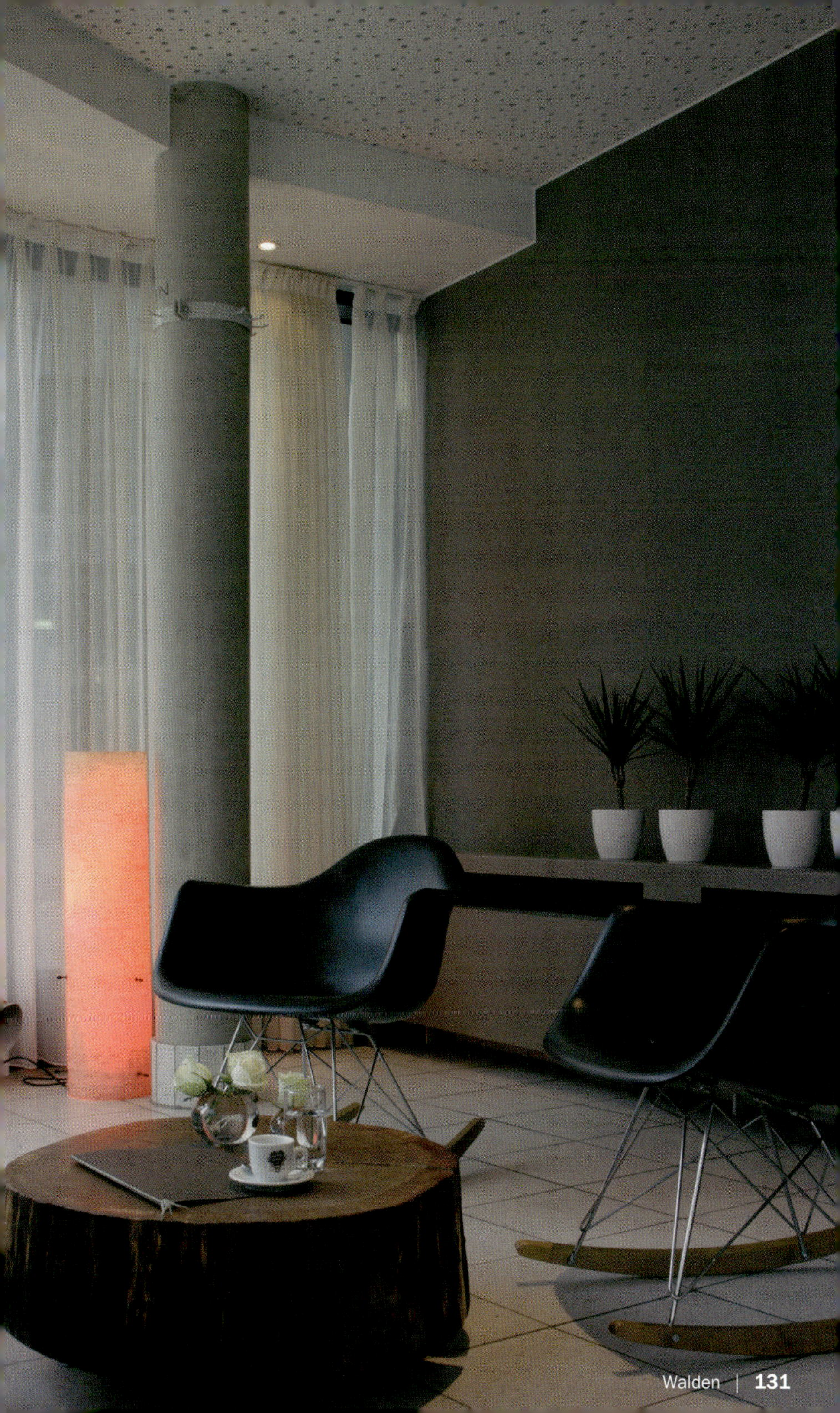

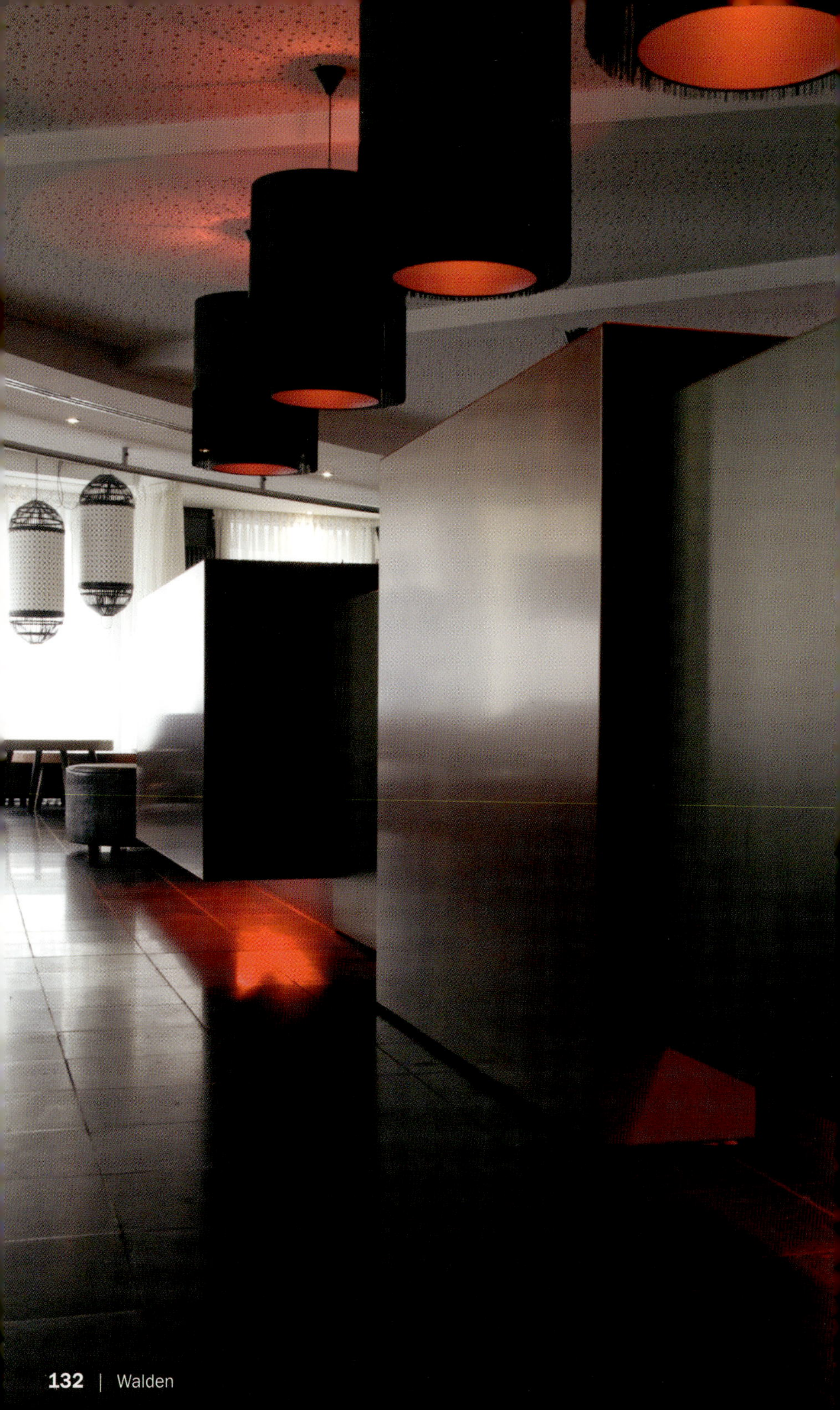

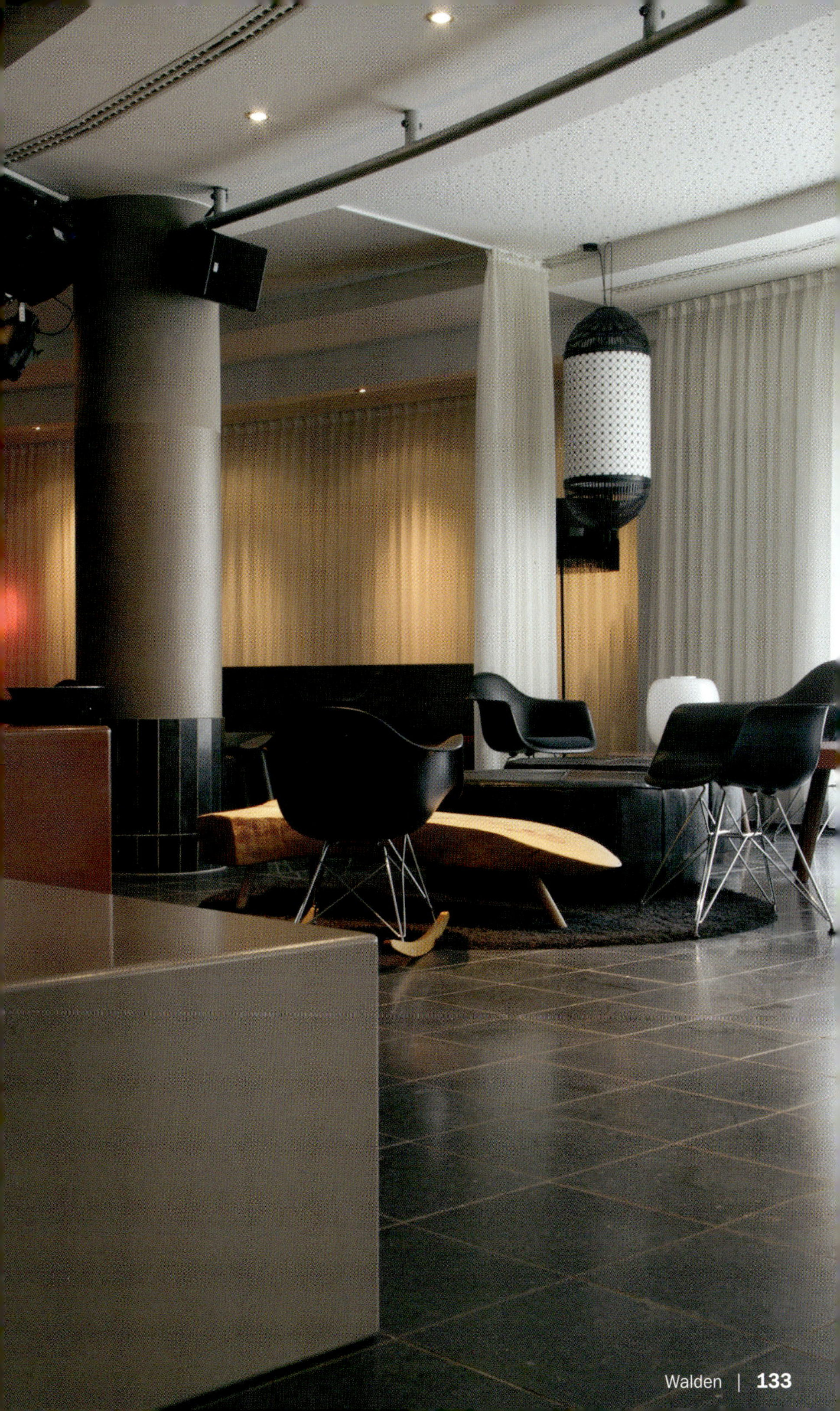

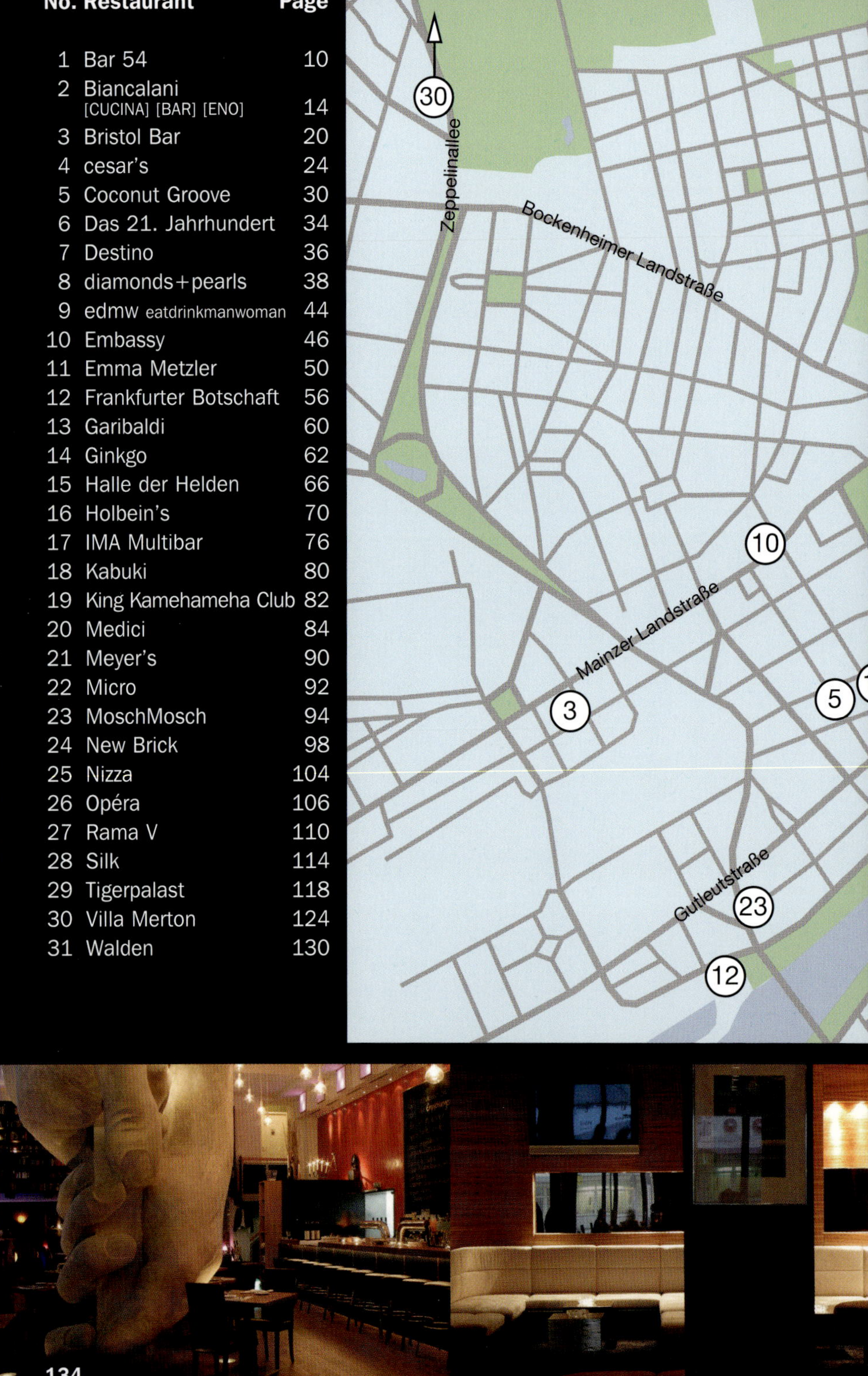

Zeppelinallee
Bockenheimer Landstraße
Mainzer Landstraße
Gutleutstraße
30
10
3
5
1
23
12

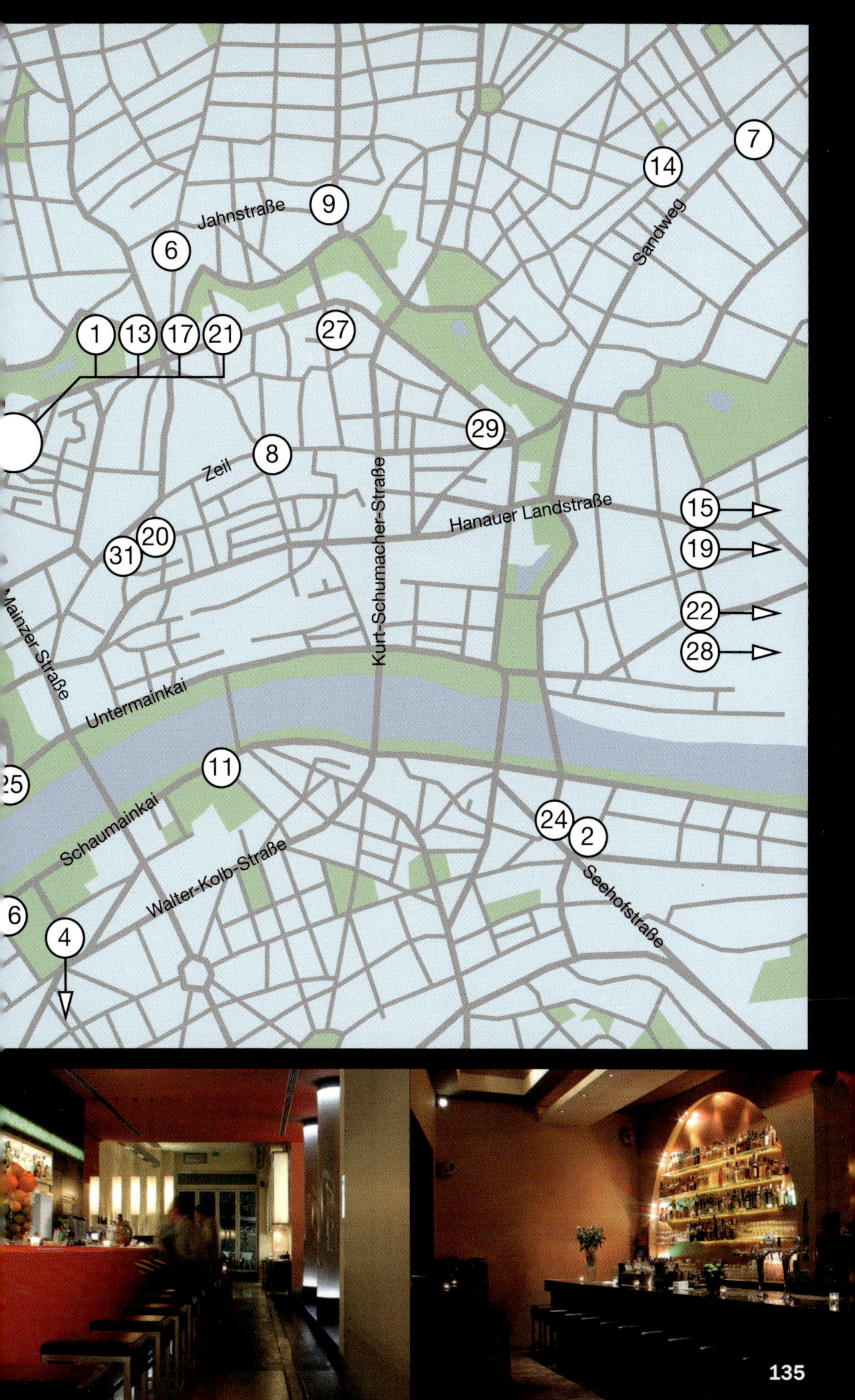

Jahnstraße
Sandweg
Zeil
Kurt-Schumacher-Straße
Hanauer Landstraße
Mainzer-Straße
Untermainkai
Schaumainkai
Walter-Kolb-Straße
Seehofstraße

Cool Restaurants

Size: 14 x 21.5 cm / 5 $\frac{1}{2}$ x 8 $\frac{1}{2}$ in.
136 pp, Flexicover
c. 130 color photographs
Text in English, German, French, Spanish, Italian or (*) Dutch

Other titles in the same series:

Amsterdam
ISBN 3-8238-4588-8

Barcelona
ISBN 3-8238-4586-1

Berlin
ISBN 3-8238-4585-3

Brussels (*)
ISBN 3-8327-9065-9

Cape Town
ISBN 3-8327-9103-5

Chicago
ISBN 3-8327-9018-7

Cologne
ISBN 3-8327-9117-5

Côte d'Azur
ISBN 3-8327-9040-3

Hamburg
ISBN 3-8238-4599-3

Hong Kong
ISBN 3-8327-9111-6

Istanbul
ISBN 3-8327-9115-9

Las Vegas
ISBN 3-8327-9116-7

London 2nd edition
ISBN 3-8327-9131-0

Los Angeles
ISBN 3-8238-4589-6

Madrid
ISBN 3-8327-9029-2

Mallorca/Ibiza
ISBN 3-8327-9113-2

Miami
ISBN 3-8327-9066-7

Milan
ISBN 3-8238-4587-X

Munich
ISBN 3-8327-9019-5

New York 2nd edition
ISBN 3-8327-9130-2

Paris 2nd edition
ISBN 3-8327-9129-9

Prague
ISBN 3-8327-9068-3

Rome
ISBN 3-8327-9028-4

San Francisco
ISBN 3-8327-9067-5

Shanghai
ISBN 3-8327-9050-0

Sydney
ISBN 3-8327-9027-6

Tokyo
ISBN 3-8238-4590-X

Toscana
ISBN 3-8327-9102-7

Vienna
ISBN 3-8327-9020-9

Zurich
ISBN 3-8327-9069-1

To be published in the
same series:

Dubai   Moscow
Copenhagen   Singapore
Geneva   Stockholm

teNeues